Dyslexia, Literacy and Inclusion

Dyslexia, Literacy and Inclusion

CHILD-CENTRED PERSPECTIVES

SEAN MACBLAIN
LOUISE LONG
JILL DUNN

Los Angeles | London | New Delhi
Singapore | Washington DC

SAGE

Los Angeles | London | New Delhi
Singapore | Washington DC

SAGE Publications Ltd
1 Oliver's Yard
55 City Road
London EC1Y 1SP

SAGE Publications Inc.
2455 Teller Road
Thousand Oaks, California 91320

SAGE Publications India Pvt Ltd
B 1/I 1 Mohan Cooperative Industrial Area
Mathura Road
New Delhi 110 044

SAGE Publications Asia-Pacific Pte Ltd
3 Church Street
#10-04 Samsung Hub
Singapore 049483

Commissioning editor: Amy Jarrold
Editorial assistant: George Knowles
Project manager: Jeanette Graham
Production editor: Nicola Marshall
Copyeditor: Rosemary Campbell
Proofreader: Isabel Kirkwood
Indexer: Anne Solomito
Marketing executive: Dilhara Attygalle
Cover design: Wendy Scott
Typeset by: C&M Digitals (P) Ltd, Chennai, India
Printed in India by: Replika Press Pvt Ltd

MIX
Paper from
responsible sources
FSC
www.fsc.org FSC® C016779

Library of Congress Control Number: 2014946599

British Library Cataloguing in Publication data

A catalogue record for this book is available from the British Library

ISBN 978-1-44629-842-8
ISBN 978-1-44629-843-5 (pbk)

At SAGE we take sustainability seriously. Most of our products are printed in the UK using FSC papers and boards. When we print overseas we ensure sustainable papers are used as measured by the Egmont grading system. We undertake an annual audit to monitor our sustainability.

To my mother and father who gave to me the joy of learning, my wife Angela for her continued love and support, and our children Marty, Nat, Nibs and Hayz.

Sean MacBlain

For the children and young people of the city of Belfast and to the visionaries and 'peace-makers' that have brought them a brighter future.

Louise Long

For Ian, Holly and Katy who make everything worthwhile.

Jill Dunn

CONTENTS

List of figures and tables   xi
About the authors   xii
Acknowledgements   xv
Foreword   xvii

Introduction   **1**
  Sean MacBlain, Louise Long and Jill Dunn

  The aims of the book   1
  Perspectives on dyslexia   3
  Pupil well-being and well-becoming   6
  Why we need to understand child-centred approaches   8
  The organisation of the book   10
  How readers can get the best from the book   12

**PART 1   NEW HORIZONS FOR PUPILS WITH
            DYSLEXIA**   **15**

**1   Changing experiences in childhood: challenges for
     the 21st century**   **17**
  Sean MacBlain

  Chapter aims   17
  Introduction   17
  Dyslexia and the changing nature of childhood   19
  Emerging curricula: current and proposed initiatives   23
  The changing nature of schools: implications for dyslexia   28
  Summary   37
  Recommended reading   37
  References   37

2 Child-centred literacy pathways: pupils' perspectives   **39**
Louise Long

Chapter aims   39
Introduction   40
Exploring critical literature on pupil voice   41
Metacognition in the context of voice   42
Innovative methodologies for exploring the views of young learners   45
An illustrative case study: the views of young learners   46
Implications for transforming practice   52
Summary   55
Recommended reading   55
References   56

3 Meeting the needs of children with dyslexia and developmental literacy difficulties: holistic approaches   **59**
Sean MacBlain

Chapter aims   59
Introduction   59
The nature of emotional intelligence   66
Developing emotional intelligence   72
Self-efficacy and its relevance   74
Summary   77
Recommended reading   78
References   78

PART 2 BUILDING CAPACITY TO RAISE LITERACY STANDARDS FOR CHILDREN WITH DYSLEXIA AND DEVELOPMENTAL LITERACY DIFFICULTIES   **81**

4 Child-centred approaches to the identification and assessment of dyslexia and developmental literacy difficulties   **83**
Sean MacBlain and Louise Long

Chapter aims   83
Introduction   83
Formal and informal assessment   84
Low achievement   94
Underachievement   95
Advancing inclusivity for pupils with EAL who have dyslexia   95
Dyslexia and comorbidity: coexistence with other developmental disorders   99

Summary	105
Recommended reading	105
References	106

5   Raising literacy standards: perspectives on best practice   109
Sean MacBlain, Louise Long and Jill Dunn

Chapter aims	109
Introduction	109
Key principles of working with children with dyslexia and literacy difficulties	110
Identifying best practice in Early Years settings	113
Identifying best practice in primary schools	115
Fostering and advancing partnerships: home, school, community and child	121
Teachers in training: challenges for schools	123
Summary	126
Recommended reading	126
References	127

6   Advancing inclusive cultures for literacy learning in the mainstream primary school   131
Louise Long

Chapter aims	131
Introduction	131
The educational context	132
Professional learning communities	133
Collaborative modes of inquiry	138
An illustrative case study	141
Implications	147
Summary	149
Recommended reading	149
References	150

PART 3   LITERACY IN CONTEMPORARY SETTINGS   155

7   New literacies in the classroom: forging culturally responsive curricula   157
Jill Dunn

Chapter aims	157
Introduction	157

New literacies   158
Following children's interests   164
Accessing the views of children   171
Summary   174
Recommended reading   175
References   175

PART 4   CONCLUSIONS   **179**

8   Contemporary Challenges: Looking To The Future   **181**
Sean MacBlain, Jill Dunn and Louise Long

Chapter aims   181
Introduction   181
Child centredness: implications for practice in the
    21st-century classroom   182
Key principles in providing for children with dyslexia
    in the inclusive classroom   186
Mentoring teachers in training: implications and
    challenges for schools   190
Summary   192
Recommended reading   192
References   192

Appendix: Useful Websites   194
Index   199

LIST OF FIGURES AND TABLES

Figure

2.1 Consultation, cognition and capacity building   44

Table

3.1 Case study – Michael (Wechsler Intelligence Scale for
     Children IV – composite scores)   62
3.2 Case study – Michael (literacy scores)   62
4.1 Case study – Alex (results from my most recent assessment)   91
4.2 Case study – Alex (results from my previous assessment)   91

ABOUT THE AUTHORS

Sean MacBlain is Reader in Child Development and Disability at the University of St Mark and St John. Before taking up his current position Sean worked as a Senior Lecturer in Education and Developmental Psychology at Stranmillis University College, a College of Queen's University Belfast. Prior to working as an academic, Sean worked as an educational psychologist in Belfast and Somerset, and continues in this field in his own private practice, *SMB Associates SW LTD* (enquiries@ seanmacblain.com). Sean's research interests include the professional development of teachers and Early Years practitioners and the social and emotional development of children and young people with special educational needs and disabilities. Sean is married to Angela and lives in Devon, England.

Louise Long is a senior lecturer in education at Saint Mary's University College Belfast where she coordinates a number of Masters modules in special educational needs and pastoral issues, as well as postgraduate programmes on child development. She is engaged in the supervision of M-level research dissertations. Louise is a chartered educational psychologist and has previously worked as an Education and Library Board psychologist, primary school teacher and Further Education lecturer. From September 2012 to November 2013 Louise was seconded to the post of assistant project manager (research) on a DE-funded project, which aimed to build capacity in literacy and dyslexia in Northern Irish primary schools. Louise's research interests are in inclusive teacher learning, dyslexia and pupil well-being. She has published extensively in national and international peer-reviewed journals and has contributed to international books on teacher education. In the last five years Louise has procured funding for a number of research projects on inclusion and dyslexia.

Jill Dunn is a senior lecturer in Stranmillis University College, Belfast. She was a primary school teacher working in Foundation Stage and Key Stage 1 classrooms before moving into teacher education. Jill teaches widely across the BEd and PGCE Early Years programmes. However, her main interests lie in the teaching of literacy in the early years. Jill completed her EdD in 2013 and her dissertation focused on children's views on using popular culture to teach writing. She has been involved in a number of funded research projects on literacy and is currently involved in an evaluation of iPads in the Early Years. Jill lives in Lisburn, Northern Ireland with her husband Ian and two daughters Holly and Katy.

ACKNOWLEDGEMENTS

The authors would like to offer their thanks to Amy Jarrold who, from the outset, was supportive and encouraging and who allowed the idea for this text to take shape. Our thanks must also go to Miriam Davey whose support has been much appreciated.

Sean would like to acknowledge the support he has received from his colleagues at the University of St Mark and St John, in particular Dr Ian Luke – Dean of the Faculty of Education, Health and Welfare, Kathy Jarrett – Programme Leader for Primary PGCE, Sally Eales – Academic Lead for Primary Initial Teacher Training, and Anne Purdy – a fellow specialist in the field of dyslexia. Sean also wishes to acknowledge the support he has had in the past from his colleague Sharon James whose understanding of children and children's literature is of the highest order. Finally, Sean wishes to acknowledge the depth of insight he gained into dyslexia whilst working in the Language Development Centre (LDC) at Millfield School (Edgarley Hall) from his colleague DJH – the most inspiring of practitioners.

Louise wishes to express her gratitude to the children, schools and families who participated in the research activities that helped to inform her contributions to this book. Her thanks are also extended to the staff of the Writing Centre and the Library at Saint Mary's University College, Belfast for their guidance and professional and personal support. Standing Conference on Teacher Education North and South (SCoTENS) informed the illustrative case study in Chapter 2.

Louise wishes to say a big thank you to her children, Ellen and Sarah, for their patience and sense of perspective. Finally, she wishes to extend her warmest regards to her friend J; she knows that he was with her every step of the way.

Jill has been very fortunate throughout her career in teaching and teacher education to learn from, and to continue to learn from, many wonderful people including colleagues in the education profession, student teachers, parents, and of course the children themselves. Jill would like to thank colleagues who read and gave advice on draft copies of chapters, and she would particularly like to thank those teachers, parents and children who gave her permission to draw on her teaching and research experiences for inclusion in this book.

FOREWORD

This book makes an important and timely contribution to the literature on inclusion generally as well as improving understanding specifically in relation to the development of literacy for children with dyslexia. All children have a right to an education that enables them to develop to their fullest potential and to do so in an environment that supports and engages with them and their parents. Since it is widely recognised that good literacy is a crucial component in an effective education that enables children to fulfill their potential and to contribute to and benefit from the societies in which they live, it is important that children who experience particular challenges in this area are provided with the support they need to develop and learn. This book aims to inform practice in the area of literacy and dyslexia by providing educators with practical, yet evidence-informed strategies to support children both academically and emotionally.

Dyslexia is a learning difficulty that affects children across the boundaries of gender, race and socio-economic status. There is a common misconception and misrepresentation of the condition as the property of pushy middle-class parents who brandish it as an excuse for their children's underachievement and use it to skewer resources towards their child. However, this book not only refutes such assertions but does so in a way that recognises that appropriate support is not just the entitlement of all but is especially important for children living in homes characterised by poverty, deprivation, neglect and/or lack of positive social and emotional modelling and support. Too many of these children fail to have their dyslexia recognised and dealt with as their primary presenting problems in school are often attributed to poor behaviour and lack of motivation. Too many also end up in 'bottom' sets and disengage from education or become disaffected and drop out. This book provides educators with understanding and skills that can enable them to identify every child's academic and social and emotional needs in this area and meet them effectively, promptly and inclusively, avoiding the adverse consequences that may flow when they are missed.

From the perspective of children's rights, it is commendable that there is an overarching focus on putting the child at the centre of practice and recognising the role that adults have to play in ensuring that every child reaches their potential and benefits from an inclusive education. Of note is the emphasis in a number of chapters on ensuring that children's views are sought and taken seriously in the decisions that affect them. This can be particularly important for children with dyslexia since their difficulties with learning and communication can have a negative impact on their self-esteem. Several of the chapters provide concrete examples of ways in which adults can engage with children in practical and engaging ways that will not only improve the learning experience but also enable children to develop their communication skills further. Likewise, the emphasis on engagement with the child's home provides further strategies for supporting parents to support their child's learning and development.

One of the most appealing features of the book is the way in which it blends accessible yet thorough summaries of the research evidence with practical exercises that prompt reflection and which will undoubtedly contribute to informing and improving professional practice. Moreover, all of this is considered across a wide range of contemporary issues and challenges ranging from the use of digital media to the particular challenges for EAL children. The wealth of both practical and scholarly experience of the three authors shines throughout the book as does their commitment to ethical practice. It will, I am sure, be a very welcome and much-used resource for those educators who are working to ensure that all children with dyslexia receive the support for literacy to which they are entitled.

Professor Laura Lundy
Director, Centre for Children's Rights,
School of Education,
Queen's University, Belfast.

INTRODUCTION

Sean MacBlain, Louise Long and Jill Dunn

The aims of the book

Literacy is central to the classroom, home, and local and wider community experiences of children and young people. Reading and writing are reciprocally related to children's holistic well-being and sustained 'well-becoming' in terms of their social, emotional and cognitive development, academic progression and overall sense of fulfilment in life and work. In most cases, the reading and writing processes are successful, but in some cases they fail. These failures in reading and writing are usually expressed through inaccurate and dysfluent word reading and/or spelling and are commonly termed *dyslexia* (Breznitz, 2012). Dyslexia can be conceptualised as a developmental language disorder that manifests itself in atypical literacy development (Snowling, 2000). For the purposes of this book, the term *developmental literacy difficulty* frequently appears alongside the term dyslexia. A developmental literacy difficulty refers to reading and writing that progress along normal lines of development but at a slower rate than would be expected given the learner's chronological age. The authors propose that approaches to assessment and intervention for both dyslexia and developmental literacy difficulties are underpinned by the same principles, which are as follows: identifying the child's strengths and weaknesses and tailoring intervention pathways to his/her unique learning profile.

However, the aim of this book is to move beyond an examination of the nuts and bolts of teaching reading and spelling to learners with dyslexia and developmental literacy difficulties to explore inclusive practices that embrace affective, metacognitive and social dimensions to literacy education, and empower parents, teachers, communities and most importantly, learners. The authors welcome a view of inclusion that encompasses diversity in a broad sense. However, this book is concerned with inclusion in terms of removing barriers to participation and raising standards in pupils with special educational needs (SEN) in literacy. Reid (2011) rightly noted that recent years have witnessed a growing global willingness among practitioners and policymakers to develop knowledge and expertise in dealing with dyslexia in the classroom. However, the authors propose that there is still much to be done to raise awareness of the essence of, and need for, child-centred approaches to raising standards in literacy in early years and primary contexts.

The basic claim of this book is that child-centred and culturally fair approaches to assessment and intervention are at the core of raising literacy standards in learners with dyslexia and developmental literacy difficulties. The book provides a text that is contextualised within two intertwining frameworks concerned with enhancing the quality of the life experiences of children and young people in general and, in particular, learners with SEN in literacy. One is the 'Every Child Matters' (ECM) agenda (DCSF, 2004) in terms of accountability and best practice in promoting the following for children and young people: staying safe, being healthy, enjoying and achieving, experiencing economic well-being and making a positive contribution. The other is the Rose Report (Rose, 2009); an enlightened and comprehensive review that makes the case for high quality, inclusive provisions and evidence-based, personalised learning pathways for children with dyslexia. This book is designed for students, practitioners and lecturers in Higher Education Institutions from the disciplines of education, psychology, sociology, nursing, speech and language therapy, and paediatric medicine. The book aims to inspire those professionals who work in the best interests of children to embrace more sensitive approaches to dealing with dyslexia and developmental literacy difficulties by placing children at the heart of everything they do in research and in practice. It is hoped that, in particular, the book will enhance knowledge and understanding in teacher educators, teachers and education specialists, of the holistic needs of children with additional needs in literacy in early years and primary contexts, as well as 'best-fit' child-centred teaching and learning methodologies. Moreover, the authors hope that this new and renewed knowledge and understanding of dyslexia and developmental literacy difficulties will empower practitioners to enable all young learners with SEN in literacy to reach their full potential, academically and aesthetically, so that they can experience a 'sense of being valued and belonging' in schools, homes, communities and society as a whole. Thus, self-efficacy is a key principle that will be addressed within this text.

The chapter turns now to set the scene for an overview of some contemporary perspectives on dyslexia by citing the views expressed over five decades ago by two celebrated pioneers in the field of dyslexia and literacy, Gillingham and Stillman (1966) who in the fifth edition of their seminal programme offered the following:

> ... children who have never failed are wonderful to observe. Their assurance and joy in achievement are even more thrilling than is the happiness of the remedial cases who have failed and are now realising success. For those who have once failed bear deep in the shadowy places of their thought the lurking fear that some new demand may be made upon them which they cannot meet. They have deeply ingrained in their unconscious minds that most devastating of all lessons – that failure can follow earnest effort. It is this insecurity, which the children, selected in the Kindergarten and taught according to their needs, never have to suffer. (p. 21)

Perspectives on dyslexia

> When teachers ask if the child they have referred to me has dyslexia, I first ask them what they understand by the term dyslexia. I'm never quite sure if we have a shared understanding of what it means to be dyslexic. Most teachers, in my experience, see dyslexia as a learning difficulty that is primarily concerned with reading and spelling. I find many parents to be the same, though intuitively they have a far better understanding of the emotional difficulties their children are experiencing, but then that's not surprising. I think teachers can gain an enormous amount from listening carefully to what children with dyslexia say about their literacy learning experiences and to what parents of children with dyslexia say about their child's emotional needs. (Interview with an Educational Psychologist)

It can be argued that dyslexia has been one of the most contentious and hotly debated disorders within the field of education and one that still remains clouded by confusion, uncertainty, and perhaps most of all, controversy. For the purposes of this book, the authors are endorsing a recent independent review, *Identifying and Teaching Children and Young People with Dyslexia and Literacy Difficulties* (Rose, 2009). This review drew upon a large evidence base and took as its working definition that dyslexia is a disorder primarily affecting reading and spelling development, usually associated with impairments in phonological processing, verbal processing speed and verbal short-term memory. The working definition also acknowledged that other features that affect educational attainment could accompany dyslexia (comorbidities), though these are not in themselves characteristics of dyslexia. Snowling (2012) noted that the evolution of this viewpoint of dyslexia can be traced back to the landmark Isle of Wight study differentiating specific from general reading difficulties (Rutter and Yule, 1975), through the now classic argument of Stanovich (1994) that questioned the utility of the 'discrepancy definition of dyslexia, to the contemporary view of dyslexia as a phonological deficit' (Vellutino et al., 2004). Against this backdrop, a set of definitions will now be presented to highlight that 'dyslexia' is not a disorder with clear-cut boundaries or with a single cause and that the utility of 'dyslexia' as a diagnostic label is debatable.

Only a few years ago, Everatt and Reid (2009) cited in Reid (2009, p. 3) offered the following:

> there is still no clear explanation that is universally accepted of what exactly constitutes dyslexia. Identification is still riddled with controversies despite the emergence of a number of new tests to identify dyslexia ... Indeed, there is still an ongoing debate on the value of dyslexia as an identifiable syndrome.

More recently, Reason and Stothard (2013, p. 12) made reference to Professor Dorothy Bishop, who, in her keynote address to the British Psychological Society at their Annual Conference questioned how useful the term 'dyslexia' was when taking a theoretical or clinical stance by offering the following:

> She considered the commonalities between the various labels such as dyslexia, dyscalculia, dyspraxia, dysphasia and ADHD and autism. They had complex causations from a mixture of multiple genetic and environmental sources and there was much overlap. It did not make sense to single out specific labels. Her suggestion was

that we should use 'neurodevelopmental disability' as a generic term and then add descriptors indicating areas of major difficulty. This would not force us to slot a person into a diagnostic category.

Others have also addressed the theme of how useful the term dyslexia is. Buckler and Castle (2014, p. 199) have, for example, commented as follows:

> ...dyslexia is not to be viewed as a 'difficulty': it is only a difficulty if the teacher is unable to match appropriate activities with the child's specific needs. Indeed, despite dyslexia synonymously being referred to as a 'specific learning difficulty', the British Dyslexia Association would prefer to use the term 'specific learning difference': that children with dyslexia learn differently to other children, yet as we have consistently maintained ... all children learn differently as they are all individual.

 Exercise

Consider the pros and cons of teachers disregarding the term 'dyslexia' and instead using the term 'neurodevelopmental disability' when talking with parents of pupils in their class who have severe and persistent difficulties in literacy.

 Useful link

Readers might wish to visit the following link *'Diagnosing Dyslexia'*. This link offers a range of insights into the experiences of children, young people and adults who have dyslexia: http://www.youtube.com/watch?v=M1tA-5hfKJk

Yet another essential consideration in any discussion on current perspectives on dyslexia and developmental literacy difficulties is an understanding of how literacy is changing in our rapidly expanding technological society. Lankshear and Knobel (2011) suggest that teaching pupils to decode, encode and comprehend printed alphabetic texts was part of the time-honoured instructional methods prior to the 1970s. However, they suggest that 'new' literacies are made of different stuff since established social practices have been transformed and continue to emerge at a rapid rate. This has resulted in new ways of producing, distributing, exchanging and receiving texts by electronic means. The multimodal nature of these texts results in meaning being expressed through a combination of modes such as spoken and written language, images, icons, sounds, layout and animation (Flewitt, 2013). This is a wider challenge for education in general to move on from conventional literacies that populate formal education in the classroom and to embrace new and powerful cultural tools so that we can shape the learning environments in which our children grow up (Kucirkova, 2013). However, it is also a very important issue in considering how we can best meet the needs of children with dyslexia and developmental literacy difficulties so that they are prepared for communication and literacy in a digital future which is evolving rapidly.

Pupil well-being and well-becoming

Recently, Whitebread (2012, p. 15) commented as follows:

> Within schools and other educational contexts, emotions are sometimes seen as a distraction, as an aspect of human behaviour, which has to be coped with, but which is essentially irrelevant to the business of learning. In fact, everything we now know about the developing child powerfully suggests that this is a misguided and potentially highly damaging view.

Some years earlier Bigge and Shermis (2004, p. 5) rather worryingly pointed towards a perceived lack of attention given to theories of education and learning by many teachers and the impact this has on their teaching. At the time, they clearly felt confident enough to write as follows:

> teachers who do not make use of a systematic body of theory in their day-to-day decisions are behaving blindly; little evidence of long-range rationale, purpose, or plan is observable in their teaching. Thus, teachers without a strong theoretical orientation inescapably make little more than busy-work assignments. True, some teachers operate in this way and use only a hodge-podge of methods without theoretical orientation. However, this muddled kind of teaching undoubtedly is responsible for many of the current adverse criticisms of public education.

Around the same time, Jarvis (2005, p. 204) also rather worryingly pointed towards the lack of attention given by most teachers to research in their professional field:

> Education differs from comparable professions, such as medicine and psychology, in that although there is a thriving field of professional research, it takes place largely in isolation from professional practice. It is a rare doctor that does not pursue the medical research literature at least occasionally, and it would be unusual for a psychologist not to at least dip into current psychological literature – this is a requirement if they have chartered status ... but teachers largely ignore education research.

Such views are concerning and emphasise the importance of teachers striving to not only develop their management of children's behaviours and follow predesigned 'top-down' curricula, but, perhaps more importantly, critically engaging with the relevance and effectiveness of their own practice and why they teach as they do. This is especially important where children are failing in their learning; in primary schools this mostly revolves around the acquisition of literacy. For children with dyslexia a pressing need is for their teachers to understand the condition, know how it affects individuals and have internalised a range of relevant and purposeful interventions that are effective and that lead to success. For children to gain success and feel good about themselves as learners teachers must also intuitively feel part of this process and properly understand how to address the individual needs of each of those pupils who are failing to acquire literacy. Theory, therefore, should inform practice. Less than a decade ago Hartas (2006, p. 28) commented as follows:

> There is ... another, less obvious and acknowledged side to dyslexia. That of behavioural/social and emotional difficulties that are triggered by the frustration and low self-esteem that children with dyslexia typically experience. ... Some young children with dyslexia are vulnerable socially, especially those whose learning difficulties are compounded with restricted expressive and receptive language. In order for these children to be successfully included in the mainstream, they need support that integrates language, literacy and social skills development.

Contemporary research highlights the potential of digital technology in engaging and motivating children in their literacy learning. Research also demonstrates that technology has a significant role to play in developing children's identity as effective learners in the classroom through its potential to offer stimulating and varied pathways into literacy that are empowering for all young learners, including those that experience difficulties in learning (Flewitt et al., 2014). Many children with literacy difficulties experience low self-esteem yet digital technology has the potential to allow children to form 'new identities' as a good speller or an improving reader. Therefore, it is crucial that teachers consider the research evidence for the potential of digital technology in empowering all children in their literacy learning since the technology on its own is neutral. It is teachers who will shape and create the learning environment through the use of the technology and allow the potential transformation and enrichment of learning (Kucirkova, 2013), while also allowing children who struggle with literacy the possibility to experience that sense of achievement and success.

Why we need to understand child-centred approaches

Schools should be enabling all learners to reach their potential by placing pupils' needs at the centre of all that they do in regard to policy and practice. Moreover, schools ought to be promoting cultures of achievement and ambition, and equality of opportunity, and have high standards for promoting the welfare, well-being and 'well-becoming' of all learners. Child-centred educational provisions are about ensuring that every child receives a high-quality educational experience and appropriate support to enable him/her to overcome any barriers to learning. Less than a decade ago the United Nations declared the entitlement to literacy to be one of our most basic human rights (MacBlain et al., 2005, p. 54). However, children who experience difficulties in the acquisition of literacy are seriously disadvantaged and in too many cases fail to realise their academic potential or acquire necessary qualifications, and, perhaps most importantly of all, they develop low self-esteem coupled with poor self-efficacy and feelings of failure. Consider the following example cited in MacBlain (2014, pp. 176–7):

 Example

Years ago, when I (Sean) was training teachers to gain a postgraduate diploma that qualified them to teach children with dyslexia, I was struck by one particular case that has never left me. As part of the course, which was validated by the Royal Society of Arts and the

British Dyslexia Association, teachers taking the course had to work with a primary aged child, a secondary aged child and an adult, all of whom had significant problems with literacy. One of the teachers began working with an elderly lady in her late sixties who was, for all intents and purposes illiterate – she had never learned to read or write. She was intelligent and had a lovely sense of humour. When the teacher began working with her it became clear that this lady had one aim in her mind – to open a bank account, acquire a cheque book and go to the local toy store and buy a large red tractor for her little grandson of five years of age *using her cheque book*. The teacher began working with her, teaching her initially how to write her name in capital letters and then her signature. As the weeks progressed, this lady learned how to write her address, how to write the letters up to one hundred, the name of the toy store, and so on. The teacher then took her to the bank where she opened a bank account. A week later she received her cheque book and after many, many trials writing out the amount of '*Twenty eight pounds and 50 pence only*' on spare paper and practising her signature she set out with the teacher to the toyshop where they collected the large red tractor from the shelf and approached the checkout. With the teacher standing right behind her the grandmother then produced her cheque book, asked the till attendant how much the tractor was, and then wrote a cheque for the correct sum.

This example clearly demonstrates how difficulties in the acquisition of literacy can have hugely adverse effects upon the lives of individuals throughout childhood and even into late adulthood. This was an important learning experience for the teacher in this example and with her own student group with whom she shared the experience subsequently.

At the centre of children's activities in primary schools is the acquisition of literacy. For those who experience difficulties the impact can be devastating. Indeed, it is hard to understand how so many children can attend primary school for years and yet transfer to secondary education with poor literacy and in some cases an inability to read even the simplest of texts. Perhaps this emphasises the paramount need for starting where the child is rather than where the curriculum states they should be. Child-centred approaches have always been premised on the view that all children are different and education should be based on the needs of the individual child. Teachers need to be in tune, not only with children's needs, but also with their interests and wider experiences within their home and community settings. The literature documents the growing gap between children's experiences of school literacies and real-life literacy practices of home and community. The Cambridge Primary Review (Alexander, 2009) reports that while children value home as being a private place they want bridges between their family and academic lives. The Committee on the Rights of the Child, General Comment No. 12 recognises the significance of the teacher's role and states that they need an understanding of the socio-economic, environmental and cultural context of children's lives (UN, 2009). The reality is that technology surrounds us and the technology industry is targeting children more and more (Ernest et al., 2014). With the emerging availability of cheaper and more portable technology, children have greater and more sustained access to a wide range of media and are using it daily for their own purposes and developing their early literacy skills in the process. Of course, this technology can be both helpful and harmful and the government is currently funding a major study led by Imperial College London into the health risks of mobile phones and other wireless technologies (Triggle, 2014). However, whether you are a techno-sceptic or a techno-enthusiast it is time to move on from this dichotomised conflict (Kucirkova, 2013) and recognise the potential for bridging the home–school literacy gap, capitalising on what children are familiar and comfortable with and recognising the possibilities of digital technology in more child-centred approaches to the teaching of literacy for all children.

The organisation of the book

The book is divided into four main sections.

Part 1: New horizons for pupils with dyslexia

Chapter 1 explores the changing nature of childhood, families and cultures and the impact of these upon children with dyslexia and developmental literacy difficulties. In this chapter, the reader is introduced to a number of current and proposed initiatives including the *Statutory Framework for the Early Years*, issues relating to proposed assessment at 11 and the increased emphasis upon the teaching of phonics. The changing nature of schooling in the UK and the implications this has for children with dyslexia and developmental literacy difficulties is also examined.

Chapter 2 explores challenges and potentials in eliciting and giving influence to the voice of children with dyslexia and developmental literacy difficulties. In this chapter, Louise makes a compelling argument that creative methodologies are a child-centred approach to increasing pupil participation and a shared understanding of pupils' strengths and needs. Capturing children's views in this way should ultimately enhance classroom practice, and the authenticity and richness of data yielded from empirical studies.

Chapter 3 addresses the importance of emotional intelligence and its relevance to children experiencing difficulties with the acquisition of literacy. The chapter also explores how developing emotional intelligence can impact positively upon children with dyslexia and developmental literacy difficulties, with a key focus being an examination of the importance of self-efficacy and its relevance to this group of children.

Part 2: Building capacity to raise literacy standards for children with dyslexia and developmental literacy difficulties

Chapter 4 considers child-centred approaches to the identification and assessment of dyslexia and developmental literacy difficulties. In this chapter, Sean and Louise examine how to develop purposeful assessment approaches that build a profile of the pupil's strengths and needs in partnership with parents and communities, and relevant professionals from health and education. Contemporary issues in advancing culturally fair assessment processes for pupils with English as an Additional Language (EAL) and in diagnosing co-morbidity are discussed.

Chapter 5 provides a detailed analysis of the critical ingredients of child-centred learning pathways for children with dyslexia and developmental literacy difficulties. Here, all the authors offer rich and fruitful suggestions for advancing inclusive literacy practices in early years and primary contexts, and for promoting home-school-pupil-community partnerships.

Chapter 6 broadens the focus of the book so far to provide a discussion on capacity building in schools and the potential of professional learning communities for advancing inclusive school cultures. In this chapter, Louise presents evidence to support the argument that the information gathered from pupils with additional needs in literacy about their teaching and learning arrangements, when used in combination with collaborative modes of school improvement, forms an empowering and learner-centred way to develop a language of possibility for transformation.

Part 3: Literacy in contemporary settings

Chapter 7 explores the rapidly changing nature of literacy and what it means to be literate in the 21st century and the impact of this on children with dyslexia and developmental literacy difficulties. The chapter emphasises the importance of tuning into children's interests in order to motivate them to learn and to make education meaningful in contemporary classrooms. Readers are invited to reflect upon the United Nations Convention on the Rights of the Child (UNCRC) Article 12 and consider why, and how, we might listen to children's voices about learning. Consideration is also given to the importance of recognising children's home literacy experiences and, particularly, the importance of utilising these to enhance the literacy experiences of children with dyslexia and developmental literacy difficulties.

Part 4: Conclusions

The book concludes with a final chapter, 'Contemporary Challenges: Looking to the Future', which addresses the challenges we are currently faced with and the nature of some of the key challenges that will face practitioners, children and families in the future. More specifically, this last chapter explores the implications for child-centred practice with children with dyslexia and developmental literacy difficulties in the 21st-century classroom. In doing so, key principles in providing for children with dyslexia in the inclusive classroom are identified and the importance of fostering and advancing partnerships between home, school, community and the child are emphasised and discussed, together with an examination of issues central to the mentoring of teachers in training and the implications and challenges these will entail.

The chapters are organised as follows:

- Chapter aims;
- An exploration of critical literature and empirical studies related to the aims of the chapter;
- Appropriate and focused exercises and discussion points;
- Illustrative case studies from early years and primary contexts that should help readers to transmit new knowledge and understanding into practice; and
- Summary of key points emerging from the chapter.

How readers can get the best from the book

Whilst this text can be read from beginning to end it can also be used as a resource. Students who are exploring assessment in early years contexts, for example, may wish to focus their reading on Chapter 4 whilst those wishing to explore the concept of professional learning communities will concentrate their reading on Chapter 6. An initial reading of the text will allow the reader to locate particular areas of interest relevant to their own thinking and professional practice.

Readers are provided with a number of examples throughout the text, which act as important reference points for their own thinking and experience as well as the ideas and issues, raised within each chapter. A number of exercises are also offered throughout with the intention that readers use these to reflect not only on the content of the text but also on their own personal observations and interpretations of professional practice.

References

Alexander, R. (ed.) (2009) *Children, their World, their Education. Final Report and Recommendations of the Cambridge Primary Review*. London: Routledge.

Bigge, M.L. and Shermis, S.S. (2004) *Learning Theories for Teachers* (6th edn). Boston: Pearson.

Breznitz, Z. (2012) *Fluency in Reading: Synchronisation of Processes*. New York: Psychology Press.

Buckler, S. and Castle, P. (2014) *Psychology for Teachers*. London: Sage.

Department for Children, Schools and Families (DCSF) (2004) *The Children's Act*. London: DCSF.

Ernest, J.M., Causey, C., Newton, A.B., Sharkins, K., Summerlin, J. and Albaiz, N. (2014) 'Extending the Global Dialogue about Media, Technology, Screen Time, and Young Children', *Childhood Education*, 90(3): 182–91.

Flewitt, R.S. (2013) 'Early Literacy: A Broader Vision', TACTYC Occasional Paper 3. Available at: http://tactyc.org.uk/occasional-paper/occasional-paper3.pdf (accessed 27 May 2014).

Flewitt, R., Messer, D. and Kucirkova, N. (2014) 'New Directions for Early Literacy in a Digital Age: The iPad', *Journal of Early Childhood Literacy*, published online 20 May 2014. DOI: 10.1177/1468798414533560.

Gillingham, A. and Stillman, B.W. (1966) *Remedial Training for Children with Specific Disability in Reading, Spelling, and Penmanship* (5th edn). Cambridge, MA: Educators Publishing Service, INC.

Hartas, D. (2006) *Dyslexia in the Early Years: A Guide to Teaching and Learning*. London: Routledge.

Jarvis, M. (2005) *The Psychology of Effective Learning and Teaching*. Cheltenham: Nelson Thornes.

Kucirkova, N. (2013) 'Response to By-passing the Debate: Beyond the '"Technology Question"' in the Early Years by Associate Professor Suzy Edwards, TACTYC, 2013'. Available at: http://tactyc.org.uk/pdfs/Response-Kucirkova.pdf (accessed 27 May 2014).

Lankshear, C. and Knobel, M. (2011) *New Literacies* (3rd edn). London: Open University Press.

MacBlain, S.F., Hazzard, K. and MacBlain, F.M. (2005) 'Dyslexia: the Ethics of Assessment', *Academic Exchange Quarterly*, 9(1).

MacBlain, S.F. (2014) *How Children Learn*. London: Sage.

Reason, R. and Stothard, J. (2013) 'Is There a Place for Dyslexia in Educational Psychology Practice?' *Debate*, 146, March: 8–13.

Reid, G. (ed.) (2009) *The Routledge Companion to Dyslexia*. New York: Routledge.

Reid, G. (2011) *Dyslexia* (3rd edn). London: Continuum International Publishing Group.

Rose, J. (2009) *Identifying and Teaching Children and Young People with Dyslexia and Literacy Difficulties*. Available at: http://webarchive.national-archives.gov.uk/20130401151715/http://www.education.gov.uk/publications/eOrderingDownload/00659-2009DOM-EN.pdf

Rutter, M. and Yule, W. (1975) 'The Concept of Specific Reading Retardation', *Journal of Child Psychology and Psychiatry*, 16: 181–97.

Snowling, M.J. (2000) *Dyslexia* (2nd edn). Malden, MA: Blackwell.

Snowling, M.J. (2012) 'Changing Concepts of Dyslexia: Nature, Treatment and Comorbidity', *Journal of Child Psychology and Psychiatry*, 53(9): e1–e3. DOI: 10.1111/j.1469–7610.2009.02197.x

Stanovich, K.E. (1994) 'Annotation: Does Dyslexia Exist?', *Journal of Child Psychiatry*, 35: 579–95.

Triggle, N. (2014) 'Mobile Phone Child Health Risk Investigation', BBC News, 20 May 2014. Available at: http://www.bbc.co.uk/news/health-27475515 (accessed 29 May 2014).

UN (2009) *Committee on the Rights of the Child: General Comment No 12: The Right of the Child to be Heard (CRC/C/GC/12)*. Geneva: United Nations.

Vellutino, F.R., Fletcher, J.M., Snowling, M.J. and Scanlon, D.M. (2004) 'Specific Reading Disability (Dyslexia): What Have We Learned in the Past Four Decades?', *Journal of Child Psychology and Psychiatry*, 45: 2040.

Whitebread, D. (2012) *Developmental Psychology & Early Childhood Education*. London: Sage.

PART 1

NEW HORIZONS FOR PUPILS WITH DYSLEXIA

CHANGING EXPERIENCES IN CHILDHOOD: CHALLENGES FOR THE 21ST CENTURY

Sean MacBlain

Chapter aims

- To explore the changing nature of childhood, families and cultures and the impact of these upon children with dyslexia and developmental literacy difficulties.
- To introduce the reader to current and proposed initiatives including the *Statutory Framework for the Early Years*.
- To explore issues relating to proposed assessment at 11 and the teaching of phonics.
- To explore the changing nature of schooling in the UK and the implications for children with dyslexia and developmental literacy difficulties.

Introduction

This chapter opens by emphasising the variation in social contexts within which children with dyslexia and developmental literacy difficulties grow up. The effect of such variation upon the learning experiences of this group of children can be highly significant. Whilst many children with dyslexia grow up in affluent and stable families, others may find themselves born into families characterised by, for example, little interest in education, few if any reading materials, an over-emphasis upon watching television, lack of parental support for their children's school, and so on. Other children with dyslexia and developmental literacy difficulties may grow up in families where substance abuse is common and where parents are struggling to find enough income to provide adequate meals and suitable diets. At the time of writing this text the number of such children in the UK is not unsubstantial and is rising (MacBlain, 2014). Whilst all of these factors will impact significantly upon the progress of any young child, in the case of children with dyslexia and developmental literacy difficulties the impact may even be greater.

Families today are very different to those of previous decades. Schools are also changing in quite radical ways, with most children in England now being educated in *Academies* and *Free Schools*, where previously they were educated in schools that fell under Local Authority control. The means by which teachers are being prepared to enter the profession is also changing, with the developing model by which they are prepared to teach in England being one whereby they receive the majority of their training within schools as opposed to Higher Education Institutions (HEIs). In other parts of the UK, for example, Northern Ireland and Scotland, the training of teachers remains predominantly within HEIs. This clearly has major implications for the way in which children with dyslexia and developmental literacy difficulties will be taught in the future as the nature of their teachers' training will be significantly different and will depend to a much greater extent upon the expertise, and level of commitment to special educational needs, that exists within the schools where teachers are being trained. Indeed, it is likely that within a decade schooling in England will be largely unrecognisable to those who were schooled in the fifties and sixties.

What is becoming increasingly clear is the emerging and hardening reality that the experiences of pupils in schools who struggle with the acquisition of literacy, are vastly different. Much of their progress will, in reality, depend to a significant extent upon the type of school they attend, the quality of training their teachers have had, and, perhaps most importantly, the nature of the family experiences they have had during the early years. For children with underlying cognitive difficulties associated with dyslexia, the experiences they have in their families during their early years will be especially significant. It is during this crucial period of development that many of the building blocks are laid for future social and emotional development and the beginning stages of resilience are started.

Dyslexia and the changing nature of childhood

Family context and its impact

Families are changing at an unprecedented rate. With this change, comes significant variation in the level and quality of support offered to children. Many researchers and academics now prefer to use the term 'household' as opposed to 'family' to account for the complex nature of social units within which children grow up. It has been estimated, for example (MacBlain and MacBlain, 2004), that in 2001 there were over 3 million children growing up in households in Great Britain with a lone parent. In 2002, it was further estimated (National Statistics, 2003) that a fifth of dependent children in Great Britain were living within families headed by a lone parent. Rates of divorce have also been increasing at what many consider to be an alarming speed. Nearly two decades ago Rowntree (cited in Brown, 1999, p.66) alerted us to the fact that, 'If recent trends continue, more than a third of new marriages will end within twenty years and four out of ten will ultimately end in divorce'. Whilst many children who grow up in lone-parent families succeed and go on to do well academically, there are many who do not. Having adequate levels of effective support in developing their literacy skills when very young is extremely important. Not having this can be highly detrimental, and in the case of children with underlying specific learning difficulties this can be a major barrier to future learning and the realisation of their potential.

The effects upon children growing up in lone-parent households remain open to question, with much debate continuing to be exercised as to the actual impact upon children's learning. Just over a decade ago, Buckingham (2000, p. 65), for example, drew attention to the financial impact upon lone-parent families and poor employment prospects for some single parents, when he offered the following:

> Single-parent families are much more likely to live below the poverty line, and to be dependent on state benefits; while lone mothers are less likely to be employed than those in two-parent families.

More recently, the newspaper columnist James Chapman, writing in the popular British newspaper *The Daily Mail* (18 April 2011), remarked as follows:

> Some 46 per cent of children are born to unmarried mothers, according to research by the Centre for Social Justice. The think-tank said a child growing up in a one-parent family is 75 per cent more likely to fail at school...

Such comments need to be scrutinised, for it is undoubtedly the case that many children growing up in lone-parent families are happy and go on to succeed and live fulfilled lives. However, it must also be recognised that for many children with dyslexia who grow up in lone-parent families, there are additional and significant challenges for them stemming from financial hardship, lack of opportunities and, in some cases, high levels of deprivation.

What is clear is that poverty is a major issue in the lives of many children. This is not of course restricted to lone-parent families, for there are also very many families with two parents who are now experiencing significant financial hardship, which is impacting upon their children's lives, and learning. In 2009, Cullis and Hansen (2009, p. 13), for example, rather worryingly commented as follows:

> Recent research shows that every £100 of additional income in the first nine months of life makes the difference of about a month's development by age five. The poorest families cannot afford books, computers, equipment and extracurricular activities and their children's education is also more likely to suffer from poorer nutrition, household overcrowding and stress.

Clearly, children with literacy difficulties and, more particularly perhaps, those with dyslexia who grow up in the 'poorest' families will typically fail to have access to computers at home, or to reading materials and learning activities designed to complement and further what they do at school; the implications for how effectively these children then become included in high achieving and academically inspiring schools appears obvious. In a report entitled *Deprivation and Risk: The Case for Early Intervention* (Action for Children, 2010), Dr Ruth Lupton wrote:

> The relationship between deprivation and educational attainment is striking. Across the UK, children from the poorest homes start school with more limited vocabularies and greater likelihood of conduct problems and hyperactivity ... During primary school UK children fall further behind, and even the brightest children from the most disadvantaged backgrounds are overtaken by the age of 10 by their better-off peers who start off behind them... (p. 12)

In his annual report, *Unsure Start: HMCI's Early Years Annual Report 2012/13 Speech 2014* Sir Michael Wilshaw, Her Majesty's Chief Inspector (Ofsted), offered the following in regard to young children:

The poorest children are less likely to follow instructions, make themselves understood, manage their own basic hygiene or play well together. By age 5, many children have started reading simple words, talking in sentences and can add single numbers. But far fewer of the poorest can do these things well. Children from low-income families are far more likely than their better-off peers to lag behind at age three … Too many do badly by the end of primary, and carry on doing badly at the end of secondary. (Wilshaw, 2014, p. 3)

Sir Michael went on to emphasise the cost to the nation:

If the gap isn't closed, the costs to our nation will run into billions. The Sutton Trust estimates that the UK's economy would see cumulative losses of up to £1.3 trillion in GDP [Gross domestic product] over the next 40 years if the country fails to bring the educational outcomes of children from poorer homes up to the UK average. (p. 3)

Here, readers may wish to reflect upon the cost to the nation of the number of highly able and talented children with dyslexia who fail to reach their potential because they also have to contend with lack of opportunities deriving from their social and cultural contexts.

The emergence of the digital child

Now consider the nature of childhood today as compared with that of 20 or even 10 years ago. Most children now have mobile phones. From an early age they can access social websites almost daily, communicate with others who live many miles away, even in different countries and, through digital technology, gain access to aspects of the adult world that years ago would have been considered unthinkable. For most children growing up in the 21st century, much of the literacy they encounter and 'consume' is through digital technologies (see Chapter 7). In many respects, children have become consumers of written information. Unlike decades ago when almost all of the literacy encountered by children was in school and had a clear academic purpose, that of working towards examinations, much literacy now encountered by children is predominantly of a social nature. Today, children need reading and writing not just for the purposes of formal education but also as a means of social communication. The implications for children struggling with literacy are obvious. For many children with dyslexia and developmental literacy difficulties their limited skills with, for example, 'texting' and responding to written messages from others will have particular implications, and may even, in some cases, cause these children to feel excluded from social groupings.

 Example

Peter is the eldest of four children and lives with his mother in a small rural village. He is in his final year of primary education and will transfer to his local secondary school in a few months' time. When Peter was six years of age his father left the family home and he has been raised by his mother along with his twin sisters and his youngest sibling Jack who is now six years of age. Peter is described by his teacher as a *'bright child who struggles with most aspects of school work ... most weeks he turns up at school without his PE kit, often without a pen or pencil ... he is always getting into trouble for not completing homework or for leaving it at home, this has meant that he regularly has to stay behind to complete work he should have done at home'*. Since starting school Peter has struggled with reading and spelling. At a chronological age of 11 years and 6 months his reading age has been recently calculated by the SENCo to be 8 years and 6 months and his spelling age as 7 years 10 months. Peter's handwriting is very poor and his teacher has commented that *'times tables continue to be a mystery to Peter... I have almost given up with these, he just does not seem to be able to retain them'*. Peter has always found family life a struggle, especially after his father left. Since then, his mother has had to devote much of her time to looking after Peter's younger siblings. The time Peter could spend with his mother was further limited by the fact that she had to work on a part-time basis, occasionally during evenings and weekends, to earn money for the family as Peter's father had been contributing very little in the way of additional finances. Peter has, for some time, wanted a mobile phone and was given one for his last birthday. Though he treasures his new phone he has found great difficulty reading the messages his friends have sent him – he is frightened to ask anyone to read them for him.

 Exercise

Consider the wider difficulties facing Peter.

1 What steps might his teacher take to support Peter's mother in addressing issues relating to his social and emotional development?

2 How might an improvement in Peter's social and emotional
   development contribute to improved progress in his literacy skills?
3 Would it be of any value for his teacher to help him develop his
   skills with communicating by text on his new mobile telephone?

Emerging curricula: current and proposed initiatives

Statutory Framework for the Early Years

In September 2012, the UK government introduced the new *Statutory Framework for the Early Years Foundation Stage* (DfE, 2012), which is now mandatory for all Early Years providers, that is, maintained and non-maintained schools and independent schools, and all providers on the *Early Years Register* (there may be some exemptions to this final group). The new Framework is premised on the view that '... every child deserves the best possible start in life and the support that enables them to fulfil their potential' (DfE, 2012, p. 2). This view is echoed in the framework document *Learning to Learn* (Department for Education in Northern Ireland [DENI], 2013), which sets out the way forward for Early Years education and learning in Northern Ireland and aims to ensure that:

> ...every child can access high quality early learning experiences that equip them to develop improved cognitive, social and emotional skills and which lay important foundations for future learning and development. (p. 6)

The UK *Statutory Framework* embraces the view that children not only develop quickly but that the life experiences they have following birth and up to their commencement of formal schooling at five years of age are of major importance and have a significant impact upon later development and learning. Such a view is not new and has been well documented over generations by such philosophers as Rousseau, Froebel and Steiner (Gray and MacBlain, 2012; MacBlain, 2014). What is new, however, is the increased focus that government has placed upon all providers to offer young children provision that is both *effective* and *purposeful*, and that can be judged as central to their social and emotional development. Not surprisingly, good and positive parenting is also seen as being a key factor central to children's development in the early years. However and importantly, a clear emphasis is put on the importance of children being able to access high quality learning. But, what does 'high quality learning' actually mean for those children with dyslexia, many of whom will be faced with years of struggle in the areas of reading, spelling and writing?

The *Statutory Framework for the Early Years Foundation Stage* proposes four overarching principles, which should be central to practice in Early Years settings:

- every child is a **unique child**, who is constantly learning and can be resilient, capable, confident and self-assured [Readers should refer to the section on developing emotional intelligence in Chapter 3 in this volume];

- children learn to be strong and independent through **positive relationships**;

- children learn and develop well in **enabling environments**, in which their experiences respond to their individual needs and there is a strong partnership between practitioners and parents and/or carers; and

- **children develop and learn in different ways and at different rates**. (DfE, 2012, p. 3)

Now consider the following exercises:

 Exercise

Consider how realistic the above principles are for Early Years practitioners working with children from severely disadvantaged and dysfunctional homes.

1 What steps might teachers or Early Years practitioners take to ensure that young children from severely disadvantaged backgrounds who present with difficulties in the initial stages of literacy acquisition are properly supported?
2 What barriers might prevent teachers or Early Years practitioners from identifying reading problems in young children whose first language is not English?

Assessment at 11

There has been a recent and growing emphasis, especially in England, on assessment, with the Coalition government in the UK specifying a rapid return in the next few years to more formal examinations. There is also much greater emphasis being placed upon formal assessment, even in the Early Years, as a means of trying to raise national standards in literacy and numeracy. Such views are, of course, driven by ideologies, and it is worth, at this point, reflecting upon a number of relevant historical/political factors as a way of contextualising the debate surrounding formal assessment and examination in the UK, and especially at the age of 11 when most children finish the primary phase of their education.

In 1918, the *Fisher Act* made education compulsory for children from 5 to 14 years of age and passed responsibility for secondary education over to the state. In 1944 the *Butler Act* raised the school leaving age from 14 to 15 and formalised the division between primary and secondary schools at the age of 11. A particular feature of this Act was its creation of a system whereby children from age 11 could attend a Grammar, Technical or Secondary Modern School depending upon their academic performance as assessed through a formal examination, which became known as the '*Eleven Plus*'.

Two decades later, in 1965, the then Labour government in England released *Circular 10/65* in which it called upon Local Education Authorities to commence a process whereby they would begin converting secondary schools into the new *Comprehensive system*. Thus began the process of doing away with the then existing system of Grammar and Secondary Modern Schools as well as the *Eleven Plus* examination (MacBlain, 2014). At the time this was hugely controversial, and whilst many opposed the closure of Grammar Schools, others celebrated their demise and embraced the new Comprehensive system in which all children were to be educated alongside each other in the same school.

There are still many older individuals in the UK who assert with a certain amount of pride that they attended a Grammar School. Some may perceive this as an indication of their higher level of intelligence, as entry to Grammar Schools was traditionally through open competition, which involved passing the *Eleven Plus* examination. Equally, there are also significant numbers of older individuals who will still recall with sadness and a degree of pain and embarrassment their failure to pass the *Eleven Plus* examination and gain a place at a Grammar School. Many of this latter group may even recall their feelings at being separated from older siblings or friends because they had to attend different schools. They may also talk about how their life chances were adversely affected; most notably, perhaps, in a failure to go on to university. There will also be those individuals who, having failed to gain a place at Grammar School, have spent many years trying to prove to themselves and others that, in fact, they were as able as their peers who did gain a place at a Grammar School. Sadly, for many children, this situation continues in some areas of the UK, perhaps most notably in Northern Ireland where Grammar Schools are very much a part of the education system, with success in examinations at age 11 still being the means of entrance to these schools. The implications for children with dyslexia are clear, for their dyslexia will typically present additional challenges for them when engaging with these examinations. Readers may wish to reflect upon how many children in the past failed to gain access to Grammar Schools and how many continue to do so in parts of the UK, for example Northern Ireland, because of their dyslexia and what the emotional and social impact has been upon their development.

The increasing emphasis on phonics

There is no doubt that the teaching of phonics has enjoyed a significant comeback in the last decades prompted by the continued poor levels of literacy in the UK. This said, its re-emergence in primary schools and Early Years settings has been surrounded by controversy, with opinions being sharply divided as to its importance in the teaching of reading and spelling for all children. Teachers have been introducing children to phonics for decades if not generations in a whole variety of ways and with differing levels of emphasis. Whilst many children have acquired knowledge of phonics as a means of supporting their acquisition of literacy, there are also those who have learned to read, spell and write with little, if any, input in this area from their teachers.

The extent of the controversy surrounding the teaching of phonics to young children, and especially beginning readers, has also been demonstrated in the popular media. Hannah Richardson, the News Education reporter for an online BBC News report in January 2014, revealed the extent of the controversies surrounding the teaching of phonics in schools in England, in particular the apparent insistence of employing this method with young 'able readers':

> The Department for Education wants English schools to use the reading system, which requires children to blend common sounds into words. But Durham University researcher Andrew Davis says those already starting to read are likely to be put off.

Drawing further upon the views of Andrew Davis, Richardson then reported as follows:

> He says: 'To subject either the fully fledged readers, or those who are well on their way, to a rigid diet of intensive phonics is an affront to their emerging identities as persons.

'To require this of students who have already gained some maturity in the rich and nourishing human activity of reading is almost a form of abuse.' He agrees that phonics can be very useful for teaching reading, but argues it should not be rigidly imposed on all. He added that a strict approach to Synthetic Phonics, 'threatens the interests of a minority of children who arrive at school already able to read'.

In contrast to Davis' views, however, Richardson also reported on the views expressed by another academic, Dr David Waugh, also at Durham University, as follows:

He said there were many myths about teaching synthetic phonics and that the Rose Review which had promoted the idea had emphasised 'phonics being taught in the context of a broad, rich language curriculum, with lots of experience of good quality literature'.

'While I have reservations about the use of pseudo words in tests, I do feel that the emphasis upon developing children's phonic knowledge has brought important benefits … After years of many teachers having few ideas about how to teach reading beyond listening to children read, we now have structured strategies in place and teachers are trained to teach reading rather than simply to listen to it,' said Dr Waugh.

A key point emphasised here by David Waugh is the apparent lack of understanding and low skills base that too many teachers in the past appear to have had in regard to the complexities of teaching, and especially in being able to address the individual learning needs and learning styles of children they encounter. Readers may wish to reflect upon how many teachers working with young children have any in-depth understanding of the direct impact upon reading and spelling of poor working memory, poor perceptual skills, or deficits in the area of processing speed, which are areas of weakness common to many children with dyslexia.

The tensions that exist around the teaching of phonics have been further emphasised by the National Association for the Teachers of English (NATE). Reflecting the feelings of the Association's members, Hannah Richardson then went on to comment as follows:

A spokesman for … NATE … said that it had published a survey of its members last month and had found concerns about an 'over-emphasis' on phonics, which it warned 'can do more harm than good'. In particular, there were concerns about children being confused by the teaching of made-up phonetic 'non-words'.

'Our research concluded that the government case for an exclusive focus on 'systematic synthetic phonics' in early years instruction is poorly argued and unsupported by the evidence cited in the government's own documentation,' said the NATE spokesman.

A Department for Education spokeswoman said: 'Too many children are not reaching the expected levels of reading at a young age, do not catch up, and then struggle in secondary school and beyond.

'Research shows overwhelmingly that systematic phonics is the most effective way of teaching reading to children of all abilities, enabling almost all children to become confident and independent readers.

'Thanks to the phonics check 177,000 six-year-olds will this year get the extra reading help they need to catch up with their peers'.

It can be seen from the above that there is a sharp divergence in thinking when it comes to the teaching of phonics and, especially, the degree of emphasis that government places upon it within primary schools and Early Years settings.

 Exercise

Take time to reflect upon the arguments for and against the teaching of phonics and whether or not the debate has become overly simplistic, and then address the following questions:

1 Is the controversy surrounding phonics really less about what method of teaching reading is best for young children and more about a lack of understanding amongst many teachers of how to teach reading to children presenting with specific learning difficulties such as dyslexia?
2 How much emphasis would you put on teaching phonics to children starting school who can already read with some degree of fluency?

The changing nature of schools: implications for dyslexia

As emphasised earlier, the nature of the schools that children with dyslexia and developmental literacy difficulties attend and the type and quality of education their schools offer are central to the progress they will make. Despite a general consensus on the curriculum offered to children in the UK, however, there exists significant variation in the type of learning experiences that children receive. Schools vary enormously and the degree of variation is increasing. This is particularly the case in England with the recent rise in the number of *Academies, Free Schools* and *Faith Schools*. These 'newer' types of school now co-exist alongside already established *independent* or 'private' schools.

A hotly debated issue, especially in England, is that of the location of schools, or as it is popularly referred to, the 'post-code lottery', where some schools are viewed by parents as being much better because they are geographically situated in areas characterised by high levels of affluence and by parents with very high aspirations for their children. This has frequently raised the contentious issue of 'class', with accusations being made in some quarters that too many children with dyslexia are failing to gain entry to highly aspiring academic schools because of their poor academic attainments due mainly to their poor literacy skills and with places all too often going to children whose parents can afford to have them privately tutored. Recently (April 2012), Alison Kershaw, writing in the UK i-Newspaper, *The Independent*, drew attention to the following views expressed by Dr Mary Bousted, general secretary of the Association of Teachers and Lecturers (ATL):

> Dr Mary Bousted ... said stratified schools are 'toxic' for deprived youngsters. ... 'We have, in the UK, schools whose intakes are stratified along class lines. We have schools for the elite; schools for the middle class and schools for the working class. Too few schools have mixed intakes ... The effect of unbalanced school intakes is toxic for the poorest and most dispossessed. And whilst teachers and school leaders strain every sinew in these schools to raise aspiration and achievement, they struggle always against the effects of poverty, ill health and deprivation and children in these schools routinely fail to make the educational progress achieved by their more advantaged peers.' ... She claimed that the Government has cut funding for Sure Start centres, scrapped the education maintenance allowance for poorer teenagers, removed protected funding for school meals, cut council budgets and made tax reforms that are likely to hit low- to middle-income families ... 'Schools cannot vanquish these inequalities; they can ameliorate them, but in vastly unequal societies only the brightest will escape the lasting effects on inequality.'

It is of course important to acknowledge that the comments offered by Dr Bousted are not accepted by everyone and may not be accepted by all of the members of the union she represents. However, it is worth readers considering how children with dyslexia might be affected not only by their parents' socio-economic status but, perhaps more importantly, by the very nature of the schools they attend.

In June 2013, Ofsted published a report *The Most Able Students: Are They Doing as Well as They Should in Our Non-selective Secondary Schools?* that has raised many important issues regarding how more able children in 'non-selective state' secondary schools are progressing. The report offered the following:

> This survey investigated why so many of our brightest students in non-selective state secondary schools, including academies, fail to achieve their potential compared with students who attend selective and independent schools ... We also examined why relatively few students from non-selective state schools apply to, or gain places at, the most prestigious universities. The survey focused on two key questions.
>
> • Are the most able students in non-selective state secondary schools achieving as well as they should?
>
> • Why is there such disparity in admissions to the most prestigious universities between a small number of independent and selective schools and the great majority of state-maintained non-selective schools and academies? (Ofsted, 2013, pp. 6–7)

The report went on to emphasise the fact that too many of the most able children and young people in these schools were underperforming in state non-selective schools and offered the following rather worrying findings:

> Too many of our most able children and young people are under-performing in our non-selective state secondary schools. Many of these able students achieve reasonably well when compared with average standards but, nevertheless, fail to reach their full potential. This is most obvious when we consider the pupils who did well in both English and mathematics at primary school and then examine their achievement at GCSE five years later. At the national level:
>
> • Almost two thirds (65%) of high-attaining pupils leaving primary school, securing Level 5 in both English and mathematics, did not reach an A* or A grade in both these GCSE subjects in 2012 in

non-selective secondary schools. This represented over 65,000 students.

- Just over a quarter (27%) of these previously high-attaining students attending non-selective secondary schools did not reach a B grade in both English and mathematics at GCSE in 2012. This represented just over 27,000 young people.

- In 20% of the 1,649 non-selective 11 to 18 schools, not one student in 2012 achieved the minimum of two A grades and one B grade in at least two of the facilitating A-level subjects required by many of our most prestigious universities. (Ofsted, 2013, p. 5)

When one considers that a significant number of schools appear to be failing many more able children then one is also drawn to ask how, in reality, are these same schools supporting their pupils with dyslexia, many of whom will be intellectually very able but affected adversely by underlying problems associated with their dyslexia. Indeed, in regard to very able children with dyslexia who might be gifted and talented, Hartas (2006, p. 15) has commented as follows:

Able young children with dyslexia are likely to experience difficulties with short-term memory and hand-eye co-ordination, as well as frustration emanating from not being able to show their good intellect in their academic work. Motor skills, especially fine motor skills, often lag behind cognitive abilities, particularly in gifted children … Regarding their self-esteem, gifted young children with dyslexia tend to be highly self-critical in that they evaluate themselves on what they are unable to do, rather than on their substantial abilities, impacting on their sense of self-worth and emotional maturity and adjustment … (p. 15)

Hartas goes on to emphasise the need for Early Years practitioners to take particular note of a number of characteristics that can alert them to learning difficulties in their very able children as follows:

- presenting potential without necessarily being motivated

- showing a marked discrepancy between oral and written language

- having a low self-esteem and being self-critical

- displaying a short attention span and

- disguising their ability to alleviate peer pressure (p. 15)

We now turn our focus to the type of schools within which the majority of children in the UK are educated.

Academies

The number of Academies in the UK is growing and with this growth has come a separation from Local Authority control and the benefits that Local Authorities have offered in the past and might offer in the future. One key issue in the establishing and development of Academies is the fact that head teachers of Academies have much greater control over their budgets and, therefore, more control over the levels of resourcing for children in their schools with special educational needs such as dyslexia. This may mean that, in practice, some head teachers of Academies will spend less on resourcing children who continue to present with literacy difficulties and divert funding away from this group of children to others who are demonstrating higher levels of academic attainment and success, which will reflect positively upon their schools. One might suggest that the advocacy role originally adopted by Local Authorities has diminished considerably.

Understanding the context within which Academies have been introduced and developed is important. In February 2013, the Department for Education website cited in MacBlain (2014, p. 225) published the following information with regard to Academies, which are independent and publicly funded:

> Academies benefit from greater freedoms to innovate and raise standards. These include:
>
> * freedom from local authority control;
> * the ability to set their own pay and conditions for staff;
> * freedoms around the delivery of the curriculum; and
> * the ability to change the lengths of terms and school days ...
>
> Some academies ... will have a sponsor ... from a wide range of backgrounds including successful schools, businesses, universities, charities and faith bodies. Sponsors are held accountable for ... improving the performance of their schools. They do this by challenging traditional thinking on how schools are run ... They seek to make a complete

break with cultures of low aspiration and achievement ... Academies receive the same level of per-pupil funding as they would receive from the local authority ... plus additions to cover the services that are no longer provided for them by the local authority ... Schools which already select some or all of their pupils will be able to continue to do so if they become academies, but schools becoming academies cannot decide to become newly selective schools ... (DfE, 2013, p. 1)

The growth of Academies in the UK has been dramatic, with just over 200 in 2010 rising to nearly 2,500 in 2012. More recently, the *Report of the Academies Commission* (Academies Commission, 2013, p. 5) emphasised the following in regard to the expansion of Academies:

The Commission believes that a fully academised system is best seen as a community of schools, each independent but working best if connected to the rest of the system. These schools would work with one another to accelerate school improvement ... Collaboration across this national community of schools should enable a balance to be struck between independence and interdependence ... Academies now range from the first early sponsored academies, set up to replace failing schools in poor areas and highly resourced strategic investments in change, to those established from 2010 as a result of the Coalition government's decisions to encourage good and outstanding schools to convert to academy status and to extend the sponsored academy programme into primary schools ... This report argues for a new phase of academy development ... to provide such support for improvement.

At the time, the Report called for a new and determined focus on implementing the Academies programme, suggesting three main imperatives in their future development, as follows:

- to ensure that there is a **forensic focus on teaching and its impact on pupils' learning** so that the gap between the vision for academies and practice in classrooms is reduced and the words 'academisation' and 'improvement' become inextricably and demonstrably linked

- to ensure that **an increasingly academised system is fair and equally accessible to children and young people from all backgrounds**

- to ensure that academies demonstrate their moral purpose and professionalism by providing **greater accountability to pupils, parents and other stakeholders. The role of governors is more important than ever in an academised system, and their scrutiny and challenge should ensure effective accountability**. (pp. 4–5)

Free Schools

These are new schools and, as yet, are largely untested. A decision to send a child with dyslexia to a Free School will bring with it a need for parents to be clear about the level of support their child will receive and the quality of training that staff, working with their child, will have already received.

The concept of Free Schools, which are an extension of the Academies Programme, has been an important feature of schooling in England. The Department for Education (DfE) website (2013) offered the following in regard to Free Schools, indicating a very high level of support given by government:

> Free Schools are all-ability state-funded schools set up in response to what local people say they want and need in order to improve education for children in their community. The right school can transform a child's life and help them achieve things they may never have imagined. Through the Free Schools programme it is now much easier for talented and committed teachers, charities, parents and education experts to open schools to address real demand within an area.

It is possible for Free Schools to be set up by a range of providers such as charities, religious groups, and parent groups. To do so, they must submit their application to the Department of Education. Start-up grants are then offered to these groups. Free Schools may offer a broad and balanced curriculum but, like other schools, are subject to inspections by Ofsted.

Following the introduction of this new concept, Graeme Paton, Education Editor for the popular UK newspaper *The Daily Telegraph*, in April 2013 drew public attention to significant increase in demand for places at these schools. He reported as follows:

Figures released by the Department for Education show that almost nine-in-10 of the schools – new primaries and secondaries established by parents' groups and charities – received more applications than places for September. Overall, an average of three pupils are competing for each place at free schools, it was revealed. The most popular school, West London Free School in Hammersmith, had 1,196 applications for just 120 places – leaving 10 pupils competing for every spare desk. Dixons Trinity Academy in Bradford had 676 applications for 112 places – a ratio of around six-to-one. Ministers insisted that the figures showed 'how popular free schools are with parents'. (Paton, 2013)

Across the UK, views are divided about the introduction of Free Schools, with some arguing that Free Schools contribute to greater segregation and division. More recently, Richard Gardner, Education Editor for the popular British newspaper *The Independent*, reported as follows:

The Government's flagship education reform faces serious questions after new figures revealed three-quarters of free schools are not full ... And this week the general secretary of the National Union of Teachers, Christine Blower, hit out at the free schools model as 'a massive waste of public resources'. (Gardner, 2014)

Like Academies, head teachers of Free Schools have much greater control over budgets and, arguably, are in more control of the level of resourcing given to those children in their schools with dyslexia and developmental literacy difficulties. Previously, the resourcing to meet individual children's needs would have been met in large part by the Local Authority. With Free Schools, and Academies, this is no longer the case, so how will children with dyslexia and developmental literacy difficulties be resourced?

Grammar Schools

Since the release of *Circular 10/65* by a Labour government in 1965, which called upon Local Education Authorities to initiate a process whereby they would start converting secondary schools into Comprehensive schools, the debate surrounding the status of Grammar Schools has raged.

With the introduction of Comprehensive Schools came a move away from testing children at the age of 11 using the hugely controversial *Eleven Plus* examination (see earlier section). The concept of Grammar Schools remains controversial and politically highly charged, as can be seen by the following, which appeared in one of the UK's most popular newspapers. In 2010 Graeme Paton, the Education Editor of the UK newspaper *The Daily Telegraph,* reported as follows:

> More than three-quarters of adults believe more academically-selective schools should be opened, particularly in inner-city areas with poor education standards, it was disclosed. Support for grammar schools has actually increased over the last four years, figures suggest. The disclosure, in a survey by ICM, comes amid growing concerns over provision for the brightest pupils in state comprehensives ... Labour introduced legislation when it came to power more than a decade ago banning the opening of any more grammars and Ed Balls, the Schools Secretary, has recently accused them of condemning many young people to 'failure' at the age of 11.

Two years later, when the new Coalition Government came to power, Graeme Paton offered the following:

> Stephen Twigg, the Shadow Education Secretary, said the party opposed an overhaul of national admissions rules that gives England's 164 state grammars the freedom to take more pupils. He accused ministers of attempting to expand academic selection 'by the backdoor' without full consultation with parents. In an attempt to trigger a Coalition split over the issue, he also said he would write to Liberal Democrat MPs seeking their support to oppose the move. The comments come just days after it emerged that the rule change could pave the way for a significant expansion in the number of grammar school places ... (Paton, 2012)

The independent sector

Independent schools, or, as they are frequently called, private schools, have been at the centre of heated debate for many years with the debate centring around accusations of inequality. Typically, these schools charge fees, class sizes are much smaller, and discipline and standards may be judged to be higher. Independent schools tend to place significant emphasis upon sport and competition and offer a wide range of additional activities and resources. Most independent schools offer excellent support for children with dyslexia. Class sizes tend to be small and teachers working with this group of children typically have appropriate specialist qualifications.

☐ Summary

This chapter initially explored the changing nature of childhood, families and cultures, and the impact of these upon children with dyslexia and developmental literacy difficulties. Readers were introduced to current and proposed initiatives including the *Statutory Framework for the Early Years*, which now affects practice of those practitioners who work with young children. Issues relating to assessment at age 11 were highlighted, as was the increased emphasis now being placed upon the teaching of phonics and controversies surrounding this. The chapter concluded by exploring the changing nature of schooling in the UK and the possible implications this might have for children with dyslexia and developmental literacy difficulties, now, and in the future.

 Recommended reading

Richardson, H. (2014) 'Able Readers Damaged by Phonics, Academic Says', *BBC News Education & Family*. http://www.bbc.co.uk/news/education-25917646 (accessed 28 January 2014).
Wilshaw, M. (2014) *Unsure Start: HMCI's Early Years Annual Report 2012/13 Speech 2014*. London: Ofsted.

References

Academies Commission (2013) *Unleashing Greatness: Getting the Best from an Academised System. The Report of the Academies Commission*. Pearson RSA.
Action for Children (2010) *Deprivation and Risk: The Case for Early Intervention*. London: Action for Children.
Brown, E. (1999) *Loss, Change and Grief*. London: David Fulton.
Buckingham, D. (2000) *After the Death of Childhood: Growing up in the Age of Electronic Media*. Cambridge: Polity Press.
Chapman, J. (2011) 'The Collapse of Family Life: Half of Children See Parents Split by 16 as Births Outside Marriage Hit Highest Level for Two Centuries', *Daily Mail*, 18 April.

Cullis, A. and Hansen, K. (2009) *Child Development in the First Three Sweeps of the Millennium Cohort Study*, DCSF Research Report RW-007.

Department for Education (DfE) (2012) *Statutory Framework for the Early Years Foundation Stage: Setting the Standards for Learning, Development and Care for Children from Birth to Five*. Runcorn: DfE.

Department for Education (DfE) (2013) 'What is an Academy?' Available at: http://www.education.gov.uk/schools/leadership/typesofschools/academies/b00205692/whatisanacademy (accessed 20 February 2013).

Gardner, R. (2014) 'Scandal of the Empty Free Schools', *The Independent*, 24 April.

Gray, C. and MacBlain, S.F. (2012) *Learning Theories in Childhood*. London: Sage.

Hartas, D. (2006) *Dyslexia in the Early Years: A Guide to Teaching and Learning*. London: Routledge.

Kershaw, A. (2012) 'School Intake "Segregated by Class"', *i-Newspaper, The Independent*, 4 April. Available at: http://www.independent.co.uk/news/education/education-news/school-intake-segregated-by-class-7618824.html (accessed 18 April 2013).

MacBlain, S.F. (2014) *How Children Learn*. London: Sage.

MacBlain, S.F. and MacBlain, M.S. (2004) 'Addressing the Needs of Lone-Parent Pupils', *Academic Exchange Quarterly*, 8(2): 221–5.

National Statistics (2003) *Social Trends*. London: Stationery Office Books.

Office for Standards in Education (Ofsted) (2013) *The Most Able Students: Are They Doing as Well as They Should in Our Non-selective Secondary Schools?* London: Ofsted.

Paton, G. (2010) 'Grammar Schools "Should be Expanded"', *Daily Telegraph*, 9 February.

Paton, G. (2012) 'Labour Seeks Lib Dem Support to Oppose Grammar Schools', *Daily Telegraph*, 16 January.

Paton, G. (2013) 'Nine-in-10 of the Coalition's Free Schools "oversubscribed"', *Daily Telegraph*, 10 April.

Richardson, H. (2014) 'Able Readers Damaged by Phonics, academic says', *BBC News Education & Family*. Available at: http://www.bbc.co.uk/news/education-25917646 (accessed 28 January 2014).

Wilshaw, M. (2014) *Unsure Start: HMCI's Early Years Annual Report 2012/13 Speech 2014*. London: Ofsted.

CHAPTER 2

CHILD-CENTRED LITERACY PATHWAYS: PUPILS' PERSPECTIVES

Louise Long

Chapter aims

- To provide a synopsis of the legislative and policy context for consulting with children and young people with special educational needs (SEN).
- To explore contemporary research and scholarship pertaining to 'pupil voice'.
- To advance the use of creative methodologies as an enabling child-centred tool for eliciting and representing voice in pupils with dyslexia and developmental literacy difficulties.
- To examine critically the professional prerequisites, potentials and ethical issues in eliciting voice in children and young people with dyslexia and developmental literacy difficulties.
- To consider the implications of increasing the authenticity and effectiveness of consultations with pupils who have dyslexia and developmental literacy difficulties for advancing inclusive policy and practice in literacy teaching-learning.

Article 12 of the United Nations Convention on the Rights of the Child (1989) offered the following:

State Parties shall assure to the child who is capable of forming his or her own views the right to express those views freely in all matters affecting the child, the views of the child being given due weight in accordance with the age and maturity of the child. For this purpose, the child shall in particular be provided the opportunity to be heard in any judicial and administrative proceedings affecting the child, the views of the child being given due weight in accordance with the age and maturity of the child.

Introduction

Eliciting, listening to, and giving consideration and influence to what children and young people say about their educational experiences and learning pathways have been integral to legislation and policy for nearly thirty years now (DENI, 1998, 2005; DfES, 2001b, 2002, 2004; UN, 1989). Unabatedly, pupil empowerment through participation has become an increasing part of the educational discourse. However, this discourse has often been characterised by rhetoric in that what is visible in schools are consultation practices that are tokenistic and therefore ineffective and lacking in authenticity. Empirical studies and critical literature provide evidence that children and young people who have special educational needs (SEN) are being left out of decision-making processes (MacConville, 2006; Noble, 2003; Todd, 2003). This failure to involve learners with SEN illuminates the need to provide structured opportunities for those pupils who are being sidelined to convey their views and ultimately to influence the decisions that are made about their educational pathways.

Since the 1989 United Nations Convention on the Rights of the Child (UNCRC) and its ratification by the UK in 1991 and acceptance by Ireland in 1992, there has been increased commitment in research, evaluation and consultation to giving voice to children and young people, including those identified as having SEN and disabilities. Across UK regions SEN legislation and policy promotes pupil participation in the decisions that are made about their educational pathways. For example, The Education (Additional Support for Learning) Scotland Act 2004 strengthens the rights of a child and a young person with additional support needs to have his/her views taken into account in discussing, monitoring and evaluating his/her learning. The Code of Practice in Northern Ireland (DENI, 1998, para. 2.28) states that 'all reasonable efforts should be made to ascertain the views of the child or young person about his or her own learning difficulties and education, offering encouragement where necessary'. Moreover, the Supplement to the Code of Practice (DENI, 2005) stresses the duty of educationalists to make themselves aware of the wishes and feelings of children and to facilitate partnerships with learners by allowing them to exercise choices in decision-making processes. In England, The SEN Toolkit (DfES, 2001b) gives specific examples for advancing pupil participation in practice, such as consulting with pupils when target setting, developing individual education plans and choosing schools. The statutory requirement for schools to involve children and young people in decision-making at individual and strategic levels will be brought into force in England in September 2014 with the launch of the new Code of Practice (DfE, 2014).

Exploring critical literature on pupil voice

Findings from empirical studies in the field of pupil voice demonstrate that when pupils in the wider school population are consulted about their learning pathways, better academic outcomes are achieved. For example, Rudduck and Flutter (2000) found that consulting pupils on assessment and learning fostered a sense of control over learning, enhanced motivation and improved academic performance. Moreover, findings from a study that aimed to elicit the views of children and young people with and without SEN on the consultation process, highlighted that all the participant pupils wanted to be involved in decisions made about them, and, further, wanted a choice regarding the nature of that involvement: for example, venue, timing and composition of the consultation team (Woolfson et al., 2006).

Of relevance to this chapter is the research that demonstrates the benefits of consulting with children who have dyslexia and developmental literacy difficulties. For example, Riddick (1996) demonstrated that listening to the voice of pupils with dyslexia could heighten teachers' understanding of children's difficulties, which leads to more constructive attributions about their learning. Moreover, a study which examined reading self-concept in pupils with dyslexia, revealed that the views which these pupils hold about their performance are likely to affect their approach to literacy tasks in general, and, in particular, their self-efficacy belief and motivation to read (Burden and Burdett, 2005). As self-efficacy belief energises the behaviour that leads to success and, as a corollary, academic achievement (Jinks and Lorsbach, 2003), those children and young people who lack a sense of reading self-efficacy remain vulnerable to low achievement and underachievement in literacy in the absence of appropriate intervention pathways.

It is now widely recognised that if intervention programmes are to meet the holistic needs of the child or young person with dyslexia, consideration should be given to motivational and affective dimensions to reading and writing during the process of assessment (Pumfrey, 1997). Long, MacBlain and MacBlain (2007) noted that it is only by identifying and addressing the needs of dyslexic pupils in a child-centred way that this group of learners can get close to reaching their true potential and ultimately embrace adulthood with higher levels of social, emotional and academic self-efficacy. However, findings from a study which investigated the views of dyslexic post-primary pupils about their educational experiences demonstrated that while laudable work is going on in the teaching of examination techniques and study skills, meeting pupils' emotional and social needs remains secondary to academic interventions (Long et al., 2007). One important feature highlighted by this research was that the majority of post-primary pupils participating in the study reported a lack of teacher empathy about the challenges of living with dyslexia. Hales (1994) argued that even when teachers did acknowledge pupils' emotional needs, they were typically viewed as barriers to learning and teaching rather than essential factors in all pedagogical relationships.

The growing body of research on the affective dimension to literacy learning prompted Long, MacBlain and MacBlain (2007) to propose a new conceptual model for teaching literacy that mediated the boundaries between the academic and the holistic by moving beyond the mechanics of teaching reading, spelling and writing to embrace emotional aspects of literacy learning. However, it is now acknowledged that an essential component of any model of learning is a pupil's ability to reflect on his or her own learning (Hewitt, 2008). This idea of thinking about thinking is called metacognition (Flavell, 1981). It is appropriate to consider metacognition as part of a wider view of literacy learning because cognitive and affective aspects of learning are so interlinked. Sean examines the affective dimension of literacy learning in Chapter 3. Therefore, the next step in the current chapter is to examine metacognition in the context of pupil voice.

Metacognition in the context of voice

This section opens with a definition of metacognition:

> Metacognition refers to one's knowledge concerning one's own cognitive processes and products or anything related to them. It refers among other things to active monitoring and consequent regulation and orchestration of these processes in relation to the cognitive objects on which they bear, usually in the service of some concrete goal or object. (Hewitt, 2008, p. 28)

Self-regulation and orchestration of one's own cognitive processes includes the ability and desire: to attend; to concentrate; to memorise; to organise; to communicate, both verbally and in writing; to evaluate; to self-correct; and to self-instruct. Some metacognitive ability is critical for learning to read proficiently (Bee and Boyd, 2007). For example, children learning to read need to identify those words they recognise immediately and those words they do not, and they need to have some idea of what skills they need to attempt to read unfamiliar words so that they can concentrate their efforts on utilising these skills. Moreover, when reading texts containing unfamiliar words, less able and younger readers do not readily make use of decoding skills, and visual, phonic and semantic cues (Flavell et al., 1993). However, Hewitt (2008) highlighted that metacognitive strategies can be taught to pupils who struggle with literacy. For example, in a study of a number of adolescent learners identified as having poor literacy skills, Brown (1987) found that an assessment of what the learner could do with the support of an adult indicated those areas in which the learner needed help to move from external regulation to self-regulation. Another attention-grabbing finding from this research was pupils' overdependence on adult support, and Dweck (1999) described this as 'learned helplessness'.

  Reflection

Bringing the literacy lesson to a close: the plenary session

Plenary sessions are significant elements of literacy lessons. Teachers can support pupils to reflect on and communicate in words or images the extent to which they maintained motivation for the task. According to Hewitt (2008), visualisation can help pupils to see in their mind's eye the learner they would like to be. When the work becomes particularly challenging, pupils can recapture this image as a motivation to persevere with the task.

There is a metacognitive dimension to the consultation process that is both shaped by and shapes pupils' learning experiences. Evidence for the metacognitive capacity of pupils with SEN has found some support in the literature. For example, McPhillips, Shevlin and Long (2012) demonstrated that pupils with pronounced literacy difficulties are self-aware and are experts in their own learning. The young participants in this study were able to collectively identify and verbally and visually communicate their learning preferences, additional academic and emotional needs and sources of support.

Moreover, they knew the teaching and assessment strategies that enabled them to progress in literacy. Thus, the consultation process could be represented as a 'virtuous' cycle of reflection (thinking about past learning), metacognition (thinking about thinking), communication (conveying thoughts about learning and thinking), metacognitive enrichment (learning about thinking) and action (engaging with new learning experiences), which have the potential to advance effective pupil learning. Moreover, the 'conversation' between pupils and teachers using visual and verbal texts should enhance the potential for more effective classroom practice. When effective learners connect with effective teachers, the cumulative effects of the fusion of teacher and pupil potentials should build capacities in the classroom and, ultimately, raise standards (see Figure 2.1.).

However, a number of factors have been identified as obstacles to pupil voice. For example, Lundy (2007) identified teachers' scepticism about the capacity of children to engage in decision-making processes as a barrier to pupil participation. Of particular interest in the context of the commentary on consulting with pupils who have SEN is the clarion call for consideration to be given to educational professionals' values base, which can be protective of learners with SEN or enabling for pupils with SEN (Norwich and Kelly, 2006). A protectionist values base is underpinned by a belief that vulnerable learners should not be burdened with the apparent mantle of choice(s) and an enabling values base

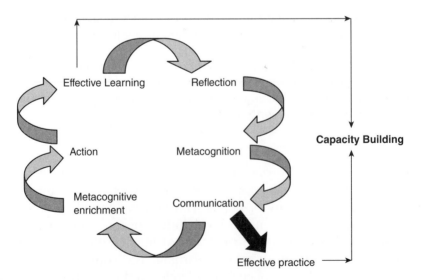

Figure 2.1 Consultation, cognition and capacity building

is underpinned by a belief that pupils with SEN have the right to, and capacity for, participation. These opposing stances can generate inter-professional and intra-professional tensions.

Hammond (2013) highlighted that pupil voice is an important principle and function of educational psychologists. However, he also cautioned that a potential barrier to pupil voice are the language-based methods that educational psychologists are using in meetings with pupils as opposed to methods that elicit voice through pupils' preferred way of communicating. Moreover, based on their experiences as practising educational psychologists, Aston and Lambert (2010) voiced their concerns about the actual role of SEN pupils in both statutory and non-statutory review meetings. They questioned if review meetings were participatory and democratic or coercive and tokenistic, as pupils were often invited along to hear and agree to targets. Fielding (2004) also raised questions about the authenticity of written representations of pupils' views when professionals are continuing to use language that is saturated by adult values.

Inherent in the debate on pupil voice is the assumption that learners who are invited to give their views on their personal and social experiences of education will be motivated and engaged and have the will and the skill to maintain interest for the duration of the consultation process. However, Curtis and his co-researchers noted that there will always be some pupils who are 'hard to reach', for example, pupils who have communication difficulties (Curtis et al., 2004). This observation highlights a barrier to representative sampling and inclusivity in research and consultation processes with young learners. Thus, creative methodologies as inclusive approaches to eliciting pupil voice are recommended.

Innovative methodologies for exploring the views of young learners

Creative methodologies are aligned with the conceptualisation of children as social agents and cultural producers, transformed by and transforming childhood. The emphasis in using creative methodologies is on 'meaning making' and the construction of knowledge as opposed to the psychological perspective of describing children's development in ages and stages. According to Leitch (2008), researchers who utilise drawings place pupils in the centre as experts in their own world, engage their creative tendencies, and create opportunities for them to communicate their social, academic and emotional worlds. Moreover, such creative activities can add an important dimension to the narrative process by eliciting insights that would be difficult to capture through speaking or writing (Chambers et al., 2011).

A review of critical literature illustrates that there is a small but growing body of published studies that have used innovative methods such as image making – drawings, posters, collage – to elicit and advocate children's views on sensitive issues, for example living with pronounced literacy difficulties (Smith and Long, 2014). In other studies, drawings were found to be particularly effective with children who have difficulties with verbal expression (Eliadou, 2011; Thomson, 2008). Moreover, Dunn, Niens and McMillan (2014) successfully utilised creative methodologies in combination with language-based methods, to yield rich data on the views of very young learners on the use of popular culture in teaching literacy. Jill gives a detailed account of this study in Chapter 7. Eliadou (2011) adroitly pointed out that utilising drawings to elicit children's views is a process that is fun, dynamic and integral to their daily lives. Thus, creative methodologies have the potential to engage and sustain the interest of learners who at one time may have been regarded as 'hard to reach' in research and consultation processes (Curtis et al., 2004). Moreover, there is a growing body of evidence illustrating that the use of drawings addresses the concern that pupils' views can be misrepresented because, as part of the research process, the participants can interpret their own drawings (Leitch, 2008; Long et al., 2012).

An illustrative case study: the views of young learners

This section describes a qualitative, small-scale study which emerged from an all-Ireland research project that used creative methodologies to elicit and later advocate the views of children with marked literacy learning needs (Long et al., 2012; McPhillips et al., 2012; Smith and Long, 2014).

The study

This study aimed to explore the 'assessment' and 'participation' stories of upper-primary pupils with pronounced literacy difficulties and to examine their views on how their participation in consultation processes might be enhanced. Four case study schools from Northern Ireland (NI) took part in the research. All the participating NI children (sample size = 22), were aged between 10 and 11 years and received school support at Stage 2 of the Code of Practice (DENI, 1998), the framework for the identification and assessment of SEN in NI. Stage 2 is school-based, whereby specific targets are set, implemented, monitored and evaluated. The study used image making in the context of focus groups as the data collection tools. All the focus groups were facilitated by one of the authors, Louise. She opened each focus group with a vignette of a young boy who had a forte for numeracy but was receiving additional support for literacy. The intention was to build a rapport with the participant pupils through discussion and to enable them to bring their own experiences to the conversation about the young boy in the vignette. This approach depersonalised the entire activity for the participant pupils and enabled them to talk openly about their own experiences of learning to read, spell and write. Louise then moved the participant pupils to the next stage in the research process and provided them with materials to make posters. Pupils worked in groups of three or four. Louise guided pupils' efforts using verbal prompts around the following themes: approachable people, teaching strategies and assessment practices, decision-making and models of additional support. These prompts were intended as a guide to stimulate discussion and to enhance reliability across focus groups. The process of engaging pupils in the creation of an image acted as a stimulus to a four-way interaction between individual pupils, the peer group, the researcher and the image. The anticipated outcome was that, as part of the technique, the completed images would generate further discussion and elaboration between the pupils on literacy learning and decision-making processes, thereby generating both visual and verbal texts. Louise asked questions around the themes listed above and, on request, annotated the images. Louise found that the images energised, illustrated and interpreted pupils' voices. The entire commentary from each session was recorded and transcribed. Louise worked with co-researchers to analyse the entire data set and identify emergent themes (Strauss and Corbin, 1990). The methodology and methods were approved by the Ethics Committee of Saint Mary's University College, Belfast.

Three core themes were derived from the data analysis. Findings demonstrated that children are *experts* in their own learning and know the pedagogies and assessment approaches that enable them to make progress in learning to read, write and spell. For example, many of the participant children would like more reading practice, more time to think about new learning and new strategies for spelling challenging words. Findings highlighted the importance of the *emotional and social dimensions* to learning, school and classroom

(Continued)

(Continued)

life. Many of the children had internalised feelings of shame and disappointment, which they attributed to failing in literacy. They identified a support network of friends and adults who encouraged them as learners and at the same time cared for them as unique individuals. The third theme to emerge from the data was that children with additional needs in literacy wanted greater *choice* and *autonomy* over areas of learning they find more difficult. For example, many of the children would like clarity and transparency in how decisions that affect them are made. A synthesis of emergent themes highlighted the need for a holistic model of literacy learning that should be situated in a pastorally sensitive milieu. Findings demonstrated that pupils with marked literacy learning needs have the capacity to be consultants in their own learning. Moreover, they would like teachers to respect and act upon their views.

The outcomes from this study add to the small but growing body of evidence that highlights the potential of image-making techniques to advance effective consultations in research and practice with children and young people with dyslexia and literacy learning needs. However, authentic and effective consultations can be achieved only when a number of prerequisites and any ethical concerns have been addressed.

The next step in this chapter is to examine the prerequisites and ethical requirements for advancing effective and authentic consultations with pupils who have SEN.

Prerequisites

The promotion of effective and authentic consultations with pupils is predicated upon coherence with the culture, ethos and values of the school and, in particular, a willingness to embed the views of children and young people (CYP) into the school's policies and practices. It is recommended that throughout consultation and research processes educationalists and researchers demonstrate attitudes and behaviours which convey to CYP that their views are important, needs are paramount and well-being and 'well-becoming' are valued. For example, patient, sincere and respectful listening should be shown throughout consultation and research processes. Moreover, CYP should be provided with safe and supportive spaces to convey their views on their educational experiences and learning pathways. Cognisance should be taken – before, during and after the consultation – of cultural and contextual factors (school, home, community) that can facilitate or hinder the efficacy of the consultation process. Educational professionals and researchers must have the confidence to make decisions throughout consultation and research activities that are informed by professional intuition and continuous reflexivity on ethical practice. They should reflect on their capacity to probe deeply, honestly and openly into underpinning theoretical perspectives, life experiences and values that could bias consultation and research processes. Moreover, there is a requirement that educational professionals and researchers remain vigilant about the power imbalance between adults and children, in other words, provide a professional check against raising aspirations but not meeting them.

Child-centred methods for eliciting voice that will enable CYP to convey their views through their preferred way of communicating should be utilised in consultation and research processes. CYP should be provided with transparent, clear and timely feedback on the outcomes of the consultation. Moreover, written and oral representations of the views of CYP should be accurate.

Ethics and practicalities

Researchers can begin gathering data when the Research Ethics Committee of their respective institutions approves the research methodology and methods. While the format of ethics forms can vary across Higher Education Institutions (HEIs), they are all underpinned by the guidance provided by recognised authorities such as the British Educational Research Authority (BERA) or the British Psychological Society (BPS). It is standard practice in HEIs to provide the Research Ethics Committee with a copy of the letter that will be sent to the research gatekeeper (e.g., the head teacher), a criminal records check for the purposes of working with children, a copy of the letter of informed consent (e.g., from the child and the child's parent or guardian) and a copy of the data collection tools (e.g., focus group questions). By way of illustration, what follows below are the protocols that one of the authors, Louise, followed to gain the informed consent of children (10–11 years) who had pronounced literacy difficulties. This research study utilised drawings in the context of focus groups as the data collection tools (Long et al., 2012; McPhillips et al., 2012).

Letters of informed consent to potential child participants were written in child-friendly language. The research team sent the letter of informed consent to children at the same time as they sent a discrete letter of informed consent to their parents or guardians. As the children in the study had all been identified as having pronounced literacy difficulties, this procedure created an opportunity for parents or guardians to read the letter of informed consent to or with the children. The letter of informed consent to children opened with the research team introducing themselves and describing, in brief, the aims of the research study. Children were informed that the research team would like to hear their ideas about how they could be helped to read, write and spell better. They were informed that as part of the study they were being asked to take part in a discussion with other children from the same school and to make a poster of their suggestions for improving their participation in consultations about their literacy learning difficulties. Potential child participants were informed of their right to withdraw at any time in the research process. As completed posters would belong to the children, they were also told that they would be able to take them away once the researcher had photographed their work. The research team informed the children that they themselves would not be photographed. They were also informed that they would not be putting their names on the completed drawings. Researchers would code each drawing by school and pupil number. Moreover, potential child participants in the study were informed that their drawings might appear in reports and publications stemming from the research project. Additional information given in the letter of informed consent was as follows:

 Example

Once the photographs of your work are uploaded to a secure PC, they will be wiped from the researcher's camera. Our conversation will be recorded on tape. Only the research team will listen to the recording. You can choose to have a different name during the discussion and artwork. We will not use the real names of people or places when we word-process what you say. In this way nobody will know who you are or who you are talking about. The recording will be destroyed when the project is finished. All electronic data will be held in our institution on a secure PC in a secure room, only to be looked at by the research team. The research team will hold the electronic data for no longer than two years. No names of children, teachers or schools will appear in anything that we write or publish about your ideas and drawings. We will ask again for your permission to take part in the research when we visit your school to have a discussion with you and do some artwork.

Please read the three statements below, and if you are happy with each of them, tick the boxes and sign your name at the bottom.

I have read about the project on reading and writing. ☐

I understand what I am being asked to do. ☐

I would like to take part in this project. ☐

Please sign your name.

The above exemplar provides a benchmark for the ethically secure use of creative methodologies. However, practical issues are introduced when using creative methodologies in research and practice. For example, from Louise's experiences of researching the views of young learners on literacy learning and teaching, it has become increasingly apparent that children with previous experience of having their views listened to are more at ease in creating and discussing drawings. Other researchers have encountered the same issues: access to and experience of using the vocabulary of learning and emotions are important variables in the research process (Wall and Higgins, 2006). However, Louise's experience has shown that even learners with less involvement in decision-making processes are able to cope well with creating images when they are given encouragement to illustrate what they really think and feel as well as reassurance that the researcher is not looking for a 'correct image'. Moreover, experience has shown that utilising image making as a tool for eliciting the voice of pupils with SEN places great demands on the researcher's interpersonal skills and sense of empathy and challenges his or her own biases about the democratic principles underpinning participatory research. It is recommended that researchers and practitioners who are considering using creative methodologies reflect carefully on their experience, training and capacity for facilitation (Leitch, 2008).

 Exercise

According to Todd (2003), the most common approach to eliciting the voice of children is just to ask them for their views, for example, asking them about their likes and dislikes, giving them a form to fill in

(Continued)

(Continued)

or administering a series of sentence completion tasks. In her view these approaches are inadequate.

In the context of Todd's pessimistic position on frequently used methods for eliciting pupil voice, think about these four questions:

1 Reflecting on your own personal or professional experiences of schools and schooling, what opportunities were pupils with dyslexia given to share their views about their additional needs and provision of these needs?
2 What could change to advance the authenticity of consultations with pupils who experience dyslexia?
3 What are the challenges to implementing these suggestions?
4 How would you respond to these challenges?

Implications for transforming practice

Eliciting, listening to, and giving consideration and influence to the views of pupils with dyslexia and developmental literacy difficulties on their learning pathways sends out a clear message to children and young people that educational professionals value them and value their academic progression. However, at a policy level there is a pressing need to promote consultations with pupils that are authentic and effective in process and outcome. Thus, the methods used to elicit voice in pupils with SEN in literacy should be child-centred, tailored to the individual pupil's preferred way of communicating, inclusive, safe and ethically secure (Leitch, 2008; UN, 2005). Findings from critical literature converge on the claim that creative methodologies meet these demands. It is acknowledged that the use of creative methodologies by academics working within HEIs will be scrutinised and monitored by Research Ethics Committees. However, teachers and other educational professionals could advance ethical practice, when utilising creative methodologies in consultations with pupils who have dyslexia and developmental literacy difficulties, by adhering to the five principles of ethical intelligence articulated by Weinstein (2011). These are the principles: do no harm, respect others, make things better, be fair, and be loving. Moreover, decisions should be made with learners and feedback given on consultation outcomes in order that issues of pupil efficacy and equity are addressed (DfES, 2001b; Messiou, 2002). This practice is aligned with the central and cyclical tenets of Lundy's (2007) interpretation of Article 12 of CRC (UN, 1989) namely, space, voice, audience and influence. Lundy (2007) elaborated on these princi-ples for eliciting voice as follows:

Space: Children must be given the opportunity to express a view.

Voice: Children must be facilitated to express their views.

Audience: The view must be listened to.

Influence: The view must be acted upon, as appropriate.

The model reflects the fact that these elements are interrelated. In particular, there is a significant degree of overlap between (a) space and voice, and (b) audience and influence. Secondly, it depicts the fact that Article 12 has an explicit chronology. The first stage is ensuring the child's right to express a view. Following on from this stage is the child's right to have the view given due weight. However, in recognition of the fact that the decision-making processes are rarely static, the model acknowledges that once the child is informed of the extent of influence, the process may begin again. Finally, the model represents the fact that Article 12 can only be understood fully when it is considered in the light of other relevant UNCRC provisions: in particular, Article 2 (non-discrimination), Article 3 (best interests), Article 5 (right to guidance), Article 13 (right to seek, receive and impart information) and Article 19 (protection from abuse) (Lundy, 2007).

Policymakers could provide funding, space, time and resources to those practitioners and researchers working with children and young people for training on Article 12 in order to advance knowledge and understanding of its content and provisos for its full and complete implementation. Integral to this training could be capacity building on inclusive methodolo-gies as well as critical analyses of case studies and ethical dilemmas. The knowledge, skills and competencies developed during training should facilitate educational professionals in ensuring that there is meaningful participation in decision-making processes for those children who have dyslexia, developmental literacy difficulties and associated developmental disorders. For example, the visual and verbal 'conversations' between teach-ers and pupils may need to be scaffolded depending on the pupil's age, levels of emotional and cognitive maturity and interest in the consultation process. Solution-focused principles should help teachers to scaffold interac-tions with pupils, and professional intuitions and ethical intelligence will be brought into play in the decisions that teachers make about the magnitude of that scaffolding (Molnar and de Shazer, 2007; Weinstein, 2011).

The final point in this section revisits the earlier argument that there is a need for a conceptual model for teaching literacy that embraces metacognition and emotions. Creative approaches to eliciting voice could well generate the third space between the academic and the holistic because they embrace psychological concepts such as metacognition and emotional intelligence (Atkinson, 2006; Goleman, 1995; Sharp, 2001). It is important that teachers have the space to develop understanding of these concepts and to consider their implications for literacy learning and teaching. However, more research is needed on the long-term impact of utilising creative methodologies to advance effective and authentic participation for pupils with dyslexia and developmental literacy difficulties that take into account the views of educational professionals and the views of young learners.

 Example

Matilda is a 10-year-old girl who has been receiving additional within-school support for literacy for three terms spanning two academic years. Matilda is interested in nature and the environment. She presents as a vibrant and highly articulate young girl. Matilda's hobbies include drama and musical theatre, and she has been awarded distinctions in her last three accredited examinations in these creative arts. Matilda has a keen eye for texture and colour. She is also a competent photographer and was featured recently in her local paper for her accomplishments in these areas. Matilda's ICT skills have been described as excellent.

It is a Monday morning, and Matilda goes into school feeling under the weather after a weekend tummy bug. The class teacher sets an independent pencil-and-paper continuous writing task on 'The Victorians'. The class teacher observes that Matilda is largely 'off task' and restless. Shortly into the activity Matilda begins to draw on her hand. Her class teacher reprimands her and immediately pens a letter to her parents to let them know that Matilda drew and coloured in a picture on her hand during literacy work. When Matilda is handed this letter, she flees from the class shouting, 'That's it, I'm out of here'.

Matilda initiated the consultation process and gave 'voice' to her needs in the way that she was able to communicate them at that point in time.

 Exercise

Draw on critical literature and your own personal and professional experiences of schools and classrooms to reflect on the following questions:

1 How should the class teacher respond to Matilda's behaviour?
2 What approaches could the class teacher utilise to get to know the Matilda that the family knows, the child that Matilda is, and Matilda's anxieties and aspirations for literacy learning?
3 What strategies could the class teacher implement to advance Matilda's level of participation in the design of this literacy task and its mode of assessment?

Summary

Enabling voice and empowering learners are central features of legislation and policy pertaining to the education of children and young people with SEN. However, educational professionals face challenges in engaging and sustaining pupils' interest in the consultation process and in genuinely illuminating and representing the realities of the educational experiences of children and young people with dyslexia and developmental literacy difficulties. Consulting with children and young people is a continuous reflective and reflexive process for educational professionals and researchers and one that should be underpinned by ethical practice. The potentials in eliciting voice through creative methodologies are that they address barriers to participation and interpretation and, ultimately, advance the effectiveness and authenticity of the consultation process. Moreover, the visual and verbal 'conversations' between teachers and pupils with dyslexia and developmental literacy difficulties heighten the potential for advancing effective learning and teaching, asserting holistic approaches to literacy teaching-learning, enhancing inclusive practice and raising outcomes in the classroom. Further research is needed that investigates the views of educational professionals, researchers and pupils on creative methodologies as an inclusive and child-centred tool for eliciting and giving influence to pupil voice.

  Recommended reading

Thomson, P. (2008) 'Children and Young People: Voices in Visual Research', in P. Thomson (ed.), *Doing Visual Research with Children and Young People* (pp. 1–20). London: Routledge.

(Continued)

(Continued)

Smith, R. and Long, L. (2014) 'Using Vocabularies of Hope to Transform the Educational Experiences of Students Identified as having Pronounced Literacy Difficulties', in P. Jones (ed.), *Bringing Insider Perspectives into Inclusive Teacher Learning* (pp 9–24). Abingdon: Routledge.

References

Aston, H. and Lambert, N. (2010) 'Young People's Views about their Involvement in Decision-making', *Educational Psychology in Practice*, 26(1): 41–51.

Atkinson, C. (2006) 'Key Stage 3 Pupils' Views About Reading', *Educational Psychology in Practice*, 22(4): 321–36.

Bee, H. and Boyd, D. (2007) *The Developing Child* (11th edn). London: Pearson Education.

Brown, A. (1987) 'Metacognition, Executive Control, Self-regulation and Other Mysterious Mechanisms', in F.E. Weinert and R.H. Kulwe (eds), *Metacognition, Motivation and Understanding* (pp. 65–106). Mahwah, NJ: Lawrence Erlbaum Associates.

Burden, R. and Burdett, J. (2005) 'Factors Associated with Successful Learning in Pupils with Dyslexia: A Motivational Analysis', *British Journal of Special Education*, 32(2): 100–4.

Chambers, F., Machalepis, M. and Martinez, M. (2011) 'Using Drawing to Explore Children's Aspirations in a Primary School', in S. Miles and M. Ainscow (eds), *Responding to Diversity in Schools* (pp. 127–35). Abingdon: Routledge.

Curtis, K., Roberts, H., Cooperman, J., Downie, A. and Liako, K. (2004) 'How Come I Don't Get Asked No Awkward Questions? Researching Hard to Reach Children and Teenagers', *Child and Family Social Work*, 9: 167–75.

Department for Education (DfE) (2014) *Special Educational Needs and Disability Code of Practice: 0–25 Years*. London: Crown.

Department for Education and Skills (DfES) (2001a) *Special Educational Needs and Disability Act*. London: DfES.

Department for Education and Skills (DfES) (2001b) *SEN Toolkit*. London: DfES.

Department for Education and Skills (DfES) (2002) *The Education Act 2002*. London: HMSO.

Department for Education and Skills (DfES) (2004) *Department for Education and Skills: Five Year Strategy for Children and Learners*. London: Crown.

Department of Education Northern Ireland (DENI) (1998) *Code of Practice on the Identification and Assessment of Special Educational Needs*. Bangor: DENI.

Department of Education Northern Ireland (DENI) (2005) *Supplement to the Code of Practice on the Identification and Assessment of Special Educational Needs*. Bangor: DENI.

Dunn, J., Niens, U. and McMillan, D. (2014) '"Cos He's My Favourite Character!"
A Children's Rights Approach to the Use of Popular Culture in the Teaching of
Literacy', *Literacy*, 48(1): 23–31.

Dweck, C.S. (1999) *Self-theories: Their Role in Motivation, Personality and
Development*. Philadelphia: Psychology Press Ltd.

Education (Additional Support for Learning) Scotland Act (2004) (Commencement
No. 3) Order 2005: Edinburgh: Scottish Parliament.

Eliadou, A. (2011) 'Using Children's Drawings to Explore Barriers to Inclusion in
Cyprus', in Miles, S. and Ainscow, M. (eds), *Responding to Diversity in Schools*
(pp. 19–31). Abingdon: Routledge.

Fielding, M. (2004) 'Transformative Approaches to Student Voice: Theoretical
Underpinnings, Recalcitrant Realities', *British Educational Research Journal*,
30(2); 295–311.

Flavell, J.H. (1981) 'Cognitive Monitoring', in W.P. Dickson (ed.), *Children's Oral
Communication Skills*. New York: Academic Press.

Flavell, J.H., Miller, P.H. and Miller, S.A. (1993) *Cognitive Development* (3rd edn).
Englewood Cliffs, NJ: Prentice Hall.

Goleman, D. (1995) *Emotional Intelligence*. New York: Bantam Books.

Hales, G.W. (1994) 'The Human Aspects of Dyslexia', in G.W. Hales (ed.),
*Dyslexia Matters: A Celebratory Contributed Volume to Honour Professor T.R.
Miles*. London: Whurr.

Hammond, N. (2013) 'Introducing Forum Theatre to Elicit and Advocate Children's
Views', *Educational Psychology in Practice*, 29(1): 1–18.

Hewitt, D. (2008) *Understanding Effective Learning: Strategies for the Classroom*.
Maidenhead: Open University Press.

Jinks, J. and Lorsbach, A. (2003) 'Introduction: Motivation and Self-efficacy Belief',
Reading and Writing Quarterly, 19: 113–18.

Leitch, R. (2008) 'Creatively Researching Children's Narratives through Images
and Drawings', in P. Thomson (ed.), *Doing Visual Research with Children and
Young People* (pp. 37–58). London: Routledge.

Long, L., MacBlain, S. and MacBlain, M. (2007) 'Supporting Students with
Dyslexia at the Secondary School: An Emotional Model of Literacy', *Journal of
Adolescent and Adult Literacy*, 51(2): 124–34.

Long, L., McPhillips, T., Shevlin, M. and Smith, R. (2012) 'Utilising Creative
Methodologies to Elicit the Views of Young Learners with Additional Needs in
Literacy', *Support for Learning*, 27(1): 1–9.

Lundy, L. (2007) 'Voice is Not Enough: Conceptualising Article 12 of the United
Nations Convention on the Rights of the Child', *British Educational Research
Journal*, 33(6): 927–42.

MacConville, R. (2006) 'Powerful Voices Conferences Draws Out Pupil Opinion
on Education and Services', *SENCO Update*, February 4–5.

McPhillips, T., Shevlin, M. and Long, L. (2012) 'A Right to be Heard: Learning
from Learners with Additional Needs in Literacy', *Literacy*, 46(2): 57–64.

Messiou, K. (2002) 'Marginalisation in Primary Schools: Listening to Children's
Voices', *Support for Learning*, 17(3): 117–21.

Molnar, A. and Shazer, S. (2007) 'Solution-focused Therapy: Towards the Identification of Therapeutic Tasks', *Journal of Marital and Family Therapy*, 13*(*4): 349–58.

Noble, K. (2003) 'Personal Reflection on Experiences of Special and Mainstream Education', in M. Shevlin and R. Rose (eds), *Encouraging Voices: Respecting the Insights of Young People Who Have Been Marginalised*. Dublin: National Disability Authority.

Norwich, B. and Kelly, N. (2006) 'Evaluating Children's Participation in SEN Procedures: Lessons for Educational Psychologists', *Educational Psychology in Practice*, 22(3): 255–71.

Pumfrey, P. (1997) 'Assessment of the Motivational and Affective Aspects of Reading', in J.R. Beech and C. Singleton (eds), *The Psychological Assessment of Reading* (pp.160–74). London: Routledge.

Riddick, B. (1996) *Living with Dyslexia: The Social and Emotional Consequences of Specific Learning Difficulties*. London: Routledge.

Rudduck, J. and Flutter, J. (2000) 'Pupil Participation and Pupil Perspective: Carving a New Order of Experience', *Cambridge Journal of Education*, 30(1): 75–89.

Sharp, P. (2001) *Nurturing Emotional Literacy*. London: David Fulton Publishers.

Smith, R. and Long, L. (2014) 'Using Vocabularies of Hope to Transform the Educational Experiences of Students Identified as Having Pronounced Literacy Difficulties', in P. Jones (ed.), *Bringing Insider Perspectives into Inclusive Teacher Learning* (pp 9–24). Abingdon: Routledge.

Strauss, A. and Corbin, J. (1990) *Basics of Qualitative Research: Grounded Theory Procedures and Techniques*. London: Sage.

Thomson, P. (2008) 'Children and Young People: Voices in Visual Research', in P. Thomson (ed.), *Doing Visual Research with Children and Young People* (pp.1–20). London: Routledge.

Todd, L. (2003) 'Consulting the Children', *Special Children*, September/October, 15–19.

United Nations (UN) (1989) *Convention on the Rights of the Child*. United Nations: New York.

United Nations (UN) (2005) *General Comment No 7: Implementing Rights in Early Childhood*. Geneva: UNICEF.

Wall, K. and Higgins, S. (2006) 'Facilitating Metacognitive Talk: A Research and Learning Tool', *International Journal of Research and Method in Education*, 29(1): 39–53.

Weinstein, B. (2011) *Ethical Intelligence: Five Principles for Untangling your Toughest Problems and Work Beyond*. CA: New World Library.

Woolfson, R.C., Harker, M., Lowe, D., Shields, M., Banks, M., Campbell, L. and Ferguson, E. (2006) 'Consulting About Consulting: Young People's Views on Consultation', *Educational Psychology in Practice*, 22(4): 337–53.

CHAPTER 3

MEETING THE NEEDS OF CHILDREN WITH DYSLEXIA AND DEVELOPMENTAL LITERACY DIFFICULTIES: HOLISTIC APPROACHES

Sean MacBlain

Chapter aims

- To explore the nature of emotional intelligence and its relevance to children experiencing difficulties with the acquisition of literacy.
- To examine how developing emotional intelligence can impact positively upon children with dyslexia and developmental literacy difficulties.
- To explore the importance of self-efficacy and its relevance to children with dyslexia and developmental literacy difficulties.

Introduction

A century ago the celebrated author D.H. Lawrence (1915, p. 24) in addressing the emotional responses experienced by children failing with literacy, wrote as follows:

Then he reddened furiously, felt his bowels sink with shame, scratched out what he had written, made an agonised effort to think of something in the real composition style, failed, became sullen with rage and humiliation, put the pen down and would have been torn to pieces rather than attempt to write another word.

Now compare Lawrence's account with the following taken from an interview by the author (MacBlain) with a young adult during the course of writing this text:

> *People have no idea how difficult it is. They don't realise how humiliating it is, having to read in front of others when you know you just can't do it or to have your written work given back to you when you know it is going to be full of mistakes ... it really hurts and it still makes me tearful when I talk about it.*

Whilst both accounts highlight the painful experiences associated with poor reading, they also reveal deeper feelings of shame, embarrassment and anger that can be associated with low levels of literacy. Here readers may be drawn to ask why such feelings, experienced at the beginning of the last century, remain evident in the 21st century. Readers may also be drawn to asking why many children in mainstream schools who are given additional support for learning and who may have individualised learning programmes can still experience significant feelings of humiliation and hurt. In a recent study, Long, MacBlain and MacBlain (2007, p. 124) drew attention to the importance of teachers working with children with literacy difficulties being properly aware of the crucial link between difficulties with acquiring literacy and emotional development and personal well-being:

> The shame and frustration that often come with living with literacy difficulties require that teachers be cognizant of the interdependent nature of academic and personal growth in the provision of individualized learning experiences.

For some time, the lack of attention given to the social and emotional side of dyslexia and developmental literacy difficulties has been recognised but not fully explored or understood. Almost a decade ago Hartas (2006, p. 28), for example, commented, in regard to children with dyslexia in the early years, as follows:

> The social and emotional consequences of dyslexia have been neglected despite accumulating evidence suggesting a strong link between dyslexia and difficulties with regard to social interactions and emotional maturity ... language and social-emotional development are interconnected ... difficulties with social adjustment, ability

to express feelings, self-confidence and self-esteem are likely to have a long-term impact on learning and academic performance.

It is of particular note that Hartas appears to be drawing particular attention to problems with social adjustment and interaction, which arise from the difficulties that can be experienced by young children with dyslexia. One is immediately drawn to the realities that face many children who may struggle within classroom situations to demonstrate their abilities because they are failing to read or write as well as their peers and this might, for example, affect their friendships and the manner in which other children perceive them and wish to interact with them. One is also drawn to thinking about older children who may have developed low self-esteem and poor self-confidence and who choose, often reluctantly, to withdraw from social situations. Interestingly, Hartas also draws particular attention to the area of emotional maturity. Readers may wish to consider the view that children with dyslexia as well as other specific learning difficulties such as dyspraxia can often present in some situations as being severely frustrated (Department of Education for Northern Ireland [DENI], 1998, p. 71) and highly sensitive (Burden and Burdett, 2005; Long et al., 2007; Ott, 1997). Some would suggest that this is, in part, due to immaturities in the development of parts of the brain. Of interest, also, is the emphasis that Hartas appears to place upon the interconnectedness between social-emotional development and language. In its broader sense, language, of course, includes written expression, which is the area that many children with dyslexia fail in. It also includes, however, such areas as 'word finding' difficulties, which is another area that many children with dyslexia can find problems with. In addition, the retention of instructions or directions given orally by others can again present problems for some children with dyslexia, making oral communication, in some situations, a very challenging business. Take the case of Michael, below.

 Example

Michael is 10 years of age and was assessed as having dyslexia when he was 8 years old. His parents, however, have remained anxious about his continued lack of progress and increasing isolation from other children, and his growing frustration, weakening self-confidence, and unhappiness about attending school. When assessed more recently

(Continued)

(Continued)

by a different educational psychologist, this psychologist reported as follows:

   … Michael presented as an articulate, pleasant and cooperative child and impressed with his willingness to attempt a number of sub-tests that clearly presented him with some difficulties. In conversation with Michael I learned that whilst he liked his teachers and was generally positive about his school he had been, at times, very unhappy. Michael told me that he often felt isolated from his friends and 'especially when they are doing something where you have to be really clever… they don't really want you in their group if you are a bit thick'.

Parental interview

Michael's mother described Michael as 'a very reserved and quiet child … his teacher says that he doesn't get involved in discussions with the others in lessons … he has such lovely ideas but when he tries to put these down on paper he really struggles … he gets really frustrated … he has always been a very sensitive child, quick to tears … his dad and I worry about him, we feel he's far more capable than his work suggests … it's almost as if the real Michael can't break out and let others see what he can really do…'.

Current level of intellectual functioning

Table 3.1   Case study – Michael (Wechsler Intelligence Scale for Children IV – Composite Scores)

Scale	Centile	Average Range
Verbal Comprehension	79	High Average
Perceptual Reasoning	55	Average
Working Memory	21	Low Average
Processing Speed	16	Low Average

Table 3.2   Case study – Michael (literacy scores)

Test	Centile	Age Equivalent
Word Recognition	16	6 years 6 months
Reading Comprehension	07	6 years 3 months
Spelling	14	6 years 3 months

It is generally accepted that two-thirds of children are considered to function within the average range of ability and this range is represented between the 16th and 84th centiles ... The 85th centile upwards represents increasingly higher ability with the 99th centile representing the top 1% of ability and the 1st centile representing the lowest 1% of ability.

Having undertaken an assessment of Michael and gained information relating to Michael's cognitive functioning, his intellectual ability and attainments in reading and spelling, the educational psychologist then went on to offer her conclusions and make a number of recommendations (see below). It is important to note that whilst she made recommendations in regard to Michael's academic performance she also made recommendations relating to his self-belief and self-esteem and the importance of developing these in regard to Michael's progress. She also placed particular emphasis upon the need for Michael to learn new strategies for managing his learning.

    ## Example (contd.)

Conclusions

The above results suggest to me that Michael is of at least average ability but with the specific learning difficulty, Dyslexia. There is a marked discrepancy between Michael's scores (see Tables 3. 1 and 3.2), which, in my view, explain many of the difficulties he experiences with formal learning. Of particular note was Michael's score on the Coding sub-test, which provides a measure of speed and accuracy of hand–eye co-ordination, short-term memory and attention skills. When scores on the Coding sub-test are taken together with scores on the Symbol Search we gain a measure of Processing Speed. Michael achieved a centile score of 16, which places him at the very bottom of the average range. This suggests to me that in formal learning situations he will experience greater difficulty than the majority of his peers with processing written symbolic information. I would suggest, for example, that Michael will take longer copying work from another source such as a White Board or textbook because he is having to give greater attention to processing individual features of the material he

(Continued)

(Continued)

is reading. This will slow him down and within formal examination conditions he will require additional time ... I noted that on the Digit Span sub-test Michael performed much better on the first part and less well on the second part ... Michael's weaker performance on the latter part of this sub-test indicates the existence of specific learning difficulties relating to Working Memory and suggests that within classroom situations he will experience difficulties following longer instructions and directions. He may, for example, appear at times to be easily distracted and as being inattentive and having poor concentration when, in reality, he is probably struggling to process and organise the verbal instructions and directions he is being given.

Michael achieved high average scores on other sub-tests indicating strengths in these areas ... Michael's literacy scores (Table 3.2) clearly indicate that he is experiencing significant difficulties in all aspects of literacy.

Recommendations

Given my assessment of Michael, I would recommend the following:

- *Increasing Michael's understanding of how he approaches new learning situations and material and especially how he organises his work schedules in relation to the type of demands these make upon him.*
- *Increasing Michael's own understanding that his specific learning difficulties/dyslexia will place greater demands upon him especially in lessons where he is involved in processing larger amounts of verbal information. Michael should understand that from time to time he will experience much greater difficulty than his peers with sustaining his concentration and attention when doing school work that Michael finds of little relevance. This will support him with developing a better sense of himself and of his true levels of ability and potential. In this way Michael will be helped to prepare himself for future transition to secondary school.*
- *Michael's handwriting is usually difficult to read. He should continue to work at developing his skills in this area especially if this is linked to his attempts at spelling new words as well as those words with which he finds particular difficulty. This will also be of particular benefit to Michael if this is done in unison with his attempts at developing his skills in the area of Information Computer Technology (ICT) and, in particular, his keyboard skills.*

- *As Michael progresses through secondary school his teachers will expect Michael to word-process the majority of his work. If he has developed good skills in this area then this will help him enormously as he prepares for his GCSE examinations.*
- *Employing ICT to support his work in the area of word recognition, reading comprehension and spelling will also be very beneficial and will offer Michael regular opportunities to record and then proofread his written work.*
- *Michael will benefit particularly from using structured literacy programmes, which emphasise the learning of new and efficient strategies for the reinforcement and consolidation of prior learning in the area of spelling. In addition, he will benefit from activities which use multi-sensory techniques and which are aimed at supporting the development of his kinaesthetic memory. This will be particularly helpful if these activities form part of his spelling programme and are linked to the development of a cursive style of handwriting.*
- *Increasing Michael's knowledge of sound/symbol correspondence and the principles that underpin this will be an essential feature of Michael's progress in spelling, as well as word recognition. He should also continue to develop his knowledge and understanding of the structural analysis of words, for example, he should increase his understanding of how words are formed using prefixes, suffixes and so on. I would suggest that he could also use the programme Letters Form Words (published by SMB Associates SW LTD: enquiries@seanmacblain.com)*
- *Given Michael's level of intellectual ability, he can be more closely involved in monitoring his own progress in developing higher order reading skills and skills in the area of spelling as well as across the wider curriculum.*
- *Whenever possible, Michael should be encouraged to set personal targets and to monitor his own progress and efforts against these.*
- *Michael can improve his reading skills through access to material, which he can read with ease, which is of high interest and which links to his natural curiosity. When engaged in paired reading with an adult he can also be encouraged to seek connections between his own ideas and those he is reading by talking about them.*
- *Michael will also continue to benefit from having opportunities where he is supported in raising his self-confidence and boosting his self-esteem, which will I believe have a very positive effect on the acquisition of higher-order reading skills. Michael's self-esteem*

(Continued)

(Continued)

> objectives could incorporate the development of those skills and aspects of his reading and writing that he wants to improve for himself. It will be important, however, for adults working with Michael to find creative and effective ways of encouraging him to take greater risks so that he can remain motivated and want to learn.
>
> • Of particular benefit to Michael will be having opportunities to use specific examples of his own personal success to convince himself that he is very capable of doing much better and that definite improvements are taking place in key skill areas. This will help him to internalise a strong self-belief that he is, in fact, improving in all aspects of literacy and numeracy and that this is due in large part to his growing confidence in his own abilities as well as his learning of new and efficient strategies, and his own direct efforts...

 Exercise

Having read the educational psychologist's recommendations:

1 What key elements should Michael's teacher include within an individualised programme to shift his reading comprehension and spelling scores into the average range?
2 What key elements should Michael's teacher include to improve his word recognition score?

The nature of emotional intelligence

In order for children to function effectively and respond purposefully to the vast array of demands made upon them as they grow, they need to be able to understand and manage their emotions (Goleman, 1996; Salovey and Mayer, 1990). However, not only do they need to make sense of their own emotions, they also need to understand those of others with whom they come into contact. To fail to do so will almost certainly bring its problems. This is especially important in those growing years whilst at school, and this has been recognised and written about for generations, by, for example, such notable philosophers and theorists as John Locke, Jean-Jacques Rousseau and

Maria Montessori, and more recently, John Holt, A.S. Neill and the contemporary American philosopher Nel Noddings. Take the following quotation offered by A.S. Neill in the 1960s, whose radical ideas on education were located within the then popular theoretical perspective, *Psychodynamics*, developed by Sigmund Freud, cited by MacBlain (2014, p. 24):

> Freud said that the unconscious was infinitely more important and more powerful than the conscious. I said, 'In my school we won't censure, punish, moralize. We will allow every child to live according to his deep impulses'.

What teachers observe on a daily basis when working with children are the children's behaviours. They do not observe actual thinking or underlying cognitive processes, only the manifestation of these as behaviours. They then make interpretations of these behaviours. In the majority of cases their interpretations will be accurate. There will be occasions, however, when interpretations may be flawed and driven by teachers' own emotional states and predetermined mindsets. In the case of children who are failing to access literacy, especially during their first years at school, teachers may attribute failure in these children to such factors as lack of concentration, ease of distractibility, poor attention span, naughtiness, and so on, when in reality these children are trying to manage significant specific difficulties relating to, for example, poor working memory, perceptual disturbance, slow processing speed, and so on. The result of inaccurate attributions may well mean that children with dyslexia are perceived, and even labelled, as a distraction to others, a nuisance, and even in some cases the 'class clown'. In such instances, not only will their learning difficulties go unnoticed but they will, almost certainly, fail to have underlying emotional states such as frustration, anxiety, and even fear, identified, as was emphasised by A.S. Neill, above.

Most practitioners working in the field of education today will be familiar with the following two terms, which are often used interchangeably when talking about children's learning and cognitive development: *emotional intelligence* and *emotional literacy*. This idea of emotional intelligence offers a most useful framework through which we can better understand the need for teachers to adopt a more holistic and child-centred approach to working with children with dyslexia and developmental literacy difficulties. To begin with, it is necessary to understand what we mean by this term emotional intelligence. Salovey and Mayer (1990, p. 189) have defined *emotional intelligence* as:

> ... the subset of social intelligence that involves the *ability to monitor one's own and others' feelings and emotions, to discriminate among them and to use this information to guide one's thinking and actions.*

These terms are particularly relevant to the emotional and social development of children with dyslexia and how these children grow up attempting to manage their own sense of achievement and progress, and in too many cases, failure. It is helpful, therefore, to look more closely at emotional intelligence and how it relates to children with dyslexia and developmental literacy difficulties.

Salovey and Mayer have proposed four key factors in developing *emotional intelligence*: perceiving emotions; reasoning with emotions; understanding emotions; and managing emotions. With the first, children begin from a very early age to develop their ability to accurately perceive emotions, for example, interpreting the body language of those around them, identifying facial expressions, and so on. In doing so, they come to learn how to observe the emotions of those around them and they do this by developing their understanding of patterns of behaviour and language. The degree to which they will come to develop their own sensitivity in this area will depend on a number of factors, most particularly perhaps, the explanations provided by adults and older siblings. As they participate in this process they will increasingly also engage in reasoning with their personal emotions and will extend their own thinking and understanding of situations, and, in the process, will develop their cognitive capacity. They can be observed, for example, to form judgements as to the appropriateness of responding to the emotions of those around them, and if so, how. Readers may wish to consider, at this point, how young children who are failing in literacy and who may have dyslexia interpret the emotions of those around them. More specifically, readers may wish to consider how these children come to internalise their interpretations of the behaviours and emotions of the key adults who are responsible for their education and how these interpretations might come to define the way in which children come to view themselves as learners.

With the third factor, individuals attach meaning to their emotions through making accurate interpretations of them. A teacher may, for example, experience a child being very aggressive towards them and they might then interpret the child's aggression simply in terms of it being an angry outburst when the child's aggression may, in actual fact, be due to feelings of embarrassment and even guilt derived from a misplaced sense of causing the original upset. Take a further example, where a teacher may experience a child being very sullen and non-cooperative, and interpret the child's behaviours in terms of the child being oppositional and rude when, in reality, the child's lack of cooperation may be due to the child feeling very embarrassed because of their fear of failing in front of their peers, coupled with an internalised sense of failure by the child. Children need to be supported in making accurate interpretations of their own emotions. This is crucial for children who are failing with reading. For this group of children, the interpretations of the emotions they feel in response to the behaviours of others around them, and especially those adults responsible for managing their learning can be of the utmost importance. They must, for example, learn to differenti- ate between the variety of emotions they feel when their teachers are responding to the frequent mistakes they make with their writing and spelling, and demonstrating, however covertly, feelings of frustration and exasperation, and in some cases, perhaps, dislike.

The final element requires an ability to manage, but more importantly to regulate feelings and emotions. Here, children need, for example, to give appropriate responses to the emotions they observe and experience in others with whom they interact. Again, readers may wish to consider the difficulties that children who continually fail with the acquisition of literacy have in regard to regulating their feelings and emotions when they find their attempts at reading, spelling and writing being perceived by adults as undesirable and something of a nuisance, or in relation to the disappointment of high-achieving parents. Salovey and Mayer (1990, p. 200) have posed an important but rather appealing conundrum:

> People who have developed skills related to emotional intelligence understand and express their own emotions, recognize emotions in others, regulate affect, and use moods and emotions to motivate adaptive behaviors. Is this just another definition of a healthy, self- actualized individual?

Making reference to the work of Mayer (co-author with Salovey referred to above) Goleman (1996, p. 48) has offered the following:

> Mayer finds that people tend to fall into distinctive styles for attend- ing to and dealing with emotions.
>
> - *Self-aware.* Aware of their moods as they are having them … When they get into a bad mood, they don't ruminate and obsess about it, and are able to get out of it sooner …
>
> - *Engulfed.* These are people who often feel swamped by their emotions and helpless to escape them … They are mercurial and not very aware of their feelings, so that they get lost in them …

> As a result, they do little to try to escape bad moods ... They often feel overwhelmed and emotionally out of control ...

> • *Accepting.* While these people are often clear about what they are feeling, they also tend to be accepting of their moods, and so don't try to change them ...

More astute teachers and Early Years practitioners will be only too well aware of when their pupils present with the second of these styles and become 'engulfed' by emotions that they do not understand but that reflect the disappointment they observe in others, and especially, the key adults in their lives. Readers may wish to reflect upon how some parents of children with dyslexia find their children swamped by feelings of failure typically characterised by avoiding doing homework, a reluctance to read, frustration and upset when faced with weekly spelling tests, and so on. When children come to *accept* their condition (the third distinctive style referred to above), then, it can be suggested, that they have gone a long way in internalising a negative self-image of themselves as failing learners.

In *An Intelligent Look at Emotional Intelligence* (2005, p. 6) commissioned by the Association of Teachers and Lecturers (ATL), Professor Guy Claxton offered the following:

> In school, young people's emotions are much more present in classrooms – and playgrounds – than they used to be. For example:

> • With what sociologists call the 'decline of deference' (and what teachers simply label as 'bad behaviour'), pupils and students bring more of their complicated emotional selves into the classroom with them.

> • Living with the consequences of 'inclusion', teachers are sometimes faced with challenging behaviour and displays of strong emotion that they struggle to know how to deal with.

Claxton (ATL, 2005, p. 9) went on to propose that *emotional intelligence* differs from more traditional perceptions of intelligence in two critical ways. First, *emotional intelligence*:

> ... values different ways of being bright. It asserts that understanding someone else's point of view, or knowing how to deal with stress, are forms of intelligence, just as useful – indeed, quite possibly more so – than being able to solve logical brainteasers fast under pressure.

Secondly, unlike popular notions that hold that intelligence is being fixed in some way, for example, with the notion of Intelligence Quotients (IQs), emotional intelligence:

> … focuses on the extent to which emotional competence can be developed. Whereas a child of 'low (intellectual) ability' tends to be seen as a prisoner of their genes, Emotional Intelligence is of interest to so many teachers because they believe they can do something to help.

This second point is an important one and directs us to seeing why the concept of *emotional intelligence* or *emotional literacy* has gained in popularity amongst Early Years practitioners and teachers not just in the UK, but across the globe. In developing the concept of *emotional intelligence* and shifting from the more traditionally held view of intelligence as something that we are born with, Early Years practitioners and teachers are increasingly recognising that what they do with children, and the way in which they do it, can have a significant impact upon the way in which children think. More particularly, this process offers teachers and Early Years practitioners the means by which they can observe and interpret more fully the ways in which children think rationally, and effectively interact with their environments and with those around them, which is really the basis of intellectual functioning (Wechsler, 1944, quoted in MacBlain, 2014, p. 137). It also draws particular attention to the challenges facing Early Years practitioners and teachers when creating effective learning environments where children feel supported in aiming high and achieving their potential, which is a far stretch from acquiring skills and developing abilities to simply allow them to 'get by' in life.

Claxton also drew attention to the importance of using some form of measurement when discussing *emotional intelligence* so that the term has greater credibility, as has been the case, for example, with the concept of Intelligence Quotient. This is important, for when we talk about 'dyslexic' children having difficulties with emotional intelligence we need to be very clear about what we are saying and implying or others may reject our judgements out of hand. Claxton proposes two ways in which this might be achieved: first, self-reporting by individuals where they might, for example, use questionnaires and interviews; and secondly, what Claxton refers to as 'performance measures' where individuals might be invited to engage in completing particular tasks, with the degree to which they are successful being observed. Claxton has drawn upon the example of one particular attempt at doing this, which was undertaken by the Israeli psychologist Reuven Bar-On who developed the 'Emotional Quotient

Inventory' (EQ-I). In creating self-report measures, which Claxton suggests are more cost effective, Claxton (ATL, 2005, p11) has commented as follows:

> The EQ-I divides Emotional Intelligence into five components, each assessed by a different sub-scale. Drawing on Howard Gardner's terminology, Bar-On calls these *intrapersonal intelligence* (which contains self-awareness, self-esteem and assertiveness); *interpersonal intelligence* (empathy, social responsibility and social awareness); *adaptability* (problem-solving, reality testing and flexibility); *stress management* (stress tolerance and impulse control); and *general mood* (happiness and optimism). Respondents indicate the extent to which they agree or disagree with a range of statements designed to tap these qualities, and the replies are statistically aggregated into scores and sub-scores in the normal psychometric ways.

It almost goes without saying that a number of those components identified by Bar-On present difficulties when it comes to defining them and agreeing on definitions, and they are even more difficult to accurately observe and record. How, for example, do we define *happiness* and what do we actually mean by the term *optimism*? Does *flexibility* mean the same to everyone and to what extent does *flexibility* depend upon the situation and the individuals involved?

Developing emotional intelligence

Recently, Hartas (2006, p. 16) commented in regard to pre-school children who were very able as follows:

> ... it is not easy to determine whether limited concentration is related to dyslexia or giftedness ... they need reassurance and the time and space to talk about their feelings. In the context of circle time and peer-mediated activities ... gifted young children with dyslexia are encouraged to display social and emotional intelligence by taking others' perspective and inferring about their thoughts and emotional states and showing good leadership qualities and good language and communication skills.

Here, Hartas is raising some very important issues in regard to how the needs of more able children can be difficult to determine and how they require carefully managed changes in their environment in order for them to develop and realise their potential. Now let us look at the case of Lauren, who, prior to starting school at the age of 5 years, was considered by those around her to be 'very advanced' and 'very bright'.

 Example

Lauren is 10 years of age and has just begun a new academic year. Though she has never refused to attend school she readily admits to feeling very unhappy when at school. This was not always the case and when she was younger she was always keen to tell everyone and especially her grandparents how much she enjoyed school. Lauren attends the local school, which is set in an affluent area. The other pupils in her class come from homes where incomes are high and where parents have high expectations for them. Though she started school in a very positive manner and was viewed by her teacher at the time as being very advanced in drawing and speaking, she has always struggled to read and spell and now, years later, tells everyone that she *'hates'* reading and that her *'worst'* lessons are when she has to *'do writing'*.

It is clear from Lauren's experiences at school that, like Michael in the earlier example, she has poorly developed emotional intelligence and that this is an important factor in her lack of progress in literacy and general development. With the agreement of her head teacher, Lauren's class teacher arranged for the school's educational psychologist to offer one afternoon when all staff can improve their understanding of the type of emotional difficulties that children with dyslexia can experience. The class teacher also arranged to meet with Lauren's mother and the Special Educational Needs Coordinator (SENCo) to agree a number of interventions. These include the following:

- Lauren's new class teacher will set aside two half-hour sessions each week with her Teaching Assistant over the next month when they can both talk with Lauren about the worries she has in regard to her problems with literacy and numeracy.
- The class teacher will introduce Lauren to a number of new strategies and model these to her Teaching Assistant who can then continue working with Lauren after the two months have passed. During her weekly sessions the class teacher will help Lauren to focus on her

strengths, for example, Lauren is very good at art and especially drawing. She will also focus on helping Lauren understand that whilst she struggles with reading, spelling and writing, this is not due to a lack of intellectual ability but because of the way she learns, emphasising to Lauren that everyone learns differently.

- Lauren's mother agrees to give some dedicated time each night to reading a book with Lauren when she goes to bed, with particular attention being given to talking with Lauren about aspects of the story (literal comprehension) and encouraging Lauren to reflect, for example, upon how the story could be different, how the characters in the story could behave differently, what elements she, herself, might add to the story if she were reading it, and so on (inferential comprehension).

Whilst Lauren is now engaging in a programme of work that will support her in making progress, it is worth considering her experiences when she was in her early years. It is also worth considering how other children manage through their primary years to cope with feelings of failure. We now turn to what has increasingly become recognised as a key factor in children's social, emotional and academic progress: *self-efficacy*.

Self-efficacy and its relevance

It should be recognised from the outset that children who struggle with literacy, can also present with a variety of personality factors as well as shades of emotional well-being. Some may, for example, present as being quite extrovert and socially skilled. Some may even present as confident and articulate. For the majority of poor readers this is not, however, the case and many of these children can be observed within schools to be inhibited and self-effacing, introverted and lacking in self-confidence. They may also, for example, internalise feelings of unworthiness and even guilt. They will, typically, be disturbed by their own lack of progress as they perceive those around them making substantial strides with all aspects of literacy, which present significant challenges for them.

These children are highly sensitive to the reactions of those around them, especially their peers, and can become very sensitive to any type of criticism levelled at them by classmates and teachers. Their interpretations of how others see them are especially important and typically more pronounced than in other children, for they are faced daily with the prospect of attempting tasks in front of their peers that will cause them significant challenges and that typically result in relatively poor outcomes, little praise and sense of achievement, and even downright failure, which they perceive to be inescapable.

Drawing upon the findings of an experimental study of college students undertaken some decades ago by Covington and Omelich (1981), Howe (1999, p. 121) summarised their results as follows:

> What happens to a child at school who encounters failure after failure … failure led to the participants having lower estimates of their ability, and in turn they became less happy, more shameful and less confident of future success. With the accumulation of further failures they became increasingly distressed, they experienced feelings of hopelessness and they became anxious to attribute their failure to external factors if it was at all possible to do so. When other strategies for maintaining self-esteem in the face of failure were no longer effective, signs of inaction and hopelessness became common.

Howe goes on to speculate how the effects of failure experienced by older college students would be much 'more devastating' on younger children.

Some decades ago Bandura (1977, 1997) introduced us to the concept of 'self-efficacy', which he saw as the belief that children had in their own abilities to do well and to exercise control over their actions in order to realise success. Bandura viewed self-efficacy as directly allied to how children think and behave, and perhaps most importantly, their emotional state. Children with weak self-efficacy may, for example, tend towards avoiding tasks that represent a challenge to them and may prefer, instead, to direct their thinking towards negative factors. They may frame their thinking in such a way as to gradually convince themselves that they are unable to achieve success. Typically, children who have weak self-efficacy may present themselves to others as having poor self-confidence. Directly related to children's capacity to achieve success are those feelings they have internalised about themselves as well as others, and the manner in which they construct their understanding of the world around them and of which they are a dialectical part.

Bandura identified four key psychological processes, which he claimed are directly influenced by the self-efficacy beliefs that individuals hold, namely, cognitive, motivational, affective and selection (Hayes, 1994, p. 477). With the first of these, the type of thinking that individuals engage in is seen as central to the way in which they behave and how their thinking alters and drives their behaviour patterns. When children, for example, are faced with a problem they will reflect upon the problem and how skilful or adept they might be in terms of solving it. In this way their thinking comes to define their chosen behaviour and actions. They may think they are unable to attempt the problem and not engage with it or they may think they can attempt it and gain some if not complete success.

With the second process, motivational, children may be very motivated to put in lots of effort to solving the problem and stick at it or they may lack motivation and give up all too readily. The third process, affective, refers to levels of anxiety and stress experienced, for example, by children when they might be faced with attempting or completing a task that may prove challenging. The final process, selection, refers to how children, for example, might or might not choose to attempt a task that is challenging. It is likely that children will attempt tasks that, whilst challenging, will be within their capability. This would suggest, as Bandura himself indicated, that when children's self-efficacy is high then they will be more likely to attempt tasks that present significant challenges. With children with dyslexia, therefore, it can be hypothesised that they will be more likely to attempt tasks such as written examinations if they have high self-efficacy. On the other hand, if they have low self-efficacy then they will be less likely and may give up too readily, thus reducing their rate of success.

Those children who experience significant struggles with literacy will attempt to understand their sense of failure in different ways. They may try to hide their difficulties from others by, for example, not volunteering to take part in particular activities, remaining detached from what is happening around them when literacy is involved, and even turning themselves into submissive and overly quiet participants. Others may present as aggressive and defiant. In very extreme cases, some children may even unwittingly adopt facial mannerisms such as ticks and nods with associated behaviours such as biting their nails excessively and even stuttering when asked questions.

Given the task of identifying personal learning goals, children with weak self-efficacy will typically perform less well than those with strong self-efficacy. They may, for example, demonstrate little interest in attempting and then completing tasks. They may also demonstrate little commitment when asked to work collaboratively with their peers. They may even demonstrate significant levels of anxiety when directed to participate in problem-based learning tasks with other students. Colverd and Hodgkin (2011, p. 36) have stressed how such children, when placed in certain learning situations, may:

> ... place limits on what they think is possible, believing a task is beyond their capability. Lack of self-belief affects their motivation

and their commitment to learning. 'I can't do this, it's boring' signals 'I don't believe I can be successful with this and therefore I don't want to take the risk – it may or may not be boring'.

Bandura proposed that a key factor in improving self-efficacy was the development of a sense of 'mastery' through experiences. Examples of this might be: observing other children succeeding at particular tasks; receiving affirming comments from significant others, such as teachers, parents and fellow students; and comprehending their own feelings and emotions. It goes without saying that developing one's self-efficacy is an important and integral part of the learning experiences of children, and especially in their early years. The implications for teachers and Early Years practitioners, therefore, in developing and strengthening self-efficacy in children are clear. Despite the obvious gains in developing self-efficacy, it can be argued that in the case of too many children with dyslexia and developmental literacy difficulties, opportunities to do so remain few and far between.

It has been recognised for decades (Harris and Sipay, 1990, p. 366) that children who are disabled in aspects of reading can be rejected not only by their peers but also by their teachers, and are frequently reported as having inferior status within their schools. Whilst Harris and Sipay recognised that inferior status may also be due to other factors such as socioeconomic status, they also emphasised that this is an important element in considering the effects of poor literacy skills. They went on to comment as follows:

> Children under the age of 7 or 8 are less likely than older students to conclude that they are low in ability and to decrease their efforts as a result of failure. After the age of 10, failure is much more likely to have seriously debilitating effects on performance … Students with low self-concepts are more likely to attribute failures to lack of ability and to explain their successes as being caused by external factors. Both attributions could lead to lowered motivation … (1990, p. 367)

☐ Summary

This chapter explored the nature of emotional intelligence and its importance and relevance to children experiencing difficulties with the acquisition of literacy. Consideration was also given to how emotional intelligence can be developed and how better emotional intelligence

(Continued)

(Continued)

can impact positively upon children with dyslexia and developmental literacy difficulties. The following chapter will now focus on child-centred approaches to identification and assessment.

 Recommended reading

Colverd, S. and Hodgkin, B. (2011) *Developing Emotional Intelligence in the Primary School.* London: Routledge.
MacBlain, S.F. (2014) *How Children Learn.* London: Sage.

References

Association of Teachers and Lecturers (ATL) (2005) *An Intelligent Look at Emotional Intelligence.* London: Association of Teachers and Lecturers.

Bandura, A. (1977) *Social Learning Theory.* Englewood Cliffs, NJ: Prentice Hall.

Bandura, A. (1997) *Self-efficacy: The Exercise of Control.* New York: Freeman.

Burden, R. and Burdett, J. (2005) 'Factors Associated with Successful Learning in Pupils with Dyslexia: A Motivational Analysis', *British Journal of Special Education*, 32(2): 100–4.

Colverd, S. and Hodgkin, B. (2011) *Developing Emotional Intelligence in the Primary School.* London: Routledge.

Covington, M.L. and Omelich, C.L. (1981) 'As Failures Mount: Affective and Cognitive Consequences of Ability Demotion in the Classroom', *Journal of Educational Psychology*, 73: 796–808.

Department of Education Northern Ireland (DENI) (1998) *Code of Practice on the Identification and Assessment of Special Educational Needs.* Bangor, N. Ireland: DENI.

Goleman, D. (1996) *Emotional Intelligence: Why It Can Matter More than IQ.* London: Bloomsbury.

Harris, A. and Sipay, E.R. (1990) *How to Increase Reading Ability: A Guide to Developmental & Remedial Methods* (9th edn). New York: Longman.

Hartas, D. (2006) *Dyslexia in the Early Years: A Guide to Teaching and Learning.* London: Routledge.

Hayes, N. (1994) *Foundations of Psychology: An Introductory Text.* London: Routledge.

Howe, M. (1999) *A Teacher's Guide to the Psychology of Learning.* London: Blackwell.

Lawrence, D.H. (1915) *The Rainbow.* London: Heinemann.

Long, L., MacBlain, S.F. and MacBlain, M.S. (2007) 'Supporting Students with Dyslexia at the Secondary Level: An Emotional Model of Literacy', *Journal of Adolescent & Adult Literacy*, 51(2): 124–34.

MacBlain, S.F. (2014) *How Children Learn*. London: Sage.

Ott, P. (1997) *How to Detect and Manage Dyslexia: A Reference and Resource Manual*. Oxford: Heinemann.

Salovey, P. and Mayer, J.D. (1990) 'Emotional Intelligence'. Available at: http://www.unh.edu/emotional_intelligence/EIAssets/EmotionalIntelligenceProper/EI1990%20Emotional%20Intelligence.pdf (accessed 20 March 2013).

BUILDING CAPACITY TO RAISE LITERACY STANDARDS FOR CHILDREN WITH DYSLEXIA AND DEVELOPMENTAL LITERACY DIFFICULTIES

CHILD-CENTRED APPROACHES TO THE IDENTIFICATION AND ASSESSMENT OF DYSLEXIA AND DEVELOPMENTAL LITERACY DIFFICULTIES

Sean MacBlain and Louise Long

Chapter aims

- To examine critically formal and informal approaches to the assessment of dyslexia and developmental literacy difficulties.
- To explore the concept of Working Memory and its relationship with language and literacy development.
- To examine critically relevant research and scholarship on the identification of dyslexia in pupils with English as an additional language (EAL).
- To examine findings from critical literature on the coexistence of dyslexia with ADHD and their implications for assessment approaches and intervention programmes.
- To explore the concept of literacy underachievement.

Introduction

In a recent article Reason and Stothard (2013, p. 10) offered what some might consider to be a rather appealing but controversial suggestion that viewing dyslexia as a continuum implies that it is '… the remit of general education' and, therefore, not'… limited to specialist teaching'. Teachers, they suggest, '… need to have the knowledge and skills that enable them to notice pupils who struggle with basic literacy and to do something about it'. Reason and Stothard go on to suggest that the question that those involved in the administration of resources need to now ask is, not 'does the child have dyslexia?' but rather, 'are the child's dyslexic difficulties so severe and persistent that they require extra resources?'

This question is central to having a better understanding of where we are now in this new century in terms of responding to the needs of children with dyslexia and developmental literacy difficulties. Given that the resourcing model applied to schools which have moved out of Local Authority control and become Academies or Free Schools has changed significantly in the past three years, the attention being given to resourcing dyslexic children must surely come under closer scrutiny.

Formal and informal assessment

The importance of having effective and purposeful assessment procedures, protocols and contexts cannot be emphasised enough. Integral to this, however, is the need to have agreed structures and careful planning. It is not enough to leave things to chance and to deal with children's difficulties and situations as they arise. Being proactive and being prepared are two essential components in successful processes. It must be remembered that parents of children with dyslexia and developmental literacy difficulties have needs as well. It is not uncommon, for example, for parents to become quite distressed when they see their child struggling to make progress and they know intuitively that there is something that is preventing them from doing so. Anxieties surrounding their child's lack of progress and, in many cases, growing unhappiness can also affect families in a number of adverse ways. Many educational psychologists, for example, will be familiar with cases where parents have contacted them for an assessment of their child and poured out feelings of frustration and anxiety, and even hopelessness, which have dominated their thinking and their own emotional lives since their child first attended formal education.

> Seeing your child struggle at school when the other children are doing well is really hard, it's really upsetting, you feel so helpless but deep down you know there is something that is stopping them make progress but no one will tell you … it affects all of us in the family.

It is the authors' contention that too many children with dyslexia fail to be identified and too many children who are identified are not identified early enough. One may frequently hear parents of children with dyslexia complaining that their child's teacher has urged them not to be too concerned about their children's progress in reading and writing as it is too early to be concerned and that dyslexia cannot be identified before the child is around 7 or 8 years of age. For many children with dyslexia, however, this can be too late and a strong sense of failure may have been internalised by the child together with a lowering of self-esteem and a growing lack of self-confidence.

Assessment takes many forms. Effective assessment, however, needs to take careful account not just of children's behaviours but also the environment within which they are learning and the nature of the teaching they are receiving. This was formally recognised in the Code of Practice (DfES, 2001a, para. 5.6), where assessment was deemed not to be a 'single process' but rather, to include the following four elements: the child's learning characteristics; their learning environment being provided by the school; the task they were completing; and the style of teaching that they were receiving.

Essentially, there are two broad approaches to assessment, namely formal and informal. With the first of these, assessment is typically undertaken using standardised tests and happens on a specific day at a specific time. For example, a child considered to be dyslexic might be given reading and spelling tests by their teacher after school or by the SENCo or an educational psychologist in a room separate to the classroom and the other children. Some reading and spelling tests can also be given to whole groups such as to classes. With the latter, assessment typically occurs over time with, for example, the teacher observing the child working in a number of situations, or regularly scrutining the type of spelling errors a child makes in different aspects of their work. This latter type of assessment can offer rich information regarding a child's performance as well as information that will not be available through standardised testing.

One frequently used informal assessment device is a Reading Inventory, where, for example, the reading style of a child is recorded – whether or not they omit words when reading, if they read word-by-word, what particular words and letter strings present problems, and so on. Such assessment, it is argued, can offer a more complete picture of a child's performance. It is now useful for readers to familiarise themselves with terminology that is frequently used by professionals when tasked with identifying and assessing children. Here are some of the most frequently used terms when standardised assessment is being carried out:

- *Percentiles*: These are frequently used by educational psychologists (see, for example, the case studies in Chapter 3). Percentiles are used to make comparisons with children of the same age or, in some cases, the same year level at school. Scores range from 1 through to 99. It is generally accepted that two-thirds of children are considered to function within the average range of ability and this range is represented between the 16th and 84th centiles ... The 85th centile upwards represents increasingly higher ability with the 99th centile representing the top 1% of ability and the 1st centile representing the lowest 1% of ability.

- *Standard scores* are scores that fall on the normal curve of distribution, which generally has a mean of 100 (or 50) and a standard deviation of 15 (or 10). A score of 100, for example, indicates an average performance. A child gaining a standardised score of 112 would fall within the average range, which lies between 85 and 115.
- *Stanines* are best understood as scales represented by 9 segments with 1 being the lowest and 9 the highest; 4, 5 and 6 represent the average range. Stanine scores tend not to be used when assessing children's academic performance.

It is worth readers taking some time to visit the following link, which offers important and useful insights into formal and informal assessment of dyslexia. It centres around a student who was diagnosed as having dyslexia in his final year at university and the types of difficulties he experienced throughout his schooling.

 Useful link

This is a short and informative video clip of two interviews. One interview is with an expert in the field of dyslexia who explains what exactly dyslexia is, the symptoms and difficulties experienced by individuals with dyslexia, and some of the ways of addressing it. The other interview is where a young man (Daniel) talks openly and honestly about his dyslexia and more specifically about the difficulties he experienced when young, throughout school and when studying at university. Daniel also talks about the type of support he received and how useful this was for him.

'Dyslexia': http://www.youtube.com/watch?v=IUbXyOjV1Cg

Identification and assessment in the Early Years

From the moment of birth, children explore not just physically but also through sight and sound. They enjoy rhyme as well as making and playing with 'silly' sounds and, later on, words and phrases. They also instinctively enjoy rhythm and can be observed actively involving themselves in nursery rhymes, clapping and tapping, and moving and dancing to the rhythms they hear. Early Years practitioners and Primary teachers know, intuitively, how important the acquisition of these skills is, and the importance of having opportunities to develop and practise them and, more importantly perhaps, learning new ones. This has been recognised for many years, as can be seen by the emphasis placed upon them by such notable thinkers as Montessori and Steiner. Young children appear to greatly enjoy all of these activities, which, as well as helping them develop their learning, also help them develop a sense of themselves and how they perceive others and are, in return, perceived by others. When young children present as having difficulties with the acquisition and internalisation of these skills then the adults working with them will need to provide them with opportunities to develop these abilities. In some cases young children who may lack stimulation from home may need a great deal of stimulation at their pre-school or nursery setting and will require careful observation of their development. If they become 'left behind' then this can affect the way they come to view themselves not just as learners but also as individuals.

Linked to the development of these connections is a need to support children in developing their vocabulary, especially when they are living in families where language lacks richness, is limited in vocabulary and their experiences of language can be limited to shouting instructions and directions. It is now recognised that children who enter Early Years settings and primary schools with large vocabularies will, typically, do better in the development of reading and writing than those who enter with a limited vocabulary. Linked to the development of early auditory development is visual and motor development. Drysdale (2009), cited in Crombie and Reid (2009, p. 238), for example, has emphasised the importance of young children interacting with shapes, colours and patterns, and having opportunities to play with and manipulate objects as a basis for future skills in reading and writing. She has commented as follows:

> Visual discrimination and recall are core skills required for processing the fine detail in print … Successful readers employ different areas on both sides of the brain to process written language … The ability to perform cross lateral movements such as crawling and skipping shows whether bilateral, whole-brain processing is taking place. Watching how children coordinate movement on, over and around objects can reveal how well they plan, organize, control and execute a sequence of movements … If reading with comprehension is to be accomplished, operation of the different skills described above must be integrated and work at speed described as 'automatic' …

Some years ago Crombie and Reid (2009, p. 71) suggested that, '...if early identification is to be effective then it is important that it focuses on pre-school children as well as children in the early years of primary school'. Much important information can be gained about a child's functioning prior to starting primary school. Children's learning and progress, at the pre-school stage, can be carefully observed and interpreted. This is, of course, dependent to a large degree on the skills and knowledge base of those who are observing, and then recording and understanding their observations (Gray and MacBlain, 2012; MacBlain, 2014). However, Crombie and Reid have drawn an important distinction, between the 'early identification of potential difficulties' and the 'early identification of dyslexia'. They go on to emphasise a number of factors that might be observed, or screened for, in very young children with potential literacy difficulties, for example, poorly developing coordination and sequencing of movements, difficulties with rhyming and alliteration and attaching verbal labels to objects, and difficulties with word finding.

> When we see a pattern of concerns, sometimes coupled with a known family history of dyslexia, we have identified a child at possible 'risk' of the later frustration and humiliation, which may result from failure to gain skills related to literacy. It is at this stage that timely appropriate interventions can make a huge difference to the child's prospects ... At this stage, there is no need to label ... but there is an obligation on the adults around to ensure that everything that can be done, is done to prevent the likely de-motivation that will result from failure to learn. (Crombie and Reid, 2009, p. 72)

Hartas (2006) further emphasises the importance of using quantitative and qualitative elements when assessing very young children, and, like Crombie and Reid, notes the importance of observation and discussions with the child's family, as well as information relating to their language development. In regard to observation, Dowling (2005, p. 30) has commented that, 'The task of really getting inside children's minds and understanding them can only properly be achieved through observing their actions and conversing with them'.

It is clear that early identification and assessment are essential. This must, however, be accurate and meaningful and must inform practice. Children who take to reading early on and who develop a strong sense of confidence in their abilities with reading, and subsequently writing, will, typically, have a head start and will, more than likely, develop a strong sense of self-confidence, self-esteem and self-efficacy (see Chapter 3). Children, who do not, may feel less able than their peers and internalise a sense of self characterised by thinking whereby they come to talk themselves into believing that they are poor readers, or worse still, not very able. Such perceived failure can have lasting effects, which, typically, are sustained throughout adolescence and adulthood (Long et al., 2007).

Identification and assessment in the primary school

It is too often asserted by some teachers in primary schools that assessment of dyslexia should not be undertaken when the child is still young or in Key Stage 1. Such thinking is misguided and will almost certainly lead to the child's difficulties failing to be properly identified and recorded and a failure in receiving appropriate and necessary provision. All too often, children have to fail before their needs are correctly identified and remedied. This can lead to all manner of problems. Take, for example, the child with dyslexia who is highly articulate and creative, good at art and design and very musical but struggles greatly with reading, spelling and writing. Their progress in literacy will be far slower than that of their friends and peers, weekly spelling tests will be a time of heightened anxiety and homework will be an area that not only causes the child considerable anxiety but also his/her parents. At times the child's parents may find themselves losing their temper and upsetting not only their child but also themselves.

Children who fail to acquire literacy when young will often develop a poor self-image, and come to view themselves as less able than their peers. They may develop secondary difficulties such as trying to avoid work that involves writing or reading, distracting others and, in more extreme cases, refusing to go to school. These children may lose confidence and instead of associating effort with outcome will internalise a notion that they simply aren't able enough to do the work. Crombie and Reid (2009, p. 72), rather worryingly, have commented as follows:

> We have not yet been able to measure the exact extent to which failure to tackle early difficulties may lead to later social problems, mental health issues and/or loss of potential, but we do know that these are significant issues ...

It is encouraging that in the past decade enormous strides have been taken in regard to early identification and assessment. These are tied very closely to the increased emphasis upon the teaching of phonics in the first years. This said, concern exists in regard to introducing all children to phonics and a more formalised literacy curriculum at too young an age. Many teachers in the UK, and especially England, which has a massive inspection service, Ofsted, feel under enormous pressure to achieve results and reach targets in literacy, often at the expense of the child's emotional and social needs.

 Example

Alex is 8 years of age and since starting school he has struggled with the acquisition of literacy. His parents have referred him for assessment by an educational psychologist. Extracts from the educational psychologist's report are as follows:

Alex presented as a pleasant and outgoing child and he impressed me with his willingness to attempt some tasks that clearly presented him with a challenge. I found Alex easy to talk to and I enjoyed his sense of humour and sense of fun. Alex worked very hard through the assessment and persevered with all of the tasks I set him. I observed Alex's pencil grip and fine motor coordination to be weak and he demonstrated a tendency to force his pencil when writing words. This said, his writing was neat and legible. I noted that Alex used print when writing ... Alex's parents reported that when in class Alex could be easily distracted and when younger had recorded a Reading Accuracy age of 5 years 6 months at chronological age 7 years and 9 months and a Reading Comprehension age of 5 years 2 months ... Of particular note was Alex's much weaker performance on the Digit-Span sub-test suggesting the existence of difficulties of a specific nature relating to Working Memory. Also of note was Alex's below average performance on the Coding sub-test. Low scores on this sub-test would suggest visual-motor coordination problems, poor pen control or absence of challenge in the task. Alex's performance on this sub-test offers further evidence for suggesting the existence of specific learning difficulties. Taken together with his weaker performance on the Block Design sub-test this would suggest the existence of some specific learning difficulties of a perceptual nature. The Block Design sub-test attempts to measure the reproductive aspect of visual-motor co-ordination, perceptual organisation ability and spatial visualisation ability or abstract conceptualising ability and generalising ability ... In summary, assessment indicates to me that he has specific learning difficulties of a dyslexic nature. Such difficulties will place greater demands upon Alex within the classroom setting and particularly in lessons when he is being asked to process larger amounts of verbal information. He will, for example, experience greater difficulty than many other children of his age with sustaining concentration and attention. This will be especially the case where he is undertaking formal learning that holds little immediate relevance for him. His difficulties with concentration should not be viewed only as a lack of motivation but more as a challenge for him, which is related to his specific learning difficulties in the area of working memory ... Alex will benefit from opportunities when he can be assisted in raising his self-confidence and self-esteem. It will be important for adults working with Alex to find creative ways of encouraging him to take greater risks. This will help him to remain motivated ... Of benefit to Alex will be opportunities where he can draw upon evidence of his own personal success to convince himself that he is capable of doing much better. This will support him in internalising a self-belief in himself and his own ability to improve. This will feed into his self-concept and self-esteem so that he sees himself as an effective learner....

Two years later Alex's parents brought him back to the same educational psychologist. Extracts from her second report were as follows:

On this occasion, Alex achieved the following reading and spelling results (Table 4.1). These should be compared with the results in Table 4.2, which Alex gained when I first assessed him.

Table 4.1   Case study – Alex (results from my most recent assessment)

Test	Standard Score	Centile	Age Equivalent
Basic Reading	72	03	6 years 9 months
Reading Comprehension	71	03	6 years 9 months
Spelling	79	08	7 years 4 months

Table 4.2   Case study – Alex (results from my previous assessment)

Test	Standard Score	Centile	Age Equivalent
Basic Reading	78	07	6 years 4 months
Reading Comprehension	80	09	6 years 7 months
Spelling	79	08	6 years 7 months

(Continued)

(Continued)

In my view Alex remains very confused by the reading and spelling process. He needs highly structured, cumulative, sequential and, especially, multisensory teaching and learning experiences that will work to address his specific learning difficulties ... When I asked Alex on this occasion to tell me the vowels he appeared very confused and responded with 't', 'u', 'e' and 'n'. Alex was still unable to tell me the alphabet in correct sequence. I would make the following suggestions, which adults working with Alex should find helpful:

- *Alex will benefit from having a much better understanding of the language of instruction in the area of literacy development. For example, he needs to know that words are made up using such elements as prefixes, suffixes and roots. He needs to familiarise himself with these so that he is using an effective strategy whereby he attempts to analyse the structure as opposed to simply guessing.*
- *Alex should follow a highly structured, sequential and cumulative programme in reading and spelling. He will benefit, particularly, from employing multisensory techniques, which work to compensate for his specific learning difficulties in the areas of working memory and processing speed.*
- *Daily reinforcement of new as well as prior learning will be important. I would suggest that Alex has a visual timetable of his week, which is broken down into segments, for example, before and after morning and afternoon breaks to help him visualise when he needs to work on particular elements of developing literacy skills.*
- *I was pleased to see that Alex was using cursive script when writing. He should be encouraged to sound out letters as he writes them and to say the actual word after he has sounded it out.*
- *Alex could be involved in making his own books.*
- *Using information and communication technology to support his learning with word recognition, reading comprehension and spelling will be very helpful and will offer Alex regular and important opportunities to record, self-check and proofread his work.*
- *Regular access to high-interest and simple reading material, which links to Alex's natural curiosity.*
- *Paired reading with adults should be encouraged, especially where he can seek connections between his own ideas and those he is reading and talk about these.*
- *Daily opportunities to develop his self-confidence.*

Exercise

Consider the lack of progress that Alex has made in the above example. Identify three factors that have contributed to him making limited progress. How important is the identification of specific learning difficulties and especially problems with Working Memory? How might these specific difficulties affect him in ways other than academic progress?

Multi-agency working

As well as recognising the importance of early identification, Crombie and Reid (2009, p. 71) also emphasised the importance of agencies working together where children are considered to have potential learning difficulties. Like others (MacBlain, 2014), they have emphasised the importance of involving parents in the identification process:

> The school should not be the only agency involved in early identification. If integrated assessment is to be effective, structured and collaborative planning is necessary. This collaboration needs to involve teachers, parents, community workers and other professionals such as home teachers, occupational therapists, psychologists and speech and language therapists.

Working with parents

Despite a growing recognition over the last decades of the importance of involving parents in the identification and assessment of children with dyslexia, it is all too often the case that parents can be left out of the picture. It is not unusual, for example, to hear parents sharing their frustration about how they are not being listened to by their child's teacher or by the school. Parents need to work in tandem with their child's teacher, particularly where their child is presenting difficulties with their learning. This said, it is vitally important that parents are listened to and not seen as overly anxious or wanting to be too involved in their children's learning and the delivery of the curriculum. Recently, MacBlain (2014, p. 178) cited a review of special educational needs and disability in England undertaken by Ofsted (2010) in which they visited early years private, voluntary, independent and maintained primary and secondary schools, including independent and non-maintained special schools, as well as residential schools, further education colleges and independent specialist colleges:

Following their review Ofsted highlighted the fact that the term 'special educational needs' was too widely used … the inspectors reported on schools, which, they observed, identified children as having special educational needs when their needs were, in actual fact, not significantly different to the majority of the other children. The report concluded that whilst these children were underachieving, this was, in part, due to the fact that the provision offered by schools was 'not good enough' and that expectations of these children were 'too low'.

This relatively recent finding by Ofsted is worrying and, as was the case with Alex in the last example, suggests that many children have, over the years, failed to have appropriate teaching.

Low achievement

Though there are many factors that contribute to low achievement, it is possible to identify some key areas. In their report *Removing Barriers to Literacy*, Ofsted (2011, p. 14) commented as follows:

Of the barriers facing the youngest children … a common problem was some form of delay of their development in speech and language. In one nursery visited, for example, where almost all children were of White British origin, approximately 30% of the three-year-olds started nursery with a marked speech delay. Another common problem that placed children at early disadvantage was a disturbed start to their lives. In one nursery visited, most of the two-year-olds had already had some form of social care intervention by the time they joined the nursery.

These statistics are worrying and suggest that many children making the transition into education from home are often ill-equipped and ill-prepared for more formal learning experiences, most notably perhaps, their acquisition of literacy. The report went on to indicate, again rather worryingly, that:

Visits to the Early Years registered providers and schools confirmed the impact of the pupils' poor socio-economic circumstances. Although the children could often learn to decode print successfully in school, they were not always able to ascribe meaning to the words they could say because they did not have the experiences that the words described. This affected their progress in literacy in the longer term because it affected their comprehension of what they were reading.

Underachievement

Identifying and addressing literacy underachievement has received renewed interest in recent years (DENI, 2011). Psychometric assessment will yield a measure of the child's level of cognitive ability and, in conjunction with observational and standardised findings on the child's literacy performance, will enable a teacher or educational psychologist to evaluate if the learner has specific learning difficulties (SpLD). A robust assessment will shed light on those factors that are contributing to the learner's failure to meet his/her potential, for example, hearing loss, inappropriate teaching, motivational issues, community factors or dyslexia. The role of intelligence tests is much contested and controversial (Mortimore et al., 2012). However, outcomes from intelligence tests will help to build a comprehensive profile of the learner's strengths and weaknesses and inform diagnostic decisions and intervention programmes. The authors sound a cautionary note in that findings from intelligence tests should be interpreted as a snapshot of the learner's performance at a particular point in time and in the context of within-child and extraneous variables and contextual and cultural factors that may impact on the learner's performance (Boyle and Fisher, 2007). Moreover, a norm-referenced test of listening comprehension or observations of a mismatch between the learner's talking and listening skills and performance in reading and writing could be used in place of intelligence testing when assessing for literacy underachievement (Moll, 2012).

Advancing inclusivity for pupils with EAL who have dyslexia

Policy directives on equality, diversity and inclusion aim to advance the UK Government's vision of ensuring that vulnerable groups have access to high-quality educational experiences that will enable all learners to gain qualifications (DfES, 2001a; GEO, 2010). The presence, participation and achievement of marginalised learners require all schools, irrespective of how they are funded or managed, to identify and remove barriers to learning in increasingly diverse contemporary classrooms. The literacy of schools in the UK is English, so minority first language (L1) bilingual children are expected to learn to read and write fluently in the majority language (Mortimore et al., 2012). Thus, pupils with EAL (L2) have additional educational needs, and provisions for these needs may require additional support that should enable this group of learners to reach their full potential at each stage of development (e.g. DfES, 2001b).

Mortimore et al. (2012) rightly pointed out that increasing numbers of children are entering UK primary schools with little or no English. Learning difficulties of a dyslexic nature may be hard to identify in pupils with EAL because of the risk that the learner's difficulties will be attributed to either poor language proficiency or limited schooling (BPS, 1999). However, difficulties with acquiring a second language can mask indicators of emerging dyslexia. The kernel of the issue in the identification of dyslexia in pupils with EAL is the difficulty with separating reading difficulties per se from poor language proficiency (Elbro et al., 2012). This problem raises questions about how to deal with the obvious language bias in diagnosing dyslexia in pupils with EAL. The influences of oral language on reading comprehension and word recognition in both the mother tongue and the second language are well documented in critical literature (Gough et al., 1996; Nation and Cocksey, 2009; Snowling and Hulme, 2011).

Elbro et al. (2012) proposed that when teachers are testing the hypothesis that a pupil with EAL has dyslexia, one way around the language bias is to assess literacy skills and language foundations in the native language. Research converges on the claim that strengths and weaknesses in the linguistic codes of phonology/orthography (sounds/letter patterns), syntax and semantics are transferred between languages (Sparks et al., 1995). Thus, it is likely that an assessment of reading abilities and/or language precursors in the native language will be valid for language precursors and reading development in the second language. However, Elbro et al. (2012) also acknowledged that such an assessment might not be feasible and went on to suggest that an alternative way of dealing with the language bias is to assess those skills that predict reading development in children who are learning to read in a second language. There is a consensus in the literature that precursors of reading can be assessed reliably in pupils who are learning to read in a second language and that assessment outcomes can be highly predictive of reading development in the second language (Lipka and Siegel, 2007). These precursors for assessment primarily include letter knowledge, phoneme awareness, rapid naming and phonological short-term memory (Elbro et al., 2012). Professional intuition and integrity will come into play in the decisions made about when to exercise flexibility in the administration of standardised tests whilst concurrently obtaining reliable standard scores that will inform the design of intervention programmes.

Robust and purposeful assessment approaches demand that information is also sought, collated and synthesised on the child's learning history, including oral language proficiency in L1 and, where appropriate, literacy progress in L1. Moreover, crucial background information on the transparency of the orthography of L1 should be gathered. Mortimore et al. (2012) adroitly pointed to the evidence base, illustrating that in transparent languages (languages where single phonemes map consistently onto single graphemes), dyslexia is more likely to manifest in terms of speed and fluency difficulties, which will, in turn, hamper comprehension skills. In cases where a pupil has been exposed to continuous reading instruction in L2, information relating to his/her understanding and use of language in social and academic situations, academic motivation and degree of engagement with literacy tasks and the outcomes from curriculum-based assessment will help to provide a holistic view of the pupil's learning profile, which is essential for child-centred intervention programmes.

It is proposed that the two principles underpinning approaches to assessment and intervention for dyslexia in pupils with EAL are child centredness and cultural fairness. The authors also propose that at the primary level child-centred assessment approaches will best inform intervention programmes by prioritising the construction of a profile of the pupil's strengths and weaknesses over an identification of dyslexia. This argument corroborates findings from Mortimore et al. (2012). Culture-fair approaches to assessment and intervention place demands on teachers to gather information from the child with EAL and his/her parents on the child's life experiences and the cultural and emotional significance of those experiences. This process could well involve an interpreter and the use of enabling and innovative methodologies for eliciting the child's views, aspirations and concerns (BPS, 1999; Mortimore et al., 2012; Smith and Long, 2014).

A key concern for practitioners is to design, implement, monitor and regularly review intervention programmes that best meet the needs of the individual learner. The starting point for any intervention programme is to build on the learner's strengths. Targets for advancing the pupil's progress in literacy should match identified areas of difficulty. Child-centred educational programmes should be 'pupil-led', which means providing structured opportunities for pupil voice and choice and teachers working in partnership with pupils. Moreover, systems should be in place to support parental involvement in provision for their child's SEN. However, these systems need to be adapted to meet the distinctive strengths and needs of each family, requiring that in addition to the cultural context, understandings of SEN and parents' capacity to access resources and expertise are also taken into account (Gardner et al. 2003).

Heneveld (2007) acknowledged that teachers are at the heart of any quality improvement process, which will live or die in the classroom through varied pedagogical and assessment strategies. Based on an extensive review of critical literature, Mortimore et al. (2012) summarised best-fit learning and teaching methodologies for pupils with EAL who have dyslexia as follows:

> programmes should incorporate a combination of strategies designed to improve phonological processing skills (including verbal memory), oral language development and explicit vocabulary teaching, explicit strategies to develop comprehension skills (such as reciprocal reading), work with morphemes and strategies to improve memory and processing speed. The programme should be structured, reinforced, cumulative and multi-sensory. It should take into account the learner's cultural background and experiences, structure of L1, learner's attitudes to literacy. (Mortimore et al., 2012, p. 45)

 Exercise

Learners with dyslexia find it difficult to hear speech rhythm and speech timing and also have difficulties in perceiving musical rhythms (Goswami, 2013). These difficulties in timing could explain why learners with dyslexia struggle with phonology – the sound structure of words – across languages.

What opportunities exist for teachers to use music and poetry from the pupil's mother tongue to explicitly link musical beat structure to the beat structure of the language and, consequently, to improve the pupil's rhythmic abilities? What role could parents and the local community play in helping teachers to advance pupils' rhythmic entrainment?

 Exercise

The following video presentations should help to inform your knowledge and understanding of effective strategies for removing language as a barrier to learning.

https://www.youtube.com/watch?v=yFisuk7J9SQ (The Teachers' TV ITE Episode 1)

https://www.youtube.com/watch?v=1zp1ehWEaaQ (Heidi Hyte: Reading Horizons)

Reflecting on your personal and professional experiences of schools and classrooms, what challenges did teachers encounter in providing rich and participative literacy learning experiences for pupils with EAL? How would you respond to these challenges?

Dyslexia and comorbidity: coexistence with other developmental disorders

Dyslexia can simultaneously occur with one or more developmental disorders and such comorbidity is higher than expected by chance (Caron and Rutter, 1991; Pennington, 2006). Moreover, the effects of having two or more comorbid disorders are more serious than those resulting from a single disorder (Knivsberg et al., 1999). Dyslexia can coexist with specific language impairment (SLI), speech sound disorder (SSD) and attention deficit/hyperactivity disorder (ADHD) (Boada et al., 2012). Moll (2012) noted that approximately 50% of children with dyslexia would have a comorbid developmental disorder. Understanding why comorbidity occurs requires an understanding of the etiological and pathogenetic mechanisms that underlie sets of symptoms. Limitations of space preclude a comprehensive review of the literature here (see Boada et al., 2012).

It is proposed that as a general rule of thumb, working memory is a key overlapping deficit in all four of the aforementioned developmental disorders. The earlier multi-component model of working memory (Baddeley and Hitch, 1974) comprised the phonological loop that is responsible for holding speech-based information, the visuo-spatial scratchpad, which is concerned with visual and spatial information, and the central executive, which is concerned with the control and regulation of cognitive processes (Baddeley, 2003). The episodic buffer, which is responsible for the coordination of information from each of the components of working memory and long-term memory, is a relatively recent addition to the original model (Baddeley, 2003). Findings from empirical studies demonstrate that children who have problems with language and literacy show impairments in the capacity of working memory and, in particular, the phonological loop (Herrmann et al., 2006). Clearly, these findings have implications for assessment approaches and intervention programmes in that pupils with dyslexia will require more than well-targeted support for literacy but also explicit instruction in strategies and bypass strategies for impairments in working memory as well as appropriate modifications to the learning environment.

Strategies for the distractible learner

 Example

The following is an excerpt from the 'recommendations' section in an educational psychology report on a 9-year-old boy who was assessed as having a poor working memory.

Use a timer to indicate a period of concentrated work. Continue to build in a reward system for completed work. Develop a further system whereby Jimmy has somewhere he can file incomplete work and return to it at a later date. Differentiate by quality and not quantity. If the quality of Jimmy's written work is compromised by his distractibility, then consider alternative modes of enabling Jimmy to meet relevant assessment criteria. For example, utilising digital technologies, scribe, paired writing or writing frames. Jimmy could well benefit from having a visual timetable at his desk to aid concentration. A preferred task could follow a written task (first ... then). Lessons should incorporate visual, auditory and kinaesthetic strategies. Gain Jimmy's attention before giving instructions; for example, stand close by, develop a private cue and/or say his name. Instructions should be given one at a time or in small chunks and be reinforced visually when possible. They should also be direct, explicit and given sequentially. The teacher should frequently check that Jimmy understands what is expected of him by asking him to paraphrase what he has just said. Be prepared to repeat instructions. Teach Jimmy memory strategies, like mnemonics or acronyms to remember information and also how to use visualisation and imaging techniques to recall information. Learning poems and songs and encouraging Jimmy to recap at the end of the day should improve his retention, as should exercises where Jimmy has to repeat sequences of digits and/or letters.

Identification

Teachers and educational psychologists may diagnose dyslexia. Speech and language therapists are the experts in diagnosing SLI and SSD. Psychiatrists, paediatricians or clinical psychologists may diagnose ADHD. Thus, comorbidity can only be identified when skilled professionals from health and education agencies work collaboratively (Knivsberg et al., 1999). However, it is not easy to give a diagnosis of comorbidity. This is because symptoms overlap: the symptoms that characterise a particular developmental disorder manifest themselves differently in children at the behavioural level; that is, a developmental disorder is not a unitary condition, and symptoms may be influenced by how a child responds to and is influenced by intervention programmes (Barkley, 1990; Gillberg, 1995). Cognisant of the challenges of diagnosing comorbidity, Knivsberg et al. (1999) highlighted the importance of identifying comorbidity so that intervention programmes can be planned and implemented to address all of the child's developmental needs.

This chapter moves on now to examine assessment and intervention issues in the context of two frequently co-occurring developmental disorders: dyslexia and ADHD.

Assessment

The comorbidity between dyslexia and ADHD is well established (August and Garfinkel, 1990; Willcutt and Pennington, 2000). According to Knivsberg et al. (1999), assessment for comorbidity should include a psychiatric examination, a developmental evaluation, psychological assessment and the assessment of reading and writing abilities. The child's hearing and eyesight should be tested and his/her medical history should be ascertained and examined. Parents, teachers, children and educational psychologists are important sources of information when building the learner's profile.

In the fourth edition of the *Diagnostic and Statistical Manual of Mental Disorders* (APA, 1994), ADHD is characterised as maladaptive levels of inattention (predominantly inattentive type), hyperactivity-impulsivity (predominantly hyperactive–impulsive type) or both inattention and hyperactivity-impulsivity (combined type). Children must meet criteria for at least six of nine symptoms within each type to qualify for a diagnosis. Children also must have symptoms of the disorder before age 7 and in at least two settings.

Specifically, symptom ratings are often obtained from both parents and teachers in the form of questionnaires, with most of these using the *DSM* criteria for ADHD. Parents are also able to provide important information on the child's developmental and medical histories and descriptions of his/her adaptive and maladaptive behaviour. Long and McPolin (2009) highlighted the sense of frustration and feelings of 'not being listened to' in an informative study that investigated parental views on the assessment process for identifying the developmental disorder, dyslexia. However, Knivsberg et al. (1999) noted that it is good practice to consult with parents and teachers. Parents' knowledge about the child, familial history of ADHD and dyslexia, and their own attitudes and expectations are important when devising education plans. Teachers should be able to provide information on the child's academic progress through classroom observations, curriculum-based assessments and findings from standardised testing. Teachers should also be able to provide information on the child's motivation and attitude to learning, attention and listening skills, levels of distractibility and ability to control activity levels. Moreover, information should be sought from teachers on the child's learning preferences, self-image as a reader and relationships with significant adults and peers when at work and at play.

Moreover, child-centred assessment approaches necessitate consulting with the child about his/her hopes and aspirations, areas of difficulty, comparative strengths, sources of support, response to the teaching strategies, and attitudes to self and others (Gillberg, 1995; Smith and Long, 2014).

Gillum (2012) claimed that when educational psychologists are assessing children, their primary focus is to identify the nature of their strengths and difficulties, the learning environment in which they find themselves and how their difficulties could be resolved. The phonological deficit theory has dominated the discourse on dyslexia for many years now. However, several other language and cognitive processing factors have been associated with the expression and severity of dyslexia. The best studied of these include verbal working memory, semantic and syntactic linguistic skills, and rapid serial naming/processing speed (Peterson et al., 2009). Thus, educational psychologists assessing for dyslexia carry out normative testing in literacy *and* associated cognitive skills. An adapted version of the framework for literacy testing appears below (BPS, 1999):

Phonics – child's knowledge of letter sound correspondences and word attack skills.

Fluency – child's reading speed.

Semantics – the study of meaning inherent in words, phrases, sentences and texts.

Learning opportunities – the instructional environment of the classroom.

The educational psychologist, through standardised testing in word and non-word reading accuracy, word and non-word reading speed, spelling, reading comprehension and listening comprehension, will assess the components of literacy learning: phonics, fluency and semantics. A piece of independent writing will enable the educational psychologist to evaluate the child's writing speed, handwriting, grammar, punctuation, syntax and choice of vocabulary, and, further, will enable an analysis of spelling errors

(Long and Clarke, 2008). Moll (2012) recommended that the following cognitive skills are assessed: rapid automatised naming (RAN), verbal short-term memory, verbal long-term memory, working memory, phonological skills, visuo-spatial skills, sequencing, speed of processing and language skills. The educational psychologist will probe whether the child's literacy learning and cognitive processing difficulties are persistent, severe, clustered and non-responsive to appropriate intervention.

The educational psychologist is also concerned with evaluating the child's learning environment (BPS, 1999). Thus, the educational psychologist will consider factors such as classroom environment in terms of teacher control and atmosphere, and teacher expectations, which should be high but realistic and effectively communicated to the learner, looking at whether the learner is receiving informed feedback and instruction on the thinking skills required for a particular task. The educational psychologist will interrogate whether the teacher is using data on the learner's progression to inform future planning and is modifying the curriculum to accommodate the learner's specific needs. Moreover, the educational psychologist will consider whether the pupil understands classroom tasks and teacher explanations, and whether the pupil is motivated and interested and has plenty of opportunities to practise with appropriate materials (Yesseldyke and Christenson, 1987).

This section concludes with a summary of what constitutes an effective and purposeful diagnostic assessment:

> The purpose of any assessment is to prove a hypothesis. It may be the only reliable means for discovering hidden qualities, strengths and weaknesses in the learner by measuring individual differences in a number of areas and must provide a balance between testing and observation. An overall profile must be compiled using information from the learner, teachers, other professionals, parents/ carers and, most importantly, the learner and be discussed by all. It should give the learner equal opportunity to demonstrate knowledge, identify barriers to achievement and also preferred learning styles that can be used when planning an effective teaching programme. Background information should include medical and, where appropriate, developmental milestones. The assessment should take place in undisturbed surroundings at a suitable time for the learner with consideration given to breaks, mealtimes, emotional state, fatigue, health and anxiety. The language used in any report must be appropriate for all who might need to read it. (Mortimore et al., 2012, p. 31)

Intervention

Gillberg (1995) claimed that a key factor in successful intervention is the provision of open, honest and specific feedback to parents. Moreover, Gillum (2012) recommended that educational psychologists outline to parents, children and teachers the important distinction between a neurological label and a child or young person's observed special educational needs. However, it is helpful to provide parents with written information on ADHD and dyslexia. The child's parents should also be made aware of professionally recognised non-statutory services and organisations wherein they can talk in supportive contexts. This opportunity to be listened to with unconditional regard should alleviate parental frustrations and any feelings of guilt and, as a consequence, contribute to meaningful engagement between teachers and parents (Knivsberg et al., 1999; Long and McPolin, 2009).

Earlier in this chapter, an illustrative example of a pupil's profile was provided that included a table of scores from standardised testing. In the context of providing parents with clear and specific feedback on the outcomes from an assessment, this section will move on now to examine the merits of utilising standard scores as opposed to age equivalents and centile scores. Standard scores from norm-referenced literacy tests enable direct comparison with standard scores from other curricular areas at different times in a child's school career. Centiles between 25 and 75 are considered to be within the average range. This is because they are normally distributed and tend to cluster around the average. However, centiles around the average range are volatile in that slight variations in standard scores between 90 and 110 produce large variations in the percentile rank. Thus, care needs to be exercised when they are being interpreted (McLoughlin, 1993). An age-equivalent score is simply the median raw score for a particular age level. There are inherent psychometric problems associated with age equivalents that seriously limit their reliability and validity. Bracken (1988) recommended that these scores should not be used for making diagnostic decisions.

McLoughlin et al. (1994) regarded the most important part of the assessment process to be the quality and nature of the feedback that is given to the learner. However, Long and McPolin (2009) demonstrated that parents of children who had a psychological assessment for dyslexia would like the educational psychologist and the parents to explain the outcome of the assessment to the child together. This finding has implications for the formation of a working model that streamlines the practice of educational psychologists to ensure that parents and professionals work together for successful feedback arrangements.

As discussed earlier in this chapter, children with additional learning needs require an education plan that is well targeted, child-centred and tailored to their individual needs. These education plans should be monitored and regularly reviewed. Knivsberg et al. (1999) rightly pointed out that early intervention is crucial for any developmental disorder, and in the comorbidity of dyslexia and ADHD, it should be possible to intervene in the preschool years, as the symptoms of both are present. Children who have dyslexia and ADHD benefit from structured teaching in structured environments and opportunities for one-to-one teaching for part of the school day (Gillberg, 1995). These one-to-one sessions could be used for structured multisensory literacy teaching and for pastoral support that enhances the child's overall sense of well-being (Long, 2012). A well-targeted behaviour management programme should form part of the child's overall education plan. Some children will also benefit from social skills training. This training can be offered in small groups or through holistic, child-centred and cross-curricular pedagogies such as circle time, role play and drama (Long and McPolin, 2010). Computer-based training should be offered, as children find it fun and motivating (Knivsberg et al., 1999). Drug treatment for ADHD and dietary intervention will fall under the auspices of relevant health professionals. Paired reading at home, where appropriate, could form part of parents' contribution to the intervention programme (Smith and Long, 2014).

☐ Summary

This chapter sought to explore the manner in which children with dyslexia and developmental literacy difficulties can be identified in the Early Years and primary school. The importance of multi-agency working was emphasised, and particularly, the involvement of parents with professionals. The chapter also identified and examined a range of key factors that lead to low achievement and underachievement and explored the particular needs of children with dyslexia whose first language is not English. The concept of comorbidity in regard to identification and assessment was examined along with the implications this has for practice.

   Recommended reading

Crombie, M. and Reid, G. (2009) 'The Role of Early Identification', in G. Reid (ed.), *The Routledge Companion to Dyslexia*. Abingdon, Oxon: Routledge.

Hartas, D. (2006) *Dyslexia in the Early Years: A Guide to Teaching and Learning*. London: Routledge.

References

American Psychiatric Association (1994) *Diagnostic and Statistical Manual of Mental Disorders* (4th edn). http://positivechange.org/how-we-work/appreciative-inquiry-ai/ Washington, DC: APA.

August, G.J. and Garfinkel, B.D. (1990) 'Comorbidity of ADHD and Reading Disability among Clinic-referred Children', *Journal of Abnormal Child Psychology*, 18(1): 29–45.

Baddeley, A.D. (2003) 'Working Memory and Language: An Overview', *Journal of Communication Disorders*, 36: 189–208.

Baddeley, A.D. and Hitch, G. (1974) 'Working Memory', in G.H. Bower (ed.), *Recent Advances in Learning and Motivation* (Vol. 8, pp. 47–90). New York: Academic Press.

Barkley, R. (1990) *Attention Deficit Hyperactivity Disorder.* New York: Guildford.

Boada, R., Willcutt, E. and Pennington, B. (2012) 'Understanding the Comorbidity between Dyslexia and Attention-Deficit/Hyperactivity Disorder', *Top Language Disorders*, 32(3): 264–284.

Boyle, J. and Fisher, S. (2007) *Educational Testing: A Competence-based Approach.* Hoboken, NJ: Wiley.

Bracken, B.A. (1988) 'Ten Psychometric Reasons Why Similar Tests Produce Dissimilar Results', *Journal of Psychology*, 26: 155–66.

British Psychological Society (BPS) (1999) *Dyslexia, Literacy and Psychological Assessment.* Leicester: BPS.

Caron, C. and Rutter, M. (1991) 'Comorbidity in Child Psychopathology: Concepts, Issues and Research Strategies', *Journal of Child Psychology and Psychiatry*, 32: 1063–80.

Crombie, M. and Reid, G. (2009) 'The Role of Early Identification', in G. Reid (ed.), *The Routledge Companion to Dyslexia.* Abingdon, Oxon: Routledge.

Department for Education and Skills (DfES) (2001a) *Special Educational Needs: Code of Practice.* London: HMSO.

Department for Education and Skills (DfES) (2001b) *The Special Educational Needs and Disability Act.* London: The Stationery Office.

Department of Education Northern Ireland (DENI) (2009) *Every School a Good School: The Way Forward for SEN and Inclusion.* Bangor: DENI.

Department of Education Northern Ireland (DENI) (2011) *Count, Read: Succeed.* Bangor: DENI.

Dowling, M. (2005) *Young Children's Personal, Social and Emotional Development.* London: Paul Chapman Publishing.

Elbro, C., Daugaard, H.T. and Gellert, A. (2012) 'Dyslexia in a Second Language? A Dynamic Test of Reading Acquisition May Provide a Fair Answer', *Annals of Dyslexia*, 62(3): 172–85.

Gardner, F., Ward, S., Burton, J. and Wilson, C. (2003) 'The Role of Mother-Child Joint Play in the Early Development of Children's Conduct Problems: A Longitudinal Observational Study', *Social Development*, 12: 361–78.

Gillberg, C. (1995) *Clinical Child Neuropsychiatry*. Cambridge: Cambridge University Press.

Gillum, J. (2012) 'Dyscalculia: Issues for Practice in Educational Psychology', *Educational Psychology in Practice*, 28(3): 287–97.

Goswami, U. (2013) 'Dyslexia – in Tune But Out of Time', *The Psychologist*, 26(2): 106–9.

Gough, P.B., Hoover, W.A. and Peterson, C.L. (1996) 'Some observations on a simple view of reading', in C. Cornoldi and J. Oakhill (eds.), *Reading Comprehension Difficulties: Processes and Intervention* (pp. 1–13). Mahwah, NJ: Erlbaum.

Government Equality Office (GEO) (2010) *The Equality Act*. London: HMSO.

Gray, C. and MacBlain, S.F. (2012) *Learning Theories in Childhood*. London: Sage.

Hartas, D. (2006) *Dyslexia in the Early Years: A Guide to Teaching and Learning*. London: Routledge.

Heneveld, W. (2007) 'Whose Reality Counts? Local Educators as Researchers on the Quality of Primary Education', *International Review of Education*, 53(5/6): 639–63.

Herrmann, J.A., Matyas, T. and Pratt, C. (2006) 'Meta-analysis of the Nonword Reading Deficit in Specific Reading Disorder', *Dyslexia*, 12: 195–221.

Knivsberg, A-M., Reichelt, K-L. and Nodland, M. (1999) 'Comorbidity, or, Coexistence between Dyslexia and Attention Deficit Hyperactivity Disorder', *British Journal of Special Education*, 26(1): 42–45.

Lipka, O. and Siegel, L.S. (2007) 'The Development of Reading Skills in Children with English as an Additional Language', *Scientific Studies of Reading*, 11(2): 105–31.

Long, L. (2012) 'Using Creative Approaches to Promote Inclusive Cultures for Literacy Learning in Northern Irish Primary Schools'. Unpublished Doctoral Thesis, School of Education, Queen's University Belfast.

Long, L. and Clarke, J. (2008) 'Identifying Dyslexia to Initiate Action: Promoting Inclusive Practice in the Primary Classroom', *Taighde agus Teagasc*, 6: 211–28.

Long, L. and McPolin, P. (2009) 'Psychological Assessment and Dyslexia: Parents' Perspectives', *Irish Educational Studies*, 28(1): 115–26.

Long, L. and McPolin, P. (2010) 'Personal and Civic Education in the NI Primary Curriculum: Teachers' Perspectives', *Pastoral Care in Education*, 28(2): 109–29.

Long, L., MacBlain, S. and MacBlain, M. (2007) 'Supporting Students with Dyslexia at the Secondary School: An Emotional Model of Literacy', *Journal of Adolescent and Adult Literacy*, 51(2): 124–34.

MacBlain, S.F. (2014) *How Children Learn*. London: Sage.

McLoughlin, D. (1993) *Quotients and Centiles*. Belfast: BELB.

McLoughlin, D., Fitzgibbon, G. and Young, V. (1994) *Adult Dyslexia Assessment: Counselling and Training*. London: Whurr.

Moll, K. (2012) 'Dyslexia and Comorbid Disorders'. Paper presented at the Centre for Reading and Language, University of York, 3 March 2012. Available at http://www.dyslexia.bangor.ac.uk/documents/KMollLectureNotes.pdf (accessed 30 May 2014).

Mortimore, T., Hansen, L., Hutchings, M. and Northcote, A., with Fernando, J., Horobin, L., Saunders, K. and Everatt, J. (2012) *Dyslexia and Multi-lingualism: Identifying and Supporting Bilingual Learners who Might be at Risk of Developing SpLD/Dyslexia*. Bath: Bath Spa University.

Nation, K. and Cocksey, J. (2009) 'The Relationship between Knowing a Word and Reading it Aloud in Children's Word Reading Development', *Journal of Experimental Child Psychology*, 10(3): 296–308.

Office for Standards in Education (Ofsted) (2010) *The Special Educational Needs and Disability Review*. London: Ofsted.

Office for Standards in Education (Ofsted) (2011) *Removing Barriers to Literacy*. London: Ofsted.

Pennington, B.F. (2006) 'From Single to Multiple Deficit Models of Developmental Disorders', *Cognition*, 101(2): 385–413.

Peterson, R.L., Pennington, B.F., Shriberg, L.D. and Boada, R. (2009) 'What Influences Literacy Outcome in Children with Speech Sound Disorder?', *Journal of Speech, Language and Hearing Research*, 52(5): 1175–88.

Reason, R. and Stothard, J. (2013) 'Is There a Place for Dyslexia in Educational Psychology Practice?', *Debate*, 146(March): 8–13.

Smith, R. and Long, L. (2014) 'Using Vocabularies of Hope to Transform the Educational Experiences of Students Identified as Having Pronounced Literacy Difficulties', in P. Jones (ed.), *Bringing Insider Perspectives into Inclusive Teacher Learning* (pp. 9–24). Abingdon, Oxon: Routledge.

Snowling, M.J. and Hulme, C. (2011) 'Evidence-based Interventions for Reading and Language Difficulties: Creating a Virtuous Cycle', *British Journal of Educational Psychology*, 81(1): 1–23.

Sparks, R.L., Ganschow, L. and Patton, J. (1995) 'Prediction of Performance in First-Year Foreign Language Courses: Connections between Native and Foreign Language Learning', *Journal of Educational Psychology*, 87: 638–55.

Willcutt, E.G. and Pennington, B.F. (2000) 'Psychiatric Comorbidity in Children and Adolescents with Reading Disability', *Journal of Child Psychology and Psychiatry*, 41(8): 1039–48.

Yesseldyke, J.E. and Christenson, S.L. (1987) 'Evaluating Students' Instructional Environments', *Remedial and Special Education*, 8(3): 17–24.

CHAPTER 5

RAISING LITERACY STANDARDS: PERSPECTIVES ON BEST PRACTICE

Sean MacBlain, Louise Long and Jill Dunn

Chapter aims

- To highlight key principles that need to be addressed when working with children with dyslexia and developmental literacy difficulties.
- To explore factors that are at the centre of best practice in Early Years settings and primary schools in regard to reading, spelling and writing.
- To examine key factors that underpin effective working between teachers and parents.

Introduction

The educational experience that children with dyslexia have is dependent upon a vast array of variables and their progress will be determined by such factors as the beliefs that their teachers have with regard to the nature of dyslexia and whether or not it exists, the ethos of the school with respect to learning difficulties and special educational needs, including how they allocate their resources, and the extent of training of the teachers with regard to the teaching of literacy. This chapter draws together a number of key interrelated themes that underpin and drive the pursuit by practitioners, and parents, for higher standards in literacy. Beginning with the identification of key principles for working with children with dyslexia and literacy difficulties the chapter then draws the reader on to focusing upon and understanding the importance of continuity and development through the Early Years and into the primary school setting. Here, the reader is also drawn into understanding the importance of developing and maintaining effective and purposeful partnerships between Early Years settings and those working in primary schools. The chapter concludes by focusing readers' attention on the changing nature of how teachers are now being trained and how their training will change in the near future, with the implications this will have for children struggling to acquire literacy.

Key principles of working with children with dyslexia and literacy difficulties

Perhaps a most useful starting point in looking at key principles of working with children with dyslexia can be found in the original and seminal work of the much celebrated authors and practitioners, Anna Gillingham and Bessie Stillman, referred to earlier in the Introduction section of this book. In the 5th edition of their *Remedial Training for Children with Specific Disability in Reading, Spelling, and Penmanship* (1966) they commented as follows:

> There are certain types of teachers often found in this work who should never have been encouraged to attempt it ... The teacher who has been unsuccessful in discipline or clarity of instruction in regular classes is not likely to succeed with especially difficult reading problems ... The teacher who is retiring and would like to earn a little money but has no idea of entering upon this field as a work demanding prolonged preparation, often brings the whole subject into discredit. Seeing no reason for careful study just 'to help a slow child read,' such a teacher would have the child read in order to afford practice and this practice often merely serves to impress errors more deeply. (p. 13)

They go on to assert that:

> The ideal candidate ... is one who, having been previously well-trained in orthodox methods of teaching reading and spelling, has taught successfully for several years ... Whether or not she has

employed in the past what was called phonics, she discovers that our phonetic approach is new and different. Hard as it is to master this different approach, the effectiveness of the new principles makes their acquisition a real delight. (p. 13)

And here is one of the key principles of working with children with dyslexia – teaching becomes a 'real delight'. It is still true, however, even decades after Gillingham and Stillman's assertions that there are still teachers working with children with literacy difficulties who have little patience and little desire to apply themselves to careful and sustained study into understanding why their pupils fail with reading and spelling, and little appetite for developing their skills and knowledge base in this area. Equally, there are many teachers who do. There are also many teachers nearing retirement or who have already reached this stage, who offer their professional services to parents of children who are struggling with reading and spelling and who have little, if any, real understanding of the necessary principles and approaches that underpin effective teaching of children with these types of difficulties. In reality, they, all too often, offer little to the child in the way of effective remediation. Gillingham and Stillman, again offer the following:

What the child so sorely needs is a teacher expert in the appropriate techniques to train him in the reading skills step by step, not one to 'hear him read for practice,' or to break words up by means of 'functional phonics,' when he is unable to learn the words thus broken up. (1966, p. 20)

It is important for readers to fully understand that Gillingham and Stillman were emphasising the fact that teachers working with children with specific difficulties in literacy need to acquire appropriate expertise, which in most cases requires much additional, and rigorous, study.

Working with children with dyslexia, therefore, requires much more than simply listening to them read and asking them to sound out and break words down into sounds. As a necessary prerequisite, for example, teachers working with these children need to understand a number of basic principles, such as how *Working Memory* and *Processing Difficulties* affect reading and spelling (see MacBlain, 2014). In addition, they need to understand how these problems, as well as those linked to *Automaticity* and *Coordination* can impact negatively upon the acquisition of literacy, and, perhaps more importantly, self-esteem, self-confidence and self-efficacy (see Chapters 2 and 3).

In addition to the above, it almost goes without saying that there are many other factors that influence the progress of children with dyslexia. To begin with, teaching and learning should place significant emphasis upon the child developing their understanding of phonics and acquiring a sound skills base in this area. In addition, the following four factors should inform the work of teachers working with children with dyslexia. Teaching should be:

- Structured – programmes/teaching should have a purpose, clear objectives with a clear rationale, and follow a clear structure.
- Sequential – programmes/teaching should have an identifiable pattern, for example they will introduce some aspects of phonics before others and teach simpler spelling principles before more complex ones.
- Cumulative – elements within programmes/teaching should build on previous learning of specific elements.
- Multisensory – this is, perhaps, the most important element of all and involves the development of kinaesthetic memory.

It is fundamental that teaching should be rigorous whilst at the same time recognising the individual needs of the child and should be undertaken in such a way as to motivate the child. Children should not experience failure. This is where the concept of intrinsic and extrinsic motivation takes on greater importance.

Before looking more closely at best practice in Early Years settings and primary schools, it is worth looking at the findings of a relatively recent review of special educational needs undertaken by Ofsted in which they identified a number of key elements which underpinned successful learning for children with special educational needs:

- they looked to the teacher for their main learning and to the support staff for support
- assessment was secure, continuous and acted upon
- teachers planned opportunities for pupils to collaborate, work things out for themselves and apply what they had learnt to different situations
- teachers' subject knowledge was good, as was their understanding of pupils' needs and how to help them
- lesson structures were clear and familiar but allowed for adaptation and flexibility
- all aspects of a lesson were well thought out and any adaptations needed were made without fuss to ensure that everyone in class had access
- teachers presented information in different ways to ensure all children and young people understood

- teachers adjusted the pace of the lesson to reflect how children and young people were learning

- the staff understood clearly the difference between ensuring that children and young people were learning and keeping them occupied

- respect for individuals was reflected in high expectations for their achievement

- the effectiveness of specific types of support was understood and the right support was put in place at the right time. (Ofsted, 2010a, p. 47)

Whilst the above elements refer to children with special educational needs in general they are also highly pertinent to children with dyslexia and developmental literacy difficulties.

Identifying best practice in Early Years settings

Good practice in teaching in the Early Years

Early childhood research in the UK over the last 50 years has had a major impact on both policy and practice and there is a good deal of current knowledge about what works in the education of children in the Early Years (EY) (Brooker, 2011). Going back further, much has been written about the work of influential pioneers of early childhood practice such as Froebel, Montessori, Steiner, McMillan, Isaacs and Malaguzzi, and how their principles and traditions have shaped current EY practice. Indeed, Tina Bruce wrote 10 common principles of early childhood practice based on the work of these pioneer educators (Bruce, 2011). One of her principles picks up on the view from Froebel, Montessori and Steiner that early childhood is not just a phase when children are prepared for adult life. Rather, it is a stage in life that is important in its own right. Therefore, we need an appropriate curriculum and pedagogy that recognises this crucial phase of childhood and capitalises on the view that children are active and competent learners. Play-based approaches have long been recognised as an appropriate pedagogy for EY and the UK has a long tradition of play-based practice (Moyles, 2010).

Learning through play in the Early Years

The principle of young children's need and right to play is informed by research and strongly defined in Western society (Brooker, 2011).

Learning through play is enshrined in curriculum guidance in all parts of the UK. The Piagetian legacy of experiential learning and the Vygotskian perspective of socio-construction (with the adult playing an essential role in supporting the child's learning) have contributed to this shift in thinking away from more formal tasks to more active approaches to teaching and learning (Hunter and Walsh, 2014). Play is recognised as a powerful means to learning (Elkind, 2008) and Vygotsky (1978) stated that play creates zones for potential development in which children perform 'a head taller than themselves'. Play is what children do when they seek to make sense of the world they live in and research has identified the myriad benefits of a play-based approach to children's learning (see Wood, 2013). However, implementing a play-based approach can be problematic for teachers who are under growing pressure from policy-makers to prioritise literacy and numeracy activities and to prepare children for more formal learning. Recent research focuses on a new pedagogic image of playful structure which invites teachers and children to maintain a degree of playfulness in the child's whole learning experience which can bridge these potential divisions between formal and informal learning (Walsh et al., 2011). Wood (2013) supports this notion of developing a continuum between playing and learning and teaching. She argues that the two pedagogical zones that lie at either end of this continuum, adult-directed activities and child-initiated activities, both allow for elements of playful learning and allow for flexibility and responsiveness in curriculum planning. Such an approach is beneficial for the teaching of literacy in the EY.

 Exercise

Consider the following two examples of literacy in an EY classroom. The first example is adult-directed but engages children with their literacy learning in a playful way. The second example is a child-initiated activity during play. Highlight the literacy learning in both examples. Do you consider one approach to be more beneficial than the other and why?

Example 1

The teacher has been using the book *Handa's Surprise* (Browne, 1994) with her Year 1 class over a number of lessons. For this particular lesson she divides the class into groups with one group tasked with re-telling and acting out the story using masks and props. Another group is given playdough in a variety of colours and asked to create Handa's basket of fruits and then to write some adjectives for the fruit on strips of card. A third group is given a variety of real fruits and asked to work with their talking partner to talk about their favourite fruit and be able to describe the fruit. They video each other and can review and re-record their video.

Example 2

All of the props used in the lesson in Example 1 are available to the children during play. Three of the children are playing in the home corner and ask the teacher if they can cut up the fruit and make a fruit salad. They are playing African villages and have assumed the names of the children in the book and have included other names of their own. They discuss the fruit as they cut it (using some of the adjectives from the previous lesson) and continue to describe the fruit as they taste it as part of their playing out of the African village theme. Another group of children are using the animal masks from *Handa's Surprise* but have made up their own narrative around a zoo based on shared experiences of one child's birthday party at the zoo.

Identifying best practice in primary schools

Central to the purpose and vision of all schools is that every child reaches his/her potential. It is widely acknowledged that there are barriers to learning, for example special educational needs that require schools to make appropriate provision so that children can overcome them to achieve success. The authors propose that the principles of child-centred provisions for pupils with special educational needs and, in particular, dyslexia are an inclusive school culture and ethos, high-quality teaching, holistic approaches to teaching, joined-up approaches to the assessment of needs and the design and implementation of learning pathways, and meaningful home-school-pupil-community partnerships. Moreover, assessment approaches should be purposeful, learning pathways ought to be personalised, and the pupil's progress and response to intervention should be rigorously monitored and regularly reviewed. The authors propose that teachers are central to bringing these critical provisions for child-centred practices into being. For example, Heneveld (2007) acknowledged that the process of advancing best practice in the classroom requires variety in teaching strategies and assessment approaches. However, there is evidence to suggest that pacing as well as variety in teaching approaches is important in establishing more inclusive practices in meeting a pupil's individual needs (Long, 2012). Westwood (2005, p. 147) defined pacing as 'teachers varying the rate at which teaching takes place, or the rate at which pupils are required to work and produce work'. Westwood (2005) went on to acknowledge that this requires a commendable individualised approach to learning that regrettably can be challenging for teachers given constraints on resources.

Evidence from empirical studies suggests that effective teachers form classroom relationships that are characterised by patience, empathy, openness and humour (Long, 2012; Oppendekker and Van Damme, 2006). Fielding (2007) noted that central to building an authentic relationship is the teacher making a difference between the personal and the functional. When a child is viewed solely in terms of his/her function, s/he is important only as 'learner' or 'pupil', of value only to the extent that s/he fits into this function. Long (2012) found there to be a consensus amongst teachers that schools should be creating opportunities for pupils with dyslexia and developmental literacy difficulties to demonstrate their competencies and talents in sport, music and teamwork, for example, to enhance their social value and sense of belonging.

The arguments about the potentially negative affective consequences of pupil isolation are now well rehearsed: feeling excluded or alienated impacts on self-esteem and self-efficacy, and academic success in what could be described as a circular and self-deprecating cycle (Burden and Burdett, 2005; Nugent, 2008; Ott, 1997). However, findings from critical literature suggest that enabling pupils and families to play positive participatory roles in schools could prevent this circular and self-deprecating cycle – for example, buddy time (Cowie and Wallace, 2000), paired-reading (Topping, 1995), reading partnerships and parental involvement in school life (Long, 2012).

The authors propose that the latter years of primary education in particular, present teachers with significant opportunities to increase self-esteem in pupils with dyslexia and developmental literacy difficulties so that they can re-evaluate themselves as successful individuals in their own right and not in the functional role of 'pupils with SEN'. It is also proposed that as part of the wider inclusive process, schools have a duty to monitor and evaluate the systems they have put in place to validate those pupils identified with dyslexia and developmental literacy difficulties that may feel vulnerable or isolated. When effective structures are put in place, which validate pupils in terms of who they are, and who they may become in life and work, they can get closer to reaching their true potential and, ultimately, embrace adulthood with higher levels of academic self-efficacy and emotional well-being (Long et al., 2007).

An illustrative case study

In Chapter 6, one of the authors, Louise, looks at a qualitative research project that used a case-study approach to explore the utility of the verbal and visual texts produced by upper-primary pupils with developmental literacy difficulties for advancing inclusive literacy cultures. Pupils' illustrations and commentary on how the management of their literacy difficulties could be improved were presented to discrete focus groups of teachers, parents and pupils in three case-study schools. This process brought together the critical components of pupil voice, collaborative reflection and dialogue, and stimulated the generation of innovative ideas for advancing literacy education. Details on the methods and methodology that moulded the design of this study can be found in Chapter 6. For the purposes of the current chapter, some of the key findings emerging from teacher focus groups will now be presented (Long, 2012).

Teachers in the study recognised the importance of developing the metacognitive skills of pupils with dyslexia and additional needs in literacy to circumvent the possibility that they could develop a dependency on adult support (Dweck, 1999). The term metacognition means thinking about thinking – in other words, understanding how it is we learn (Flavell, 1981). For example, pupils could be encouraged to model the strategies used by a good speller, visualise how a completed piece of written work should look and develop strategies for learning spellings such as simultaneous oral spelling and cued spelling (see Kelly and Phillips, 2012). These findings resonated with Reid (2011), who argued that pupils with dyslexia should be encouraged to engage in self-assessment, for example, 'Have I done this before?' 'How did I tackle it?' Moreover, there is evidence to suggest that pupils who do well in school demonstrate this kind of task-focused behaviour (Chapman and Tunmer, 1997). Alternatively, pupils who are reluctant in learning situations and avoid challenges normally show low achievement (Midgley and Urdan, 1995).

Findings from the study highlighted that teachers utilise praise to support children with dyslexia and developmental literacy difficulties to learn that success is a result of pupils' own efforts. As Samuelsson (2008) noted, once children attribute success to their own efforts, they are more likely to be motivated to try other literacy tasks in the

(Continued)

(Continued)

future. Participant teachers agreed that praise should be public and deserved. However, Dweck (1999) demonstrated that the effectiveness of praise is determined by the praise being process-related rather than person-focused. Nonetheless, teachers in Long's study acknowledged the value of praise for raising pupils' self-esteem.

Moreover, emergent themes from this illustrative study supported the axiom that the concept of pupil well-being has multiple sites of explanation and intervention (Duckett et al., 2008). For example, participant teachers expressed agreement that rote learning offers pupils with dyslexia and developmental literacy difficulties the opportunity to experience success, which should impact on their motivational levels and self-esteem. This finding confirmed the research of Norman and Spohrer (1996), who demonstrated that traditional teaching approaches have their place and that rote learning and drill-and-practice are valuable in transforming understanding into automated skill, making the information and procedures available without conscious effort. The frequency of how often children are asked to practise has been of interest to researchers. There is a deeply engrained body of evidence in experimental psychology to provide support for distributed practice (Cepeda et al., 2009) – although its impact on education has been limited. Nonetheless, this approach has been applied successfully to children's early reading (Solity et al., 1999).

A minority of teachers in the current study expressed concerns that an emphasis on drill-and-skill in word recognition neglected the main purpose of reading, which is to communicate meaning. Thus, as well as teaching reading skills, teachers acknowledged the importance of helping learners to develop a range of comprehension strategies that will enable them to read for information and pleasure. Moreover, there is evidence to suggest that 'coaching' pupils on how and when to use reading strategies is effective in raising literacy outcomes (NICHD, 2000). Findings from the research study demonstrated that such activities should take place in literature-rich learning environments. These environments could be achieved through well-resourced school and local libraries and the presence of teachers who convey a love and enjoyment of literature. These findings substantiated the recommendations made in a recent policy document (DENI, 2011).

Findings from this illustrative study highlighted the enabling potential of ICT, including games for advancing fun approaches to literacy learning. Technological change offers the opportunity to enrich the pedagogic toolkit of teacher educators and teachers in hitherto undreamt of ways. Information and communication tools are becoming increasingly portable, flexible and powerful, and numerous studies point to the potential of these new technologies as learning tools (Moon, 2007, p. 363).

Similarly, Norman and Spohrer (1996) demonstrated that interactive multimedia technology could help motivate learners by providing information in a form that is concrete and perceptually easy to process. However, several of the pupils in the study reported that the availability of novels on film has offered an easy way to access stories without the need for reading. This finding was consistent with the work of Robertson et al. (1996).

Teachers in the current study recognised the value of child-centred education plans. Through critical reflection and dialogue, they increasingly saw their role as one of facilitator who would encourage children to recognise their strengths and build on them as they take ownership of designing and reviewing their education plans. Falvey (1994) rightly noted that these opportunities are critical for developing pupils' capacity for self-determination. Participant teachers acknowledged the importance of target setting for motivating pupils, both in terms of visually displaying curricular levels for the whole class and keeping visual records of pupils' individualised learning targets and the outcomes from review meetings. In the current study, teachers also recognised that accurate and timely formative feedback was integral to literacy education. This finding was consistent with the principles of formative feedback (Black and Wiliam, 1998).

Whilst this section has discussed the views of teachers in a recent exploratory qualitative study on promoting inclusive cultures for literacy learning in mainstream primary schools, the final point makes a comment on a theme that emerged from parent, teacher and pupil focus groups. The theme is that recreational reading is a key to developing the perception of oneself as a 'reader'. This finding was consistent with Strommen and Mates (2004), who concluded that a lifelong love of reading could be fostered in children who view themselves as participant members of a community that values recreational reading as a significant and enjoyable activity. Important variables here are the conversations that go on between parents and children about books:

> The child's immediate culture, the family, must invest itself in the process to demonstrate the pleasure by regularly reading aloud to young children, making age- and interest-appropriate books easily available as the child matures, providing a model for

(Continued)

(Continued)

children to emulate, scheduling time for family reading, and demonstrating the social nature of reading and encouraging interest through conversations about the books family members read. (Strommen and Mates, 2004, p. 189)

This finding illuminated the pressing need for future research into processes for promoting school-home partnerships for literacy education. According to a recent DENI (2011) report on literacy, a culture must be developed that strives to create an appropriate nexus between home and school by the introduction of strategies that 'blur the edges' where traditional schools stop and where outside communities begin. In Chapter 7, one of the authors, Jill, reports on a research project that examined children's views on the potential for popular culture for motivating them to engage with literacy tasks, in other words, bringing children's out-of-school literacy lives into the classroom. Tensions and potentials in home-school-community partnerships will be examined more closely in the next section of this chapter.

Overall, teachers in the study viewed metacognitive awareness and formative feedback as integral to literacy teaching. Promisingly, teachers in this study had aligned their pastoral role with their teaching role in recognition of the interwoven nature of learning and emotional well-being. What seemed to matter to the teachers in this study was creating opportunities for pupils with dyslexia and developmental literacy difficulties to experience success in literacy work. Moreover, findings suggested that literacy education offers opportunities to blur traditional boundaries between home, school and community, and, ultimately, to enhance a sense of enjoyment in the spoken and printed word for all.

 Exercise

Many teachers in the illustrative case study presented above (Long, 2012) identified contextual constraints to effective literacy learning and teaching including large classes, the demands of fulfilling the requirements of the curriculum, rigidity in school criteria for choosing learners for additional support, inherited 'grammars' for teaching children with additional needs, and prescribed schemes within schools for teaching spelling. How would you respond to these challenges?

Fostering and advancing partnerships: home, school, community and child

Findings from international critical literature and empirical studies have demonstrated that parental involvement has a positive impact on the outcomes of schooling. For example, research has illustrated the positive correlation between parental involvement and literacy and numeracy outcomes, and improvements in pupils' behaviour (Desforges, 2003; Smit and Driessen, 2009). When parents work in partnership with schools and educational practitioners they can help their children 'build a pro-social, pro-learning self-concept and high educational aspirations' (Hartas, 2008, p.139).

Governments, schools and systems have advanced models of partnership for all pupils and, in particular, pupils with SEN (Ludicke and Kortman, 2012; Porter, 2008). For example, the SEN *Code of Practice* in England and Wales (DfE 1994) and the *Code of Practice on the Identification and Assessment of Special Educational Needs* in Northern Ireland (DENI, 1998) put mechanisms in place to support parental participation. However, the revised *Code* (DfES, 2001) and the *Supplement to the Code of Practice on the Identification and Assessment of Special Educational Needs* (DENI, 2005b) recommended that teachers draw on parents' expertise about their child's academic and affective needs to inform intervention programmes and concurrently communicate to parents their respect for, and sensitivity to, their feelings and pressures. Moreover, since the implementation of special educational needs and disability legislation (DfES, 2001; DENI, 2005a), there are new services to provide parents of children who have SEN with advice and information as well as personnel that support parents to resolve disputes with local education authorities and schools.

Norwich et al. (2005) pointed out that partnership with parents of children who have dyslexia requires a continuing interplay and convergence of ideas, values and practices between general parent partnership and SEN or dyslexia-specific partnership. However, Reay (2005) highlighted that general parent-teacher relationships are often characterised by the struggle for control and definition. Furthermore, much of the research on parental involvement has discussed parents as if they are all alike, often overlooking, for example, differences between mothers and fathers, diversity in parenting styles and cultural, linguistic and socioeconomic factors (Reay, 2005; Wolfendale, 2000). In relation to SEN partnership, there is a consensus in critical literature that parents and teachers believe that partnerships are essential for supporting the learning of pupils with additional educational needs. However, there is a growing body of evidence that parents and teachers differ in how they construct parental involvement. For example, Ludicke and Kortman (2012) highlighted that teachers value and prioritise parental participation in supervising home-work and attending school events, whilst parents of pupils with additional learning needs placed more value in their involvement in implementing individualised education plans (IEPs) and in their participation in general parent-teacher meetings and additional SEN meetings.

Nevertheless, Long (2012) demonstrated that parents and teachers are in agreement that schools should be prioritising their outreach pro-grammes to 'hard-to-reach' parents. Teacher and parent participants in this study recommended advancing inclusive cultures for literacy learning by adopting flexible and blended communication tools and protocols, raising awareness amongst staff that it is their responsibility to promote parental participation and appointing a designated teacher to lead the school's strategy for promoting home-school-community partnerships. Whilst effective parental partnerships have significance in particular for the academic and social-affective progress of pupils with additional learn-ing needs (Long and McPolin, 2009; Porter, 2008), there is a gap in the literature on research studies on parent partnerships in relation to dys-lexia. One example of an informative study in this field highlighted the adverse consequences of parents and teachers failing to recognise, share and work on their differing perspectives so that joint decisions are made about the child's needs (Griffiths et al., 2004). In a more recent study, Long and McPolin (2009) demonstrated that parents of children with additional needs in literacy experience feelings of frustration when teachers do not listen to their concerns.

Moreover, the parents in this study reported that they were con-fused about procedures for the management of SEN and the patterns of language used by professionals. In those cases where the partner-ship between schools and parents became fragmented, many parents were found to seek and obtain an independent educational psychology assessment by approaching a non-statutory organisation, for example the Northern Ireland Dyslexia Centre. Long and McPolin (2009) recom-mended that Government make schools aware of the professionally recognised non-statutory community services so that, in particular, schools can avail themselves of them to accelerate educational psychology assess-ments. These agencies could also collaborate with schools in providing parents and teachers with neutral and accurate information and advice, which should help to alleviate parental frustrations about their child's rate of progress in literacy and thereby contribute to meaningful engage-ment between parents and teachers. However, Norwich et al. (2005, p. 163) rightly noted that it would be wise for sectional interests to see that what they are pursuing is linked to wider SEN interests and to the general interests of all. More recently, the Department of Education in

Northern Ireland (DENI, 2011) explicitly acknowledged the importance of schools helping *all* parents to support their children's literacy and numeracy development by using existing community-based services and resources, for example the public library.

The final comment in this section is to suggest that child-centred approaches to partnerships between parents of children who have dyslexia, teachers and local communities should utilise 'extended professionalism' (Power and Clark, 2000) as the conceptual framework that informs effective practice (Norwich et al., 2005). In extended professionalism teachers are sensitive to parents' perspectives, take them seriously and respectfully, assume that parents are concerned and interested in their children's education; and that non-involvement does not necessarily mean a lack of interest (Norwich et al., 2005, p. 163). Moreover, it is proposed that the concept of a dyslexia-friendly school is not divorced from the concept of the inclusive school that promotes a sense of belonging and being valued for all parents of children attending the school. It is also proposed that there may be distinctive and additional aspects to ever-evolving models of school-parent-community partnerships in cases where teachers or parents have expressed concerns about the academic progress and holistic well-being of a child or young person. Child-centred approaches to advancing the literacy development of a pupil with dyslexia or developmental literacy difficulties require person-centred approaches to teacher-school-community partnerships that are respectful of the dignity of the individual – professional or parent – and the diversity of resources and needs within the school and local community.

Teachers in training: challenges for schools

With the formation of the coalition government in the UK in 2010 much changed in the way in which teachers are now trained to enter the profession. Perhaps the greatest change has been the shift away from Higher Education Institutions (HEIs), namely from universities to schools. Whilst some see this as a step in the right direction, others do not. Moving the training of teachers from HEIs into schools falls within, for example, the new School Direct initiative which has significant implications for the manner in which teachers will, in the future, be trained to work with children with special educational needs and literacy difficulties.

A particular concern surrounds the way in which teachers in training who work only in one particular school may be socialised into believing that the teaching they observe in their school and the manner in which children are taught is the only way or the 'right' way. Too few teachers currently working in primary schools have a real understanding of dyslexia. Even fewer have any proper understanding of how to identify children with dyslexia and how to assess for this condition. The situation is even more worrying in post-primary schools and colleges. Prospective teachers who train in schools where there is little real understanding of dyslexia and where identification, assessment and interventions for children with this condition are wanting may fail to understand, and learn, the complexity of this condition and the important and appropriate methods they will need to teach effectively. In essence, the trainee teacher's experience and subsequent knowledge, understanding and skills will be very dependent upon the context within which they are training.

Recently (March, 2014), the British Dyslexia Association (BDA), whilst emphasising the fact that dyslexia and related specific learning difficulties make up the largest portion of disabled pupils in schools, with estimates ranging from between 15% and 20%, reported the following concerns regarding a petition to the government on their website as follows:

> In response to the Government's statement … the BDA would like to draw attention to the fact that the listed Government's interventions have so far failed to address the problem …
>
> • The new Teachers' Standards which came into effect from September 2012 do not ensure that teachers are equipped to deal with specific learning difficulties (dyslexia).
>
> • ITT [Initial Teacher Training] placements in special schools or specialist settings within a mainstream school are for general learning difficulties and do not address the need for expertise with specific learning difficulties (dyslexia).
>
> • Self help for teachers through the Continuous Professional Development Framework for teachers cannot be a substitute for specialist training…
>
> Early identification and appropriate specialist support for children with specific learning difficulties through specialist teacher training could offer significant savings over the current long term cost of literacy and psychological difficulties … (http://www.bdadyslexia. org.uk/news/initial-teacher-training.html)

It is clear that the BDA continues to express concerns in regard to the training and preparation of teachers for working with children with dyslexia and their continuing professional development, especially in those important first years of teaching. It is of note that they raise a particular concern in regard to teachers in training having some opportunities to work in special schools during their training, which they emphasise deals mainly with 'general' learning difficulties and not 'specific' learning difficulties (dyslexia). The BDA also reported the government's response to their concerns on their website as follows:

> The Government agrees that teachers should be well prepared to meet the needs of all pupils …

> The new Teachers' Standards which came into effect from September 2012 state that: 'a teacher must …. adapt teaching to respond to the strengths and needs of all pupils,' and in particular: 'have a clear understanding of the needs of all pupils, including those with special educational needs … and be able to use and evaluate distinctive teaching approaches to engage and support them.'…

> The Department currently funds the Dyslexia-SpLD Trust to develop an online Continuous Professional Development framework for teachers, which includes a self-assessment and guide for further study. We are also continuing to work with the Dyslexia-SpLD Trust to explore how we can make use of their expertise in further strengthening the recently published advanced materials on Dyslexia, Autism and Communication Needs. Ofsted routinely inspects ITT provision.

> As part of this process, it monitors and evaluates how well individual training providers train teachers to meet the needs of all pupils with SEN and disabilities including those with dyslexia and specific learning difficulties … (http://www.bdadyslexia.org.uk/news/initial-teacher-training.html)

 Exercise

Given that it is often asserted that teachers are not properly trained to teach children with dyslexia, what key elements would you consider are essential for any teacher in training to prepare them to offer appropriate teaching and learning experiences to children with literacy difficulties?

Recently, Ofsted (2010b, p. 40) drew attention to aspects of the quality of training in their report *Reading by Six: How the Best Schools Do It* in regard to how well teachers were prepared during their training at Higher Education Institutions (HEIs) to teach reading, and made specific reference to the importance of HEIs knowing which schools in their partnership groups were very effective in this area:

> In the last four years, most initial teacher education providers have revised their primary and early years training programmes. Programmes based in Higher Education Institutions now include additional sessions on teaching early literacy skills using a systematic phonics approach and the theoretical aspects of systematic phonics are covered effectively. However, the quality of school-based training is variable … not all trainees are confident to teach reading when they are in their schools. Around 8% of Ofsted's reports on initial teacher education published between February 2009 and August 2010 judged trainees' skills to be 'very good' or 'excellent'. However, while leading literacy schools provide models of good practice, not all providers know where to find the very good practice within their wider partnership of schools … In 2010, only 51% of the newly qualified teachers who responded said that their training had prepared them well to teach early reading.

☐ Summary

This chapter highlighted a number of key principles that teachers and Early Years practitioners need to address when working with children with dyslexia and developmental literacy difficulties. Key factors that underpin best practice in reading, spelling and writing within Early Years and primary schools were also explored, together with the importance of effective working partnerships between teachers and the parents, and caregivers, of their pupils.

📖 Recommended reading

Burden, R. and Burdett, J. (2005) 'Factors Associated with Successful Learning in Pupils with Dyslexia: A Motivational Analysis', *British Journal of Special Education*, 32(2): 100–4.

Wood, E. (2013) *Play, Learning and the Early Childhood Curriculum* (3rd edn). London: Sage.

References

Black, P. and Wiliam, D. (1998) 'Assessment and Classroom Learning', *Assessment in Education*, 5(1): 7–74.

British Dyslexia Association (BDA) (2014) *Initial Teacher Training Campaign*, http://www.bdadyslexia.org.uk/news/initial-teacher-training.html (accessed 10 March 2014).

Brooker, L. (2011) 'Taking Children Seriously: An Alternative Agenda for Research?', *Journal of Early Childhood Research*, 9(2): 137–49.

Browne, E. (1994) *Handa's Surprise*. London: Walker Books.

Bruce, T. (2011) *Early Childhood Education* (4th edn). London: Hodder Education.

Burden, R. and Burdett, J. (2005) 'Factors Associated with Successful Learning in Pupils with Dyslexia: A Motivational Analysis', *British Journal of Special Education*, 32(2): 100–4.

Cepeda, N., Coburn, N., Rohrer, D., Wixtead, J.T., Mozer, M. and Pashler, H. (2009) 'Optimising Distributed Practice: Theoretical Analysis and Practical Implications', *Experimental Psychology*, 56(4): 236–46.

Chapman, J. and Tunmer, W. (1997) 'A Longitudinal Study of Beginning Reading Achievement and Reading Self-concept', *British Journal of Educational Psychology*, 67: 279–91.

Cowie, H. and Wallace, P. (2000) *Peer Support in Action: From By Standing to Standing By*. London: Sage.

Department for Education (DfE) (1994) *Code of Practice on the Identification and Assessment of Special Educational Needs*. London: HMSO.

Department for Education and Skills (DfES) (2001) *Special Educational Needs and Disability Act*. London: DfES.

Department of Education Northern Ireland (DENI) (1998) *Code of Practice on the Identification and Assessment of Special Educational Needs*. Bangor: DENI.

Department of Education Northern Ireland (DENI) (2005a) *Special Educational Needs and Disability NI Order*. Bangor: DENI.

Department of Education Northern Ireland (DENI) (2005b) *Supplement to the Code of Practice on the Identification and Assessment of Special Educational Needs*. Bangor: DENI.

Department of Education Northern Ireland (DENI) (2011) *Count, Read: Succeed*. Bangor: DENI.

Desforges, C. (with Abouchaar, A.) (2003) *The Impact of Parental Involvement, Parental Support and Family Education on Pupil Achievements and Adjustment: A Literature Review* (Research Report RR433). London, UK: Department for Education and Skills.

Duckett, P., Sixsmith, J. and Kagan, C. (2008) 'Researching Pupil Well-being in UK Secondary Schools: Community Psychology and the Politics of Research', *Childhood*, 15(1): 89–106.

Dweck, C.S. (1999) *Self-theories: Their Role in Motivation, Personality and Development*. Philadelphia: Psychology Press.

Elkind, D. (2008) *The Power of Play: How Spontaneous Imaginative Activities Lead to Happier, Healthier Children*. Cambridge, MA: De Capo Lifelong.

Falvey, M. (1994) *Community-based Instruction*. Baltimore: Paul H. Brookes Publishing Company.

Fielding, M. (2007) 'The Human Cost and Intellectual Poverty of High Performance Schooling: Radical Philosophy, John Macmurray and the Remaking of Person-centred Education', *Journal of Education Policy*, 22(4): 383–409.

Flavell, J.H. (1981) 'Cognitive Monitoring', in W.P. Dickson (ed.), *Children's Oral Communication Skills*. New York: Academic Press.

Gillingham, A. and Stillman, B.W. (1966) *Remedial Training for Children with Specific Disability in Reading, Spelling, and Penmanship* (5th edn). Cambridge: MA: Educators Publishing Service, Inc.

Griffiths, C., Norwich, B. and Burden, B. (2004) *'I'm Glad I Don't Take No for an Answer': Parent Professional Relationships and Dyslexia*. Research Report on behalf of the Buttle Trust and the British Dyslexia Association: Exeter University School of Education.

Hartas, D. (2008) 'Practices of Parental Participation: A Case Study', *Educational Psychology in Practice*, 24(2): 139–53.

Heneveld, W. (2007) 'Whose Reality Counts? Local Educators as Researchers on the Quality of Primary Education', *International Review of Education*, 53(5/6): 639–63.

Hunter, T. and Walsh, G. (2014) 'From Policy to Practice? The Reality of Play in Primary School Classes in Northern Ireland', *International Journal of Early Years Education*, 22(1): 19–36.

Kelly, K. and Phillips, S. (2012) *Teaching Literacy to Learners with Dyslexia: A Multisensory Approach*. London: Sage Publications.

Long, L. (2012) 'Using Creative Approaches to Promote Inclusive Cultures for Literacy Learning within Northern Irish Primary Schools'. Unpublished doctoral dissertation, Queen's University Belfast.

Long, L. and McPolin, P. (2009) 'Psychological Assessment and Dyslexia: Parents' Perspectives', *Irish Educational Studies*, 28(1): 115–26.

Long, L., MacBlain, S. and MacBlain, M. (2007) 'Supporting Students with Dyslexia at the Secondary School: An Emotional Model of Literacy', *Journal of Adolescent and Adult Literacy*, 51(2): 124–34.

Ludicke, P. and Kortman, W. (2012) 'Tensions in Home–School Partnerships: The Different Perspectives of Teachers and Parents of Students with Learning Barriers', *Australasian Journal of Special Education*, 36: 155–71.

MacBlain, S.F. (2014) *How Children Learn*. London: Sage.

Midgley, C. and Urdan, T. (1995) 'Predictors of Middle School Students' Use of Self-Handicapping Strategies', *Journal of Early Adolescence*, 15: 389–411.

Moon, B. (2007) 'School-based Teacher Development in Sub-Saharan Africa: Building a New Research Agenda', *The Curriculum Journal*, 18(3): 355–71.

Moyles, J. (2010) 'Play: The Powerful Means of Learning in the Early Years', in S. Smidt (ed.), *Key Issues in Early Years Education* (pp. 23–31). London: Routledge.

NICHD (2000) *Report of the National Reading Panel: Teaching Children to Read.* Washington, DC: Government Printing Office.

Norman, D.A. and Spohrer, J.C. (1996) 'Learner-Centered Education', *Communication of the ACM*, 39(42): 109–16.

Norwich, B., Griffiths, C. and Burden, B. (2005) 'Dyslexia-Friendly Schools and Parent Partnership: Inclusion and Home–School Relationships', *European Journal of Special Needs Education*, 20(2): 147–65.

Nugent, M. (2008) 'Services for Children with Dyslexia – the Child's Experience', *Educational Psychology in Practice*, 24(3): 189–206.

Office for Standards in Education (Ofsted) (2010a) *The Special Educational Needs and Disability Review.* London: Ofsted.

Office for Standards in Education (Ofsted) (2010b) *Reading by Six: How the Best Schools Do It.* London: Ofsted.

Oppendekker, M.C. and Van Damme, J. (2006) 'Teacher Characteristics and Teaching Styles as Effectiveness Enhancing Factors of Classroom Practice', *Teaching and Teacher Education*, 22: 1–21.

Ott, P. (1997) *How to Detect and Manage Dyslexia: A Reference and Resource Manual.* Oxford: Heinemann.

Porter, L. (2008) *Teacher–Parent Collaboration: Early Childhood to Adolescence.* Camberwell, Australia: Australian Council for Education Research.

Power, S. and Clark, A. (2000) 'The Right to Know: Parents, School Reports and Parents' Evenings', *Research Papers in Education*, 15(1): 25–48.

Reay, D. (2005) 'Mothers' Involvement in their Children's Schooling: Social Reproduction in Action?', in G. Crozier and D. Reay (eds), *Activating Participation: Parents and Teachers Working Towards Partnership.* Stoke on Trent: Trentham.

Reid, G. (2011) *Dyslexia* (3rd edn). London: Continuum International Publishing Group.

Robertson, C. with Lovatt, P., Morris, D. and Nutall, C. (1996) 'Reading: A Pastime of the Past?', *Reading*, 30(3): 26–8.

Samuelsson, J. (2008) 'The impact of different teaching methods on students' mathematics skills', *Educational Psychology in Practice,* 24(3): 237-250.

Smit, F. and Driessen, G. (2009) 'Creating Effective Family–School Partnerships in Highly Diverse Contexts: Building Partnership Models and Constructing Parent Typologies', in R. Deslandes (ed.), *International Perspectives on Contexts, Communities and Evaluated Innovative Practices: Family–School–Community Partnerships* (pp. 64–81). Abingdon, Oxon: Routledge.

Solity, J., Deavers, R., Kerfoot, S., Crane, G. and Cannon, K. (1999) 'Raising Literacy Attainments in the Early Years: The Impact of Instructional Psychology', *Educational Psychology*, 19(4): 373–97.

Strommen, L. and Mates, B. (2004) 'Learning to Love Reading: Interviews with Older Children and Teens', *Journal of Adolescent and Adult Literacy*, 48(3): 188–200.

Topping, K. (1995) *Paired Reading, Spelling and Writing: The Handbook for Teachers and Parents.* London: Cassell.

Vygotsky, L. (1978) *Mind in Society.* Harvard, MA: MIT Press.

Walsh, G., Sproule, L., McGuinness, C. and Trew, K. (2011) 'Playful Structure: A Novel Image of Early Years Pedagogy for Primary School Classrooms', *Early Years*, 31(2): 107–9.

Westwood, P. (2005) 'Adapting Curriculum and Instruction', in K. Topping and S. Maloney (eds), *Inclusive Education* (pp.145–59). Abingdon, Oxon: Routledge.

Wood, E. (2013) *Play, Learning and the Early Childhood Curriculum* (3rd edn). London: Sage.

Wolfendale, S. (2000) 'Effective Schools for the Future: Incorporating the Parental and Family Dimension', in S. Wolfendale and J. Bastiani (eds), *The Contribution of Parents to School Effectiveness* (pp. 1–18). London: Fulton.

CHAPTER 6

ADVANCING INCLUSIVE CULTURES FOR LITERACY LEARNING IN THE MAINSTREAM PRIMARY SCHOOL

Louise Long

Chapter aims

- To explore international and national contexts for educational reform and capacity building in schools.
- To examine the concept of inclusion.
- To explore the concept of professional learning communities (PLCs).
- To examine critically collaborative modes of inquiry as levers for change in the advancement of inclusive school cultures for literacy learning.
- To consider critically the implications of the above statements for policy, research and practice in dyslexia and developmental literacy difficulties.

Introduction

It is widely accepted that education is a key to prosperity and happiness for individuals, communities and nations. Countries need high levels of literacy if they are to compete in a global information economy where the cyclical relationship between liberalisation and educational expansion can be either mutually reinforcing or lead to loss of human resource potential. In the current climate of economic malaise and ensuing austerity measures, schools are widely viewed as being in a pivotal position to help bring about prosperity by turning out highly literate, life-long learners. Thus, educators internationally face tremendous challenges of high-quality provision and accountability in raising literacy standards. However, the literature is replete with evidence suggesting that barriers to literacy learning continue to remain apparent when it comes to issues of social disadvantage, gender and 'looked after children' (DENI, 2011; DfES, 2004; Ofsted, 2011). Thus, enhancing inclusive educational practices is critical for removing these recognised barriers to participation and for raising literacy outcomes for all pupils, not just the already high-performing few (Miles and Ainscow, 2011).

Jackson et al. (2000) noted that meaningful participation in general education activities with typically developing peers, membership of a general education group and acceptance by others are the most significant benefits and outcomes of inclusion. Jones (2005), echoed Jackson et al. (2000) when she acknowledged that acceptance and belonging are central principles of effective inclusion. Jones' conceptualisation of inclusion encompasses pupil diversity, special educational needs (SEN) and disability (2005). This broad viewpoint of inclusivity is welcomed and embraced by the authors of this book. However, for the purposes of the current chapter, inclusive practices will centre on SEN in literacy. According to UNESCO (2005), advancing inclusivity is about the presence, participation and achievement of all pupils and, in particular, pupils who may be at risk of being marginalised. Heneveld (2007) articulated that such advancements require transformations in pedagogical and assessment strategies, school leadership and support systems for teachers. Moreover, community and societal support, and high-level political leadership, are also essential for educational reform (Heneveld, 2007).

The educational context

The current UK government has heralded educational reform as the great progressive cause of our time (DfE, 2010, p. 6). Findings from international evidence demonstrate that the advancement of educational reform depends upon capacity building. Capacity building can happen at three distinct but interdependent levels. Capacity can be built at the level of the individual teacher, when groups of teachers work collaboratively and at a whole-school level (Miles and Ainscow, 2011; Stoll et al., 2006).

Teachers are members of a 'learning profession' (Darling-Hammond and Sykes, 1999), which denotes connectivity between members of a community of professionals who are constantly engaged with learning. Moon (2007) acknowledged the positive consequences when professional communities work collaboratively to share learning and to act on their learning to promote pupil learning and improve pupil outcomes. Thus, developing professional learning communities (PLCs) – communities of continuous inquiry and improvement (Hord, 1997) – appears to hold a lot of promise for capacity building for sustainable advancement in a fast-changing and increasingly uncertain world.

Professional learning communities (PLCs) is a term that is now well embedded in the lexicon of international education. However, the homeland for much of the earlier research into the function and usefulness of PLCs in schools is widely acknowledged to be North America. Thus, the implications of research findings from the North American schools' context for policy and practice in the UK schools' context may be limited by the impact of contextual and cultural differences on PLCs (Stoll et al., 2006). Sigurðardóttir (2010) rightly noted that cultural and contextual factors are particularly difficult to discern and understand, let alone control. However, the launch of a report by a team of researchers based at the University of Bristol entitled *Creating and Sustaining Effective Professional Learning Communities* (Bolam et al., 2005) gave momentum to UK-based research into PLCs. England's Department for Education and Skills (DfES) in conjunction with the National College for School Leadership (NCSL) and General Teaching Council (GTC) funded this study, which reflected the importance given to addressing a lacuna in the literature relating to PLCs as a way of building capacity and increasing effectiveness in the context of UK schools. Aspects of the aforementioned study inform the discussion on PLCs that follows.

Professional learning communities

This section opens by exploring the concept and operationalisation of a PLC. There is no universally agreed definition of a PLC. However, findings from critical literature demonstrate agreement that the idea of a PLC draws attention to the possibility that an array of individuals based within and outside a school have the potential to reciprocally enhance their own learning, pupils' learning and school development (Stoll et al., 2006). Learning is *a* central theme that distinguishes a PLC from a strong professional community that has a clear collective sense of how things are done in a school (McLaughlin and Talbert, 2001).

However, the notion of community is *the* central theme in the discourse on PLCs (Stoll et al., 2006). Five features most frequently identified from critical literature probing the notion of community are: shared beliefs and understandings; interaction and participation; interdependence: concern for individual and minority views; and meaningful relationships (Westheimer, 1999). My (Louise's) experiences of teaching, researching and practising educational psychology have illuminated that in functional and progressive school communities, meaningful interpersonal relationships within and between teachers, leaders and pupils are underpinned by an ethic of care, a sense of belonging and an ethos of trust that enable risks taken and lessons learned to be shared with open minds and kind hearts, and successes to be celebrated in the spirit of togetherness (Long, 2012; Montgomery and Kehoe, 2010). So, key to the notion of community is harmony, reciprocity and healthy relationships, whereas key to the professional element in the concept of a PLC is the acquisition of knowledge and skills, reference to clients and professional autonomy (Stoll et al., 2006).

With a broader view of the three-in-one entity of the PLC, Hord (1997, 2004) highlighted five indicative dimensions: supportive and shared leadership; shared values and vision; focusing on pupil learning; supportive conditions; and shared personal practice. Louis et al. (1996) suggested similar dimensions but added reflective dialogue as one of the core conditions. However, all the dimensions that characterise a PLC should be conceptualised as a process rather than the final result of something (Huffman and Hipp, 2003). Therefore, the study of a school as a PLC is concerned with the level of the school as a learning community, in other words, a more or a less mature learning community (Stoll et al., 2006).

There is a small but growing body of international evidence that demonstrates a relationship between effective PLCs and enhanced pupil outcomes. In Australia, Andrews and Lewis (2007) found that a mature PLC improved teachers' knowledge base and made a significant impact on their classroom practice. In the UK, Stoll et al. (2006) demonstrated that post-primary schools with greater support for professional learning had higher levels of pupil progress. Moreover, in Iceland, Sigurðardóttir (2010) obtained strong evidence on the relationship between a school's level of effectiveness, including raised outcomes on national tests, and its level as a professional learning community. These findings provide reason for optimism that mature PLCs can fulfil their ultimate aim, which is to benefit pupils. Thus, capacity building should be viewed as the intermediary outcome of a mature PLC and, as such, is sandwiched between the creation of new knowledge within the organisation using collaborative inquiry and reflection and raising pupil outcomes (Bolam et al., 2005).

Example

Below are the reflective comments that a third-year BEd student shared with me (Louise) during her school-based placement experience in a large, inner-city, co-educational, Catholic primary school. With permission, they have been included in this chapter:

I found from my experiences in this school that teachers were highly collaborative in the ways in which they worked together and with the extended team of teaching assistants, external bodies and SEN support staff. This teamwork allowed for a more holistic approach to progressing children's learning. I believe that teachers in my placement school saw the value in working together for extending their own professional learning. In turn, this enhancement of their professional learning improved the quality of education they provided for the children. I was invited to attend the play, literacy and numeracy planning sessions. I found these sessions extremely informative as they enabled me to gain an insight into the amount of planning, recording, assessing and evaluation that occurs within the primary classroom. However, I also found that consistency in teachers' planning could overshadow each individual teacher's unique classroom style. Even so, it was quickly apparent to me that teachers recognised their differences in opinions as a way of stimulating innovative thinking, experimentation and better practice. Collaboration also extended to involving the local community and getting parents involved with different aspects of school life to engage them in their children's experiences in school. Overall, the warm, community ethos of the school was reflected in all that school staff did, and this sense of community was most evident in teachers' collaborative approaches and focus on ensuring an enriched learning experience for all pupils.

 Useful links

The following links offer useful insights into the building blocks for effective PLCs and their potential to progress pupils' learning:

Professional Learning Animation: Australian Institute for Teaching and School Leadership: http://www.youtube.com/watch?v=e6ZifjWftc8

Rick DuFour on the importance of PLCs: Solution Tree: http://www.youtube.com/watch?v=MnWDJFxfAKE

(Continued)

(Continued)

Rebecca DuFour on four critical questions of a PLC: Solution Tree: http://www.youtube.com/watch?v=Ds7fmtamZ5w

Seven Hills Elementary PLC Meeting: Pearson North America: http://www.youtube.com/watch?v=r2UCLZDWdyA

 Exercise

Draw on what you have learned from these virtual presentations and your own personal and professional experiences of schools to reflect on the following questions:

1 What factors can help the development of an effective professional learning community?
2 What factors can hinder the development of an effective professional learning community?
3 How would you respond to these identified barriers to developing an effective learning community?

The observations made by the student teacher in the above example resonate with Deppeler who suggested that 'collaboration enables teachers with diverse expertise to work together as equals with others in the school community and to share decision-making to address the challenges in their schools' (2012, p. 125). However, the pooling of different professional expertise through the collaborative problem solving that occurs in the context of a PLC should have impact on all pupils' learning, not just those pupils who are already high achievers. In the face of fewer resources and increasingly diverse classrooms, collaboration amongst teachers is critical for advancing more inclusive school cultures, for it is through a process of reflection, conversation and innovation that teachers' practices will become more responsive and flexible, and ultimately, reshape institutional practices (Ainscow and Miles, 2008). Deppeler (2014) reminded us that flexibility and responsiveness do not mean letting go of different professional identities or diminishing the skills and expertise that individual professionals possess. However, authentic collaboration *does* mean that multiple and diverse perspectives are included and represented in the advancement of democratic processes and inclusive educational cultures. This cultural change should be directed towards a 'transformative view of inclusion, in which diversity is seen as making a positive contribution to the creation of responsive educational settings' (Ainscow et al., 2006, p. 15).

There is considerable consensus in critical literature on the crucial role of school leadership in promoting inclusive practice (Dyson et al., 2004; Hopkins et al., 1994; Miles and Ainscow, 2011). For example, Johnson and Johnson (1989) argued that in order for schools to be working at their optimum, school leaders need to challenge traditional, individualistic approaches to teaching; inspire a clear, mutual vision of what the school should and could be; empower staff through cooperative teamwork; lead by example, using cooperative procedures and taking risks; and encourage staff members to keep striving to improve their expertise. Of particular interest in the context of the commentary on inclusive school cultures is a review of research literature on school leadership that was carried out by Riehl (2000). She acknowledged that school leaders need to attend to three broad types of task: fostering new meanings about diversity; promoting inclusive practices within school; and building connections between schools and communities.

Schools that are mature PLCs are more likely to network effectively and build connections with other schools. Deppeler (2014) rightly noted that those schools where strong PLCs exist have developed capacities for collaboration, critical reflection and open conversation to generate ideas for transformation and the advancement of vibrant, inclusive school cultures. Muijs and his co-writers articulated the prerequisites for capacity for collaboration among schools as follows: support from external experts who participate alongside their school-based partners; engagement and support from educational authorities for collaborative processes; resources to encourage key stakeholders to explore the possible benefits of networking; shared motivation for collaboration between schools; and accountability processes that encourage collaboration (Muijs et al., 2011).

 Exercise

According to Muijs et al., (2011), in the absence of the right conditions for effective collaboration between schools, any attempts to encourage schools and teachers to work in partnerships will eventually come to little more than the creation of time-consuming and ineffective meetings, which sooner or later will be discontinued.

In the context of Muijs' cautionary note, are PLCs and partnerships between schools sustainable?

Collaborative modes of inquiry

This chapter moves on now to discuss two distinct modes of collaborative inquiry – action research inquiry and appreciative inquiry (AI) – that can take place within the context of a mature PLC.

Action research inquiry

Action research projects attempt to improve practice and understanding through a combination of systematic reflection and strategic innovation. They are characterised by inquiry that is done *by* or *with* insiders to an organisation, but never *to* or *on* them (Herr and Anderson, 2005, p.3; italics in original). In the school context, practical small-scale action research projects can be used to investigate classroom practices (Elliot, 1991; Stenhouse, 1981) and drive school enhancement projects using insider knowledge (Carr and Kemmis, 1986; Miles and Ainscow, 2011).

Wall and Higgins (2006) noted that the outcomes from action research projects also have significance to the wider research community, what Stenhouse (1981) refers to as *systematic inquiry made public*. However, there is the thorny matter of why anyone should take seriously the evidence that is collected using action research projects and other collaborative modes of inquiry (Miles and Ainscow, 2011). Schon (1991) suggested that teachers could obtain appropriate rigour in the study of practice by focusing on validity and utility. Validity is the requirement that the researcher's description of the world matches what is really there, independent of our ideas and talk about it (Burr, 2003). Miles and Ainscow (2011) recommended that teachers use triangulation to address issues of validity and utility. In the research process triangulation refers to the application and combination of several research methodologies in the study of the same phenomenon (Bogdan and Biklen, 2006). The idea is that a researcher can be more confident of a finding if different methods lead to that same finding. Miles and Ainscow (2011) proposed that rigour can be obtained in collaborative inquiry when teachers discuss the evidence collected through investigations in their schools, including alternative explanations as to what lessons could be drawn from these experiences.

Appreciative inquiry

In the mid-eighties David Cooperrider and his associate at Case Western Reserve University introduced the term 'appreciative inquiry' (AI)

(Cooperrider et al., 2000). AI is the study of what gives life to systems when they are at their best. It is an organisational development method-ology based on the assumption that inquiry into dialogue about strengths, successes, values, hopes and dreams is itself transformational (Hammond, 1998). It is founded on the following sets of beliefs about human nature and human organising:

- People individually and collectively have unique gifts, skills and con-tributions to bring to life.
- Organisations are human social systems, sources of unlimited rela-tional capacity, created and loved in language.
- The images we hold of the future are socially created and, once articulated, serve to guide individual and collective actions. (Corporation for Positive Change, 2011)

Through human communication people can shift their attention and action away from problem analysis to lift up worthy ideals and produc-tive possibilities for the future. AI suggests that human organising and change, at its best, is a relational process of inquiry, grounded in affirma-tion and appreciation (Corporation for Positive Change, 2011). One way to fully understand AI is to consider the meaning of its two words. Appreciation has to do with recognition, with valuing and with gratitude. Inquiry refers to the acts of exploration and discovery. It implies a quest for new possibilities, beginning in a state of unknowing, wonder and willingness to learn. It implies an openness to change.

According to Cooperrider et al. (2000), the process of AI works through the 4-D Cycle. Based on the notion that human systems, people, teams, organisations and communities grow and change in the direction of what they study, AI works by focusing the attention on its most positive poten-tial, which is the positive core. The positive core is the essential nature of the organisation at its best; people's collective wisdom about the organi-sation's tangible and intangible strengths, capabilities, resources, poten-tials and assets. The AI approach is often worked out in practice by using the following '4-D' model:

- **Discover** – people talk to one another, often via structured interviews, to discover the times when the organisation is at its best. These stories are told as richly as possible.
- **Dream** – this phase is often run as a large group conference where people are encouraged to envision the organisation as if the peak moments revealed in the 'discover' phase were the norm rather than the exception.

- **Design** – a small team is empowered to go away and design ways of creating the organisation dreamed in the conferences.
- **Destiny** – the final phase is to implement the changes. (Cooperrider and Srivastva, 1987)

AI is a radically different approach to organisational development and the management of change, deeply conjoined with social constructionist thinking (Cooperrider et al., 2000). In the AI approach, the framework for collective action includes asking a series of questions beginning with one designed to foster an appreciation of the best of what there is within an organisation and a vision of what the institution might look like. The process continues with the participants engaging in collective dialogue over 'what should be' and finally 'what can be'. Vocabularies of hope serve to act as catalysts for this set of questions, for example, stories, metaphors, or pupils' images.

It is now widely acknowledged that collaboration in schools, which is stimulated by engagement with evidence, can transform practice through the two processes of transferring existing knowledge and generating context-specific new knowledge (Miles and Ainscow, 2011). Moreover, the presence of hitherto potentially marginalised learners could act as a stimulus to exploring a more collaborative culture that encapsulates experimentation and an ethos of mutual support between colleagues. When developing inclusive practices, Ainscow and Miles (2008) argued for the need to create spaces that allowed teachers and others to engage with new evidence in ways that 'interrupted thinking' (p. 25), and focused attention on overlooked possibilities for moving practice forward. Such approaches require education practitioners to reflect on their own ways of working, to take risks with the involvement of pupils themselves and to explore child-friendly ways of engaging all stakeholders (Miles and Ainscow, 2011). For example, Smith and Neill (2005) successfully used the AI approach in conjunction with evidence gathered from pupils to examine the possibility that pupils' poems about how to build peace between polarised communities could encourage dialogue within groups of teachers and the generation of transformative ideas for building peace in Northern Irish schools.

There is a growing body of evidence that data gathered from pupils about the teaching and learning arrangements within a school using image-based research methods is particularly powerful in drawing teachers' attention to new ways of addressing barriers to participation and learning (Smith and Long, 2014; Miles and Ainscow, 2011). The next step in this chapter is to examine a two-phased research project that used image-based research methods to gather Phase 1 data from pupils with SEN in literacy for the purposes of engaging Phase 2 participants in critical reflection and conversation and, ultimately, to generate ideas for transforming practice in literacy teaching.

An illustrative case study: using children's drawings to stimulate transformative ideas for literacy teaching

The study

Background

In Chapters 2 and 7, two of the book's authors, Louise and Jill, probe the utility of creative methodologies as an enabling child-centred tool for eliciting and representing voice in young learners. A key research project that is discussed in both these chapters used creative methodologies in the context of focus groups to investigate the 'assessment' and 'participation' stories of upper-primary pupils with marked literacy difficulties and to explore their views on how their level of participation in the assessment and remediation of their literacy difficulties might be enhanced. The outcomes from this study highlighted the need for a holistic model of literacy learning and for the provision of educational pathways that incorporate choice, voice and opportunities to allow pupils to take more responsibility for their own learning. Moreover, pupils should be provided with these pathways and opportunities in the context of nurturing and well-resourced learning environments (Long et al., 2012; McPhillips et al., 2012; Smith and Long, 2014).

However, this research was conceptualised as a precursor to a second phase that investigated what happened when the visual and verbal texts obtained from pupils in Phase 1 were used as catalysts for interpretative discussion by groups of teachers, upper-primary pupils without SEN and parents of primary pupils attending participating schools in conjunction with the appreciative mode of collaborative inquiry (Cooperrider et al., 2000). The Phase 2 study, which takes central place in this chapter, was driven by an aspiration to contribute to institutional change for pupils with additional needs in literacy. In this regard, Louise felt that the visual and verbal texts produced by the pupils in Phase 1 offered exciting possibilities for stimulating conversation and generating creative ideas for change amongst teachers, pupils and parents, in other words, some new meanings. In the second phase of the research, there were three schools, two of which had been involved in the Phase 1 study. Throughout the study, the schools were referred to as school A2, school E2 and school C1. The total Phase 2 study was underpinned by ethical principles and the ethical standards set by Queen's University Belfast (Long, 2012; Smith and Long, 2014).

(Continued)

(Continued)

Phase 2 research questions were informed and derived from Phase 1 outcomes. In Phase 2, practices from AI were used in the context of focus groups to investigate participants' perceptions of the visual and verbal texts produced in Phase 1 and to investigate what participants viewed as 'best practice teaching and learning methodologies' to use to meet the needs of learners who struggle with literacy and also to hear participants' practical propositions for change. Three focus group discussions took place in each school. Focus group one was comprised of parents of pupils with and without SEN attending the school. Focus group two was comprised of teachers of upper-primary pupils. Focus group three was comprised of upper-primary pupils without SEN. In total, 29 people participated in the focus groups. During all of the focus groups, participants were guided through a PowerPoint presentation of the images that Phase 1 children had produced. The presentation also included a number of randomly selected quotations from Phase 1 pupils' conversations. Following the PowerPoint presentation, Phase 2 focus group participants were asked a small number of the following questions:

- What are your views on Phase 1 pupils' assessment and participation stories? What strikes you most about these images?
- What can we learn from these? What is the best provision in this school in terms of meeting the needs of pupils who struggle with literacy learning?
- What practices could develop from your learning? (Long, 2012; Smith and Long, 2014)

One of the authors (Louise) facilitated the focus groups. She chose to use a minimal amount of facilitation to make sure that participants' voices remained central to focus group discussions (Morgan, 1988).

The choice of innovative methods and methodologies in this study was informed by Louise's interest in making a radical departure from the prevailing, sedimented and buried-over practices relating to the (re)construction of 'the problem' (White and Epston, 1990), the methodologies of what Foucault (1980) refers to as 'regimes of truth' (Long, 2012). Rather, the spirit of inquiry, concern and appreciation embodied within the community of each focus group provided teachers, pupils and parents of pupils attending the case-study schools with the opportunity to dialogue as creative and enlivened agents about the carnival of possible organisational futures.

Data analysis

Gergen (1999) perceived the generation of new meanings as central to the process of change and transformation within many aspects of life. Gergen (1999) likened this process to the poetic dimension of language and adopted poetry as a metaphor for the capacity of language to generate new meanings relevant to social transformation. Moreover, Gergen (1999) saw the poetic dimension as exhibiting a number of qualities which, when simulated, held the potential to realise three important functions. These were as follows:

- *The catalytic function:* the unsettling of common habits of mind, moving somebody into new spaces of meaning.
- *The imaginative function:* the stimulation of the imagination in oneself and others, the generation of a discourse that created an image of the future that excited, enticed, enthused.
- *The aesthetic function*: realised through transformative dialogue, which is akin to the concept of empathy in counselling practice (Brammer, 1998).

In the Phase 2 study, content analysis of the data was used in tandem with Gergen's framework (1999), which was deemed appropriate for interpreting the data in the study in relation to the research questions.

Findings

Due to limitations of space, it is possible to include just a few exemplars of the data gathered from focus groups to illustrate the key argument that: the evidence gathered from pupils with SEN in literacy in tandem with an appreciative mode of school improvement is an empowering way to advance inclusive school cultures for literacy teaching-learning. First, Louise will illustrate some of the dialogue from focus groups relevant to the catalytic function – the unsettling of common habits of mind. Then she will move on to illustrate some of the conversation relevant to the imaginative function – the generation of a discourse of hope that moved participants into a positive perception of the future. Finally, Louise will present some dialogue to illustrate the aesthetic function – a developing empathy amongst focus group participants.

Unsettling common habits of mind

Data analysis demonstrated that evidence gathered from pupils with SEN in literacy stimulated interesting conversations in the context of

(Continued)

(Continued)

focus groups and moved participants into new spaces of meaning. The example dialogue below illustrates how participants in the study reconceptualised homework:

> I am a firm believer in no homework … having said that, children with difficulties need more 1-to-1 reading time with their parents. (Parent 1: focus group school, C2)

> When I go home, I could practise my talents. (Child 3: focus group school, A2)

> Children should be using this time to read as widely as possible, and they should be choosing what they read. (Parent 2: focus group school, A2)

Imaginative ways to improve school-based practice

Data analysis demonstrated that the focus groups provided engaging and supportive contexts for participants to dialogue about imaginative ideas for enhancing school-based practice. For example, after much discussion, all the teachers in school A2 agreed on the following action points for enhancing literacy learning in their school:

- Changing the school's reading scheme to one that incorporates comprehension questions to encourage children to talk about what they read. This should happen in conjunction with efforts to slow down the rate at which teachers are expected to move pupils through the levels in a graded reading scheme;
- Giving teachers more autonomy to do what they feel works best for a particular class or pupil irrespective of the demands of the curriculum;
- Creating more opportunities for pupil-led learning and innovation;
- Adapting a more balanced approach to teaching spelling and reading;
- Changing the didactic format of staff meetings to enable teachers to engage in reflective dialogue and the sharing of ideas and expertise at 'a down-to-earth level';
- Timetabling one session a week to develop reading for meaning;
- Sharing learning intentions and success criteria with parents in homework diaries; and
- Providing additional support to pupils with dyslexia and developmental literacy difficulties solely in the context of the classroom.

The aesthetic function

The aesthetic function is similar to the concept of empathy in counselling practice and is at the heart of community building

(Gergen,1999). The dialogue below is viewed as fitting Gergen's description of the aesthetic dimension of the poetic:

Praise is important for raising self-esteem. It fires the pupils up. (Teacher 3: T3 and focus group, school A2)

Sometimes I award certificates if pupils meet a target. It boosts confidence and motivates pupils. They can show the certificates to parents, teachers and the Principal. It's important to make a big hoo-hah about it. (T4: A2)

Yes, you think that Primary 6 and Primary 7 are tougher than they are. But they are still children. They need praise. They need that boost. (T3: A2)

A sincere clap is appreciated … that's all that pupils need. (T1: A2)

The importance of context in collaborative inquiry-based approaches to school advancement was apparent in the current study in terms of the impact of the socioeconomic status of the local community on participants' views on the role of schools in supporting parents to advance their literacy skills and to become involved in school-based activities. These findings corroborated the work of Miles and Ainscow (2011).

Discussion

A synthesis of the emergent themes from all three of Gergen's categories illuminated the high importance that participants attached to literacy learning and, in particular, reading. For example, two of the themes emerging under the 'catalytic function' were the value that participants attached to the enabling use of technology when teaching reading to pupils with SEN in literacy and the importance of embracing these pupils as active social agents. Moreover, under the 'imaginative function' participants hoped to use reading activities to blur boundaries and build bridges between homes, schools and communities. Overall, findings pointed to a network of social, aesthetic, affective, cognitive, metacognitive, communicative, linguistic and intrapersonal effects that define the global 'reading experience' schema. Findings suggested that this schema, which is built upon experiences of reading, is intrinsically linked to pupils' well-being and 'well-becoming'. Thus, it is proposed that access to the written word in all its permutations is critical for enhancing the quality of *childhood* and for shaping the quality of *adulthood*. For this reason . it is also proposed that experiences of reading and the wider reading experience should be at the very core of the primary curriculum.

(Continued)

(Continued)

Findings from the study also added to existing conceptualisations of literacy. They suggested that approaches to literacy teaching-learning should be holistic, integrated with the development of thinking skills and formative modes of assessment, and connected with the Personal Development curriculum and pupils' life experiences (Council for Curriculum Examinations and Assessment [CCEA], 2007). Findings also suggested that the promotion of inclusive cultures for literacy learning should enable teacher autonomy and flexibility in the classroom, give greater choice and voice to pupils, and create more opportunities for home-school partnerships. The outcomes from the Phase 2 study demonstrated a need for classroom practice to be developed to achieve a more balanced approach to literacy teaching in terms of the following:

- the provision of opportunities for pupils to be independent in browsing, choosing and reading a wide variety of high-interest material and interactive literacy activities;
- the development of pupils' reading skills and the provision of opportunities for pupils to engage in reading and writing activities that are meaningful and relevant;
- the use of hard copy reading materials and digital technologies to encourage pupils to engage with literature;
- the provision of rote learning experiences and inquiry-based learning experiences;
- the use of graded reading schemes and authentic reading materials;
- the implementation of a homework policy that incorporates teacher-led homework activities and opportunities for pupils to use after-school time to read;
- the use of printed texts and visual literacy to include short films, media and multimodal texts; and
- the provision of opportunities for collaborative and independent learning.

Key findings from Phase 2 also demonstrated that dialogical modes of professional learning have tremendous potential for unsettling common habits of mind, for recognising the best of existing practices and for stimulating ideas for classroom and institutional transformation. For example, participants recognised the interwoven nature of pupil well-being and literacy success, the benefits of variety in pedagogical and assessment practices, the centrality of teachers in school enhancement processes, the roles of parents and pupils in developing inclusive literacy practices, the potential benefits of involving pupils and parents in collaborative inquiry and, furthermore, participants reconceptualised pupils as active social agents.

Overall, findings from this research project supported the central argument that learner-focused approaches to school improvement are an empowering way to develop a language of possibility for transformation. By utilising collaborative inquiry and action research, teachers can adapt their practices and, through feedback, learn more. In this way a 'virtuous' cycle is created, and classroom practices represent the views of key stakeholders within boundaries of time and resources. This is not to say that all views should be implemented, but that rich and sustained collaborative critical reflection, conversation and strategic innovation have the potential to advance vibrant and inclusive school cultures. As Lodge and Reed (2001) noted, small changes to teachers' practices can bring large benefits to both teachers and learners.

The final point in this section acknowledges that there were some limitations in the illustrative research project described in this chapter (Long, 2012; Smith and Long, 2014). These limitations may be addressed through extensive future research that draws on more case study schools and larger samples. Moreover, discussing the findings from this study and entering into further dialogue with participants may allow the strength of perceptions and views to be further explored and increase the likelihood of creating congruence between perceptions and behaviour. Future research in case study schools could be planned over a longer period of time to enable head teachers and school staff to move to Stage 4 of the 4-D model of AI (Cooperrider and Srivastva, 1987). However, at the final stage of the 4-D cycle, inequality in power across participant groups may or may not determine which ideas for the transformation of practice are enacted in practice.

Implications

Inclusive learning and teaching policies and practices are complex and multifaceted. Thus, it is not surprising that findings from critical literature have highlighted that teachers are very apprehensive about inclusive practices (Florian, 2008). Arguably, the experiences and views of all key stakeholders will influence the success of teachers' attempts to realise the inclusive vision in schools and classrooms (Jones, 2014). The outcomes from the research study highlighted in this chapter generate a sense of hope about what can be achieved when the views of those involved in and affected by the school system are integrated and utilised to support teachers' own learning and efficacy and to open up the status quo to possible innovations in literacy teaching-learning. Thus, it is proposed that policy-makers, researchers and practitioners embrace insider perspectives because they offer holistic and child-centred views on provisions for SEN in literacy. For example, insider contributions on the area of teaching literacy to pupils with dyslexia and developmental literacy difficulties could come from dyslexic pupils, their parents, teachers, school leaders and teacher educators. Jones (2014) elegantly captured the authenticity of listening to the lived experiences of pupils with SEN when she highlighted that this process provides insights into pupils' experiences that cannot be articulated in any other way. Moreover, pupil voice enables practitioners, researchers and policymakers to appreciate more profoundly how schools and schooling impact on the development of self-esteem, self-efficacy and identity in children with dyslexia and developmental literacy difficulties (Long, 2012; Long et al., 2007; Norwich, 2002). Sean examines these concepts of self in Chapter 3 of this book.

Clearly, it is vital that insider perspectives permeate teachers' initial and continued learning in order to enrich professional understandings and that training in the methodologies of action research and collaborative inquiry are embedded into pre-service and in-service teacher education programmes. Indeed, Deppeler (2014) cautioned that standards-based school reform was driven by a narrow research base that privileged 'outsider voices' and gave rise to technical recipes for practice that reduced teaching to a craft-based activity rather than a 'research-informed and research-informing profession' (Lingard and Renshaw, 2009, p. 26). However, building capacity through collaborative inquiry and action research in the context of PLCs generates context-specific knowledge and a collective whole-school sense of responsibility for advancing an inclusive culture for literacy teaching-learning. One matter for consideration is how to close the gap between collective critical dialogue, innovative thinking and classroom practice. Dialogue without action in the context of PLCs is analogous to suspending a caterpillar in the cocoon of metamorphosis. However, rigorous approaches to collaborative inquiry have the potential to empower pupils, parents and teachers to form and inform policy and practice and, ultimately, to improve schools and raise pupil outcomes.

Findings from the study featured in this chapter demonstrated what could be achieved when Higher Education Institutions (HEIs) work in partnership with schools. However, there is an urgent need for more robust and detailed research studies that critically examine the challenges and barriers to developing inclusive cultures for literacy learning in schools through research collaborations between schools and HEIs.

☐ Summary

This chapter explored the international and national backdrop for educational reform and capacity building in schools and its relationship to inclusivity and pupil outcomes. The chapter highlighted that mature PLCs enable critical dialogue and collaboration that have the potential to form, inform and transform practice, and to increase the presence, participation and achievement of all pupils. It was proposed that within the context of PLCs, teachers can advance the vision to become a research-informed and research-informing profession by engaging in collaborative modes of inquiry such as action research and AI. It was also proposed that these methodologies in conjunction with evidence gathered from pupils are an empowering and democratic way of using insider perspectives to advance vibrant and inclusive school cultures for literacy learning. Findings from an illustrative study suggested that inclusive approaches to literacy teaching-learning should promote teacher autonomy and flexibility, advance home-school partnerships and give voice and choice to pupils with dyslexia and developmental literacy difficulties. This chapter affirmed findings from critical literature that policymakers, practitioners and teacher educators should advance child-centred approaches to literacy teaching by integrating perspectives from key stakeholders on best-fit teaching and learning methodologies. Moreover, there was a call for future large-scale research on the use of AI as a learner-centred school improvement methodology.

📖 Recommended reading

Bolam, R., McMahon, A., Stoll, L., Thomas, S., Wallace, M., Greenwood, A., Hawkey, K., Ingram, M., Atkinson, A. and Smith, M. (2005) *Creating and Sustaining Effective Professional Learning Communities*. Research Report 637. London: DfES and University of Bristol.

Hord, S. (2004) 'Professional Learning Communities: An Overview', in S. Hord (ed.), *Learning Together, Leading Together: Changing Schools Through Professional Learning Communities*. New York: Teachers College Press.

Smith, R. and Long, L. (2014) 'Using Vocabularies of Hope to Transform the Educational Experiences of Students Identified as Having Pronounced Literacy Difficulties', in P. Jones (ed.), *Bringing Insider Perspectives into Inclusive Teacher Learning* (pp. 9–24). Abingdon, Oxon: Routledge

References

Ainscow, M. and Miles, S. (2008) 'Making Education for All Inclusive: Where Next?', *Prospects*, 38: 15–34.

Ainscow, M., Booth, T. and Dyson, A. (2006) 'Inclusion and the Standards Agenda: Negotiating Policy Pressures in England', *International Journal of Inclusive Education*, 10(4–5): 295–308.

Andrews, D. and Lewis, M. (2007) 'Transforming Practice from Within: The Power of the Professional Learning Community', in L. Stoll and K.S. Louise (eds), *Professional Learning Communities: Divergence, Depth and Dilemmas*. Maidenhead: Open University Press.

Bogdan, R.C. and Biklen, S.K. (2006) *Qualitative Research in Education: An Introduction to Theory and Methods*. Boston, MA: Allyn and Bacon.

Bolam, R., McMahon, A., Stoll, L., Thomas, S., Wallace, M., Greenwood, A., Hawkey, K., Ingram, M., Atkinson, A. and Smith, M. (2005) *Creating and Sustaining Effective Professional Learning Communities*. Research Report 637. London: DfES and University of Bristol.

Brammer, L. (1998) *The Helping Relationship: Process and Skills*. Boston, MA: Allyn and Bacon.

Burr, V. (2003). *Social constructionism* (2nd ed). Hove: Routledge.

Carr, W. and Kemmis, S. (1986) *Becoming Critical*. Lewes: Falmer Press.

Cooperrider, D. and Srivastva, S. (1987) 'Appreciative Inquiry in Organisational Life', in W. Passmore (ed.), *Research in Organisational Change and Development* (pp. 129–169). Greenwich, CT: JAI.

Cooperrider, D., Sorensen, P.F. and Whitney, C. (2000) *Appreciative Inquiry: Rethinking Human Organisation Towards a Positive Theory of Change*. Champaign, IL: Stripes Publishing.

Corporation for Positive Change (2011) *Foundations of Appreciative Inquiry*. Available at: http://www.positivechange.org/how-we-work/appreciative-inquiry-ai/ (accessed 16 September 2014).

Council for Curriculum Examinations and Assessment (CCEA) (2007) *Curriculum Support and Implementation Box for Key Stages 1 and 2*. Belfast: CCEA.

Darling-Hammond, L. and Sykes, G. (eds) (1999) *Teaching as a Learning Profession*. San Francisco: Jossey-Bass.

DENI (2011) *Count, Read: Succeed*. Belfast: DENI.

Deppeler, J. (2012) 'Developing Inclusive Practices: Innovation Through Collaboration', in C. Boyle and K. Topping (eds) *Inclusion in Schools: What Works?* (pp 125–38). Buckingham: Open University Press/McGraw-Hill.

Deppeler, J. (2014) 'Developing Equitable Practices in Schools', in P. Jones (ed.), *Bringing Insider Perspectives into Inclusive Teacher Learning* (pp 178–189). Abingdon, Oxon: Routledge.

DfES (2004) *Removing Barriers to Achievement: The Government's Strategy for SEN*. London: HMSO.

DfE (2010) *The Importance of Teaching*. London: TSO Ltd.

Dyson, A., Howes, A. and Roberts, B. (2004) 'What Do We Really Know about Inclusive Systems? A Systematic Review of the Research Evidence', in D. Mitchell (ed.), *Special Educational Needs and Inclusive Education: Major Themes in Education*. London: Routledge Failmer.

Elliot, J. (1991) *Action Research for Educational Change:* Buckinghamshire: Open University Press.

Florian, L. (2008) 'Special or Inclusive Education: Future Trends', *British Journal of Special Education*, 35(4): 202–8.

Foucault, M. (1980) *Power/Knowledge: Selected Interviews and Writings*. New York: Pantheon Books.

Gergen, K. (1999) *An Invitation to Social Construction*. London: Sage

Hammond, S.A. (1998) *The Thin Book of Appreciative Inquiry* (2nd edn). Plano TX: The Thin Book Publishing Co.

Heneveld, W. (2007) 'Whose Reality Counts? Local Educators as Researchers on the Quality of Primary Education', *International Review of Education*, 53: 639–63.

Herr, K. and Anderson, G. (2005) *The Action Research Dissertation*. London: Sage Publications.

Hopkins, D., Ainscow, M. and West, M. (1994) *School Improvement in an Era of Change*. London: Cassell.

Hord, S.M. (1997) *Professional Learning Communities: Communities of Continuous Inquiry and Improvement*. Austin, TX: Southwest Educational Development Laboratory.

Hord, S. (2004) 'Professional Learning Communities: An Overview', in S. Hord (ed.), *Learning Together, Leading Together: Changing Schools Through Professional Learning Communities*. New York: Teachers College Press.

Huffman, J.B. and Hipp, K.K. (2003) 'Professional Learning Community Organizer', in J.B. Huffman and K.K. Hipp (eds), *Professional Learning Communities: Initiation to Implementation*. Lanham, MD: Scarecrow Press.

Jackson, L., Ryndak, D. and Billingsley, F. (2000) 'Useful Practices in Inclusive Education: A Preliminary Review of What Experts in Moderate to Severe Disabilities are Saying', *Research and Practice for Persons with Severe Disabilities*, 25(3): 129–41.

Johnson, D.W. and Johnson, R. (1989) *Learning Together and Alone: Cooperative, Competitive and Individualistic Learning*. Boston, MA: Allyn and Bacon.

Jones, P. (2005) 'Teachers' Understandings of Pupils with Profound and Multiple Learning Disabilities and the Possible Impact of Assessment on the Classroom', *PMLD Link*, 16(3): 19–23.

Jones, P. (2014) 'Whose Insider Perspectives Count and Why Should We Consider Them?', in P. Jones (ed.) *Bringing Insider Perspectives into Inclusive Teacher Learning* (1–8). Abingdon, Oxon: Routledge.

Lingard, B., and Renshaw, P. (2009). Teaching as a research-informed and research-informing profession, in A. Campbell and S. Groundwater-Smith (eds), *Connecting Inquiry and Professional Learning in Education: International Perspectives and Practical Solutions* (pp.26-39). London: Routledge.

Lodge, C. and Reed, J. (2001) 'Transforming School Improvement Now and for the Future', *Journal of Educational Change*, 4(1): 45–62.

Long, L., MacBlain, S. and MacBlain, M. (2007) 'Supporting Students with Dyslexia at the Secondary School: An Emotional Model of Literacy', *Journal of Adolescent and Adult Literacy*, 51(2): 124–34.

Long, L. (2012) 'Using Creative Approaches to Promote Inclusive Cultures for Literacy Learning in Northern Irish Primary Schools'. Unpublished Doctoral Thesis, School of Education, Queen's University Belfast.

Long, L., McPhillips, T., Shevlin, M. and Smith, R. (2012) 'Utilising Creative Methodologies to Elicit the Views of Young Learners with Additional Needs in Literacy', *Support for Learning* 27(1): 1–9.

Louis, K.S., Marks, H.M. and Kruse, S. (1996) 'Teachers' Professional Community in Restructuring Schools', *American Educational Research Journal*, 33: 757–98.

McLaughlin, M.W., and Talbert, J.E. (2001). *Professional communities and the work of high school teaching*. Chicago, IL: The University of Chicago Press.

McPhillips, T., Shevlin, M. and Long, L. (2012) 'A Right to be Heard: Learning from Learners with Additional Needs in Literacy', *Literacy*, 46(2): 57–64.

Miles, S. and Ainscow, M. (2011) (eds) *Responding to Diversity in Schools: An Inquiry-Based Approach*. Abingdon, Oxon: Routledge.

Montgomery, A. and Kehoe, I. (2010) 'Reimagining Our School System', *The Psychologist*, 23(6): 486–7.

Moon, B. (2007) 'School-based Teacher Development in Sub-Saharan Africa: Building a New Research Agenda', *Curriculum Journal*, 18(3): 355–71. Available at: http://dx.doi.org/10.1080/09585170701590007

Morgan, D.L. (1988) *Focus Groups as Qualitative Research* (1st edn). Beverley Hills, CA: Sage.

Muijs, D., Ainscow, M., Chapman, C., and West, M. (2011). *Collaboration and Networking in Education*. Dordrecht: Springer.

Norwich, B. (2002) 'Inclusion and Individual Differences: Recognising and Resolving Dilemmas', *British Journal of Educational Studies*, 50(4): 482–502.

Ofsted (2011) *Removing Barriers to Literacy*. London: HMSO.

Riehl, C.J. (2000) 'The Principal's Role in Creating Inclusive Schools for Diverse Students: A Review of Normative, Empirical, and Critical Literature on the Practice of Educational Administration', *Review of Educational Research*, 70(1): 55–81.

Schon, D. (ed) (1991). *The Reflective Turn*. New York: Teachers College Press.

Sigurðardóttir, A. (2010) 'Professional Learning Community in Relation to School Effectiveness', *Scandinavian Journal of Educational Research*, 54(5): 395–412.

Smith, R. and Long, L. (2014) 'Using Vocabularies of Hope to Transform the Educational Experiences of Students Identified as Having Pronounced Literacy Difficulties', in P. Jones (ed.), *Bringing Insider Perspectives into Inclusive Teacher Learning* (9–24). Abingdon, Oxon: Routledge.

Smith, R. and Neill, J. (2005) 'Examining the Possibilities of School Transformation for Peace in NI from a Narrative Perspective', *Journal of Transformative Education*, 3(1): 6–32.

Stenhouse, L. (1981). What counts as research? *British Journal of Educational Studies,* 29(2): 103-114.

Stoll, L., Bolam, R., McMahon, A., Wallace, M. and Thomas, S. (2006) 'Professional Learning Communities: A Review of the Literature', *Journal of Educational Change,* 7: 221–58.

UNESCO (2005) *Guidelines for Inclusion: Ensuring Access to Education for All.* Paris: UNESCO.

Wall, K. and Higgins, S. (2006) 'Facilitating Metacognitive Talk: A Research and Learning Tool', *International Journal of Research and Method in Education,* 29(1): 39–53.

Westheimer, J. (1999). Communities and consequences: An inquiry into ideology and practice in teachers' professional work. *Educational Administration Quarterly,* 35(1): 71-105.

White, M. and Epston, D. (1990) *Narrative Means to Therapeutic Ends.* New York: Norton.

LITERACY IN CONTEMPORARY SETTINGS

NEW LITERACIES IN THE CLASSROOM: FORGING CULTURALLY RESPONSIVE CURRICULA

Jill Dunn

Chapter aims

- To explore the rapidly changing nature of literacy and what it means to be literate in the 21st century and the impact of this on children with dyslexia and developmental literacy difficulties.
- To explore the importance of tuning into children's interests in order to motivate all children to learn and to make education meaningful in contemporary classrooms.
- To reflect on the United Nations Convention on the Rights of the Child (UNCRC) Article 12 and consider why, and how, we might listen to children's voices about learning.
- To consider the importance of recognising children's home literacy experiences and utilising these to enhance the literacy experiences of children with dyslexia and developmental literacy difficulties.

Introduction

Digital technology permeates all aspects of our lives in the 21st century. Everyone is 'logged on', from the 'silver surfers' (adults in the 50+ age bracket who use the internet on a regular basis) to very young children. For the older generation, communication with distant friends and family used to be limited to occasional phone calls and letters but now it is ubiquitous due to emails, blogs, Skype, Facebook, Instagram and a myriad other websites and applications (Bates, 2011). But it is not only the older generation that is capitalising on diverse forms of technology for communication, young children are appropriating digital technology for their own purposes too. Today's children have been born into a digital world and they have no reservations when it comes to using technology. They do not ask questions about which buttons to press or worry if they might break something; they just use it, whether for playful exploration or more specific communicational needs.

New literacies

The emergence of tablet computers and touchscreen devices has brought a new shift in edutainment. This term, edutainment, was first used in the computer industry to refer to the act of learning through a medium that both educates and entertains, and with this concept that learning can be fun and fun can enhance learning, edutainment is a huge market (Rapeepisarn et al., 2006). There is a vast array of computer applications (apps) aimed specifically at young children and the nature of the interactive interface of tablet computers and their appropriate size and portability means that there has been an explosion in young children's use of touchscreen tablets. Recent data gathered in Europe suggests that 50% of Swedish children aged between 3 and 4 use tablet computers; 23% of children in Norway from 0 to 6 years old have access to touchscreens at home and 17% of families in Germany with children aged 3 to 7 have touchscreen tablets. In the UK the use of tablet computers by children increased from 2% to 11% between 2011 and 2012 and the current rate of uptake is likely to be considerably higher than this (Holloway et al., 2013). Hence, the digital landscape of early childhood is changing rapidly and influencing children's early experiences of literacy.

Children's emerging understanding of what literacy is, and is used for, will be influenced by their own and their immediate family's use of technology to read, write and communicate. Digital technology is transforming the communicational landscape and bringing fundamental changes to what it means to be literate in the 21st century. Ten years ago, Gunther Kress highlighted two key changes in literacy: the move from the dominance of writing to the new dominance of the image and the move from the dominance of the medium of the book to the dominance of the medium of the screen (Kress, 2003). There are a variety of terms used in the literature to indicate changing views of literacy: 'new literacies', 'multiliteracies', 'technoliteracy' and 'digital literacy' (see Merchant, 2009), all of which refer to the ways in which new technologies intersect with changing practices in making meaning in the modern world. There is criticism of the narrow view of literacy in our schools compared with wider literacy practices in society. Leading literacy educators have been calling for a change to the constraints of the official curriculum since the 1990s with a greater focus on real literacy practices and the multiple and multimodal texts that children are familiar with. Whilst they are sometimes referred to as new literacies, they may be new to school but they are already well established among many children and young people (Lankshear and Knobel, 2003).

The impact of new literacies on the motivation of children with dyslexia and developmental literacy difficulties

There is a body of research that recognises the negative impact of children's struggles with literacy learning and self-esteem (see Humphrey, 2003; Long et al., 2007, 2012). Children who constantly struggle with literacy throughout school very quickly begin to see themselves as failures in a system which privileges the written word. They are the outsiders, trying to get to grips with reading schemes, spelling lists and phonics and struggling to get their thoughts and ideas written down using paper and pencil. They can feel anxious, inadequate and alienated from their peers. A strong sense of failure prevails and they have not even left primary school yet. Chapter 3 in this book provides a more detailed discussion on the nature of emotional intelligence and its relevance to children experiencing difficulties with the acquisition of literacy.

 Example

Sarah is 6 years old. She is in her second year of primary school and she has been identified as having difficulties with literacy by her class teacher. Her teacher reports that she struggles to remember high frequency words and has poor word attack skills. She can tell stories very well orally but her written work is disappointing due to poor sentence structure and limited use of vocabulary. The teacher works

(Continued)

(Continued)

with her in a small group of children during reading time on a basic reading scheme and Sarah also goes out to the literacy support teacher for revision on her letter sounds. Sarah's mother reports that Sarah says she can't read and she can't write stories like her friends and she believes she is stupid because she has to go out to Mrs Perry for extra help with her literacy. However, at home Sarah loves to use her Mum's smartphone and iPad to text and email her Granny. She composes her own messages and attaches photos that she has taken. She is 'pony mad' and can search the internet to find websites about ponies and riding paraphernalia. She will use her Mum's iPad to take photos of her toy ponies and then make her own stories using storybook apps such as BookMagic with a combination of photos and text. She reads these to her Mum as bedtime stories.

 Exercise

There is much debate in the literature about what constitutes literacy. However, if we adopt Street's (1997) view that literacy is a communicative practice, can you identify how Sarah is developing skills in literacy? Discuss the potential differences in the literacy skills being developed in school and those being developed at home and how these might affect Sarah's perceptions about her own abilities in literacy.

Pahl and Rowsell (2010, p. 3) note that 'the literacy found in schools is actually just one type of literacy'. Even though children with dyslexia and developmental literacy difficulties struggle with their literacy in school they persevere in using technology for their own needs and interests in making meaning from a range of digital texts and in communicating with others. There are calls in the literature for more appropriate learning opportunities for children with dyslexia which go beyond the teaching of the mechanics of reading (see Long et al., 2007). Children need to be engaged and motivated in their learning and there is a body of literature which reports on the increased motivation, enthusiasm and engagement of children in their learning when they use tablet devices (Burden et al., 2012). This includes children with special educational needs where research indicates that technology can provide exciting and interesting experiences as well as helping to improve emergent literacy and writing (see Shamir et al., 2012).

In a recent survey of teachers of special educational needs, enhanced student motivation was the most frequently reported benefit of using tablet computers in school (Johnson et al., 2013). Whilst there are some concerns about tablet devices and overuse, misuse and distractions from learning, research overwhelmingly reports on the positive impact of tablet devices and student motivation. Therefore, there is great potential in harnessing this technology for the purposes of enhancing the motivational levels of children with dyslexia and developmental literacy difficulties and enhancing their views of themselves as literacy learners.

There is some debate that the novelty effect used to explain increases in motivation when using digital technologies may wear off as the technology becomes more established. Davies and Merchant (2014) refer to this as the allure of the new and shiny. However, there is the counter-argument that the content created for the technology, for example the range of applications (apps), is continually developing and pushing the boundaries to create novel and compelling approaches and maintain students' wonder and curiosity (Johnson et al., 2013). As this is such a new area, with a rapidly expanding number of apps (over 1 million reported apps in both Apple's App Store and in Android's Google Play store as of September 2014), the issue of novelty effects, motivation and the use of tablet devices is a growing area for future research.

The affordances of new literacies

An affordance is the quality of a particular object which allows an individual to perform certain actions. So in the case of the use of tablet devices, we want to know what are the particular qualities of this technology that allow children to develop literacy skills and how are these different from the skills which they develop when engaging with more traditional literacy practices using paper and print? Merchant (2015) argues that it is rapidly becoming difficult to talk about literacy without reference to new technology, and the research evidence suggests that integrating digital technology in the classroom requires the development of new literacy skills, strategies and dispositions, since these technologies transform the way that children will learn.

If we take the example of e-books, we can see that many of these books aimed at young children allow the reader to use audio support while reading, to turn on text tracking and to record themselves reading the text and play it back. Children can access the definition of chosen words by tapping on them and can add notes if they choose to do so. There are lots of choices in this interaction with the e-book and this is what makes reading more individualised, interactive and engaging, which can potentially engage struggling readers (Larson, 2010). The benefits for children with dyslexia and developmental literacy difficulties lie in the opportunities to make choices in their engagement with texts. They can choose to use audio support as often as they wish before choosing to read the text unaided. They can also choose to record themselves reading and thus see themselves acting as real readers. Some children with dyslexia can lose their place in the text when reading and the use of text tracking can be beneficial in maintaining place whilst allowing the flow necessary for reading in context. Using a dictionary can be frustrating for some children with dyslexia due to their difficulties with sequencing the alphabet. Therefore, the instant access to word definitions simply by tapping on words can aid their efforts to make meaning without interrupting their enjoyment of the text. These choices in the level of support give children independence in making meaning from the text without heavy reliance on adult assistance, and can potentially engage those readers who are reluctant to read for pleasure.

There is a growing range of apps that allows children to create their own stories using a combination of text, pictures and symbols. These can be organised in a variety of attractive formats through some simple choices by the child. Built-in cameras provide opportunities for children to capture photographs and videos to include in their stories, which facilitates collaboration between children and allows them to create more meaningful texts. Visuals play a very important role in learning, with pictures consistently trumping text and oral information. This is called the pictorial superiority effect (Stenberg, 2006). Pictures are more easily remembered than text, they are more likely to be stored and much more likely to be retrieved. There is a new but growing body of neuroscientific research evidence that suggests that text should be paired with visual information to aid children's learning (Frey and Fisher, 2010).

Many children, especially children with dyslexia, view writing as very hard work due to a combination of possible factors such as poor speed of writing, insecurities about spelling, difficulties organising ideas and embarrassment about the appearance of their work resulting in low self-esteem as a writer (Kelly and Phillips, 2011). There is too much emphasis placed on narrative, essay-type writing in primary school and children need to experience a much broader range of forms of writing as well as self-chosen texts linked to children's own interests and purposes. Healy Eames (2002) reports that children with dyslexia want writing to be purposeful and serve real communicative functions and be linked to their interests. The use of tablet devices facilitates this with the camera allowing children to include chosen and meaningful photographs very easily in their stories. There are options to tell stories orally to a set of selected drawings or photographs. These can be told a number of times, allowing children time to rehearse their story until they have it the way they want it. Children have choices in using a keyboard to type text or using a microphone option for converting speech to text. This is valuable for children with dyslexia who have a very poor speed of writing due to poor automaticity in letter formation and short-term memory difficulties in remembering and organising what they want to say. This combination of speaking, listening, touching and seeing provides a multisensory approach which is advocated for children with dyslexia. Visual, auditory, tactile and kinaesthetic modalities are all engaged, leading to stronger connections in the brain and thus enhancing memory and learning (Singleton, 2009). These technical capabilities and creative apps transform the writing process for children with dyslexia, assisting them in composing meaningful texts and seeing themselves as real writers.

 Example

Emily is 8 years old and has recently been diagnosed with dyslexia. She has always struggled with written work and finds it very difficult to write stories in school due to a poor ability to structure her ideas and to get them down on paper in time. She is also very embarrassed by her poor spelling. These have all led to her avoiding written activities in public situations such as school or other groups outside of school such as Brownies. However, her Mum has bought her an iPad and encouraged her to dictate stories on it using the microphone option. An older cousin introduced Emily to the app Pic Collage which allows the creation of collages of photos, stickers, text and frames. Emily recently had a jewellery-making birthday party and she enjoyed looking at all the photos that her Mum took of her and her friends making bracelets. So with the help of her cousin she created a collage which included photos of her party, stickers and dictated text. She was able to arrange the collage very easily and choose backgrounds and borders which complemented the theme of a birthday party. The complete collage 'told the story' of the birthday party through a variety of modes including pictures, text and design and Emily printed these off and gave them to her friends.

 Exercise

Merchant (2006) argues that traditional relationships between readers, writers and texts are radically changing. Twenty years ago Emily would only have been able to write her story of her birthday party on paper using a pencil. However, tablet devices allow children

(Continued)

(Continued)

to create a multimodal text that is no longer contained by the limits of a page. Some of the features of written language are that meaning is conveyed in the absence of a shared physical context between the writer and the reader and that it makes thoughts and emotions permanent. Can you discuss how Emily's multimodal text conveys meaning and brings permanence to her thoughts and emotions?

 Useful links

The following links offer further useful insights into some of the aspects of digital literacy discussed in this chapter:

Professor Jackie Marsh's talk entitled 'How Do UK Children Use ebooks?': http://www.youtube.com/watch?v=v6mYbUON3OQ

A brief demonstration of Oliver Jeffers 'Heart and the Bottle' iPad picture book app: http://www.youtube.com/watch?v=Wc3fghSJvBM

A report on how the digital divide starts in the early years: http://www.literacytrust.org.uk/talk_to_your_baby/news/3561_digital_divide_starts_in_the_early_years

---

Following children's interests

We have already made the point earlier in this chapter, that it is crucial to engage children in their learning by following their interests and thus making the curriculum more meaningful for them. This is true for all children and especially important for children with dyslexia and developmental literacy difficulties as their difficulties with literacy can easily turn them off learning. It has always been the central tenet of early childhood that the starting point for learning should be the child – what they know and what they can do. In her hugely successful book, Julie Fisher (2013) argues that the current government's mantra that children in the Foundation Stage should be 'made ready for school' should be turned on its head and, instead, schools should be 'made ready for children'. She highlights the expertise of children's first educators, their parents, and she advocates an appreciation of the learning that has gone on at home. She believes that it is up to teachers to make children's new learning environments in school equally relevant and worthwhile. Lilian Katz (2010) also believes that one of the basics for every young child is that they are involved in activities which are real and significant, intriguing and absorbing to them.

The value of popular culture in the classroom

There is a growing literature which recognises the central role that popular culture plays in many young children's lives. Jackie Marsh, who has written widely on this topic, suggests that popular culture is 'the range of texts, artefacts and practices that are popular with large numbers of children and are either produced commercially or produced and circulated amongst children themselves' (Marsh, 2010a, p. 13). Children are immersed in popular culture from birth and it is evident in children's conversations, play, drawing and writing, irrespective of adults' approval (Ashton, 2005). Research has demonstrated that children will naturally bring their outside interests regarding popular culture into the classroom (Kissel, 2011). Wohlwend (2013) argues that children do not simply watch or read the messages in popular films, television programmes or video games, rather they live immersed in these texts due to what she calls the 'omnipresent flow of transmedia', which are the franchises anchored by children's media that spin off a whole range of consumer goods. Marsh et al.'s (2005) Digital Beginnings Research Report on young children's use of popular culture, media and new technologies states that popular culture is part of young children's social and cultural practices as they grow up in their homes and communities. Childhood in the 21st century is littered with popular culture icons and shaped by, what Marsh et al. refer to, as the 'fashions and passions of media'.

  Example

Harry gets out of bed (Disney *Cars* duvet cover) in the morning wearing his Spiderman pyjamas. He has his breakfast out of his favourite Shrek bowl looking at the *Monsters University* characters on the cereal box. He sets off for school with his Buzz Lightyear rucksack containing his pencil case with a mishmash of pencils and rubbers from the recent films *Frozen* and *Cloudy with a Chance of Meatballs*. He is going to his friend Molly's birthday party after school where the party tableware will be themed on *Despicable Me 2*. He has bought

(Continued)

(Continued)

Molly a Minion action figure set (characters from *Despicable Me*). She is also getting a Hello Kitty card and wrapping paper. Harry likes *Despicable Me 2* but he really wants Mario and Sonic at the Olympic Winter Games for his next birthday.

Concerns have been raised in the literature over the past 10 to 15 years about the dramatic differences between children's early literacy experiences at home (including popular culture) and the literacy they are confronted with when they begin their school lives. The failure to acknowledge children's home literacy experiences and everyday uses and enjoyment of popular culture is stifling the possibility of children's potential to make meaning from their social and cultural worlds. These are lost opportunities for teachers and research indicates that many settings reflect very little of children's home practices (Marsh, 2010b). Children's literacy experiences at home include a vast array of experiences with books, comics, television, gaming, film and many more popular culture artefacts. However, early childhood classrooms offer limited opportunities for children to engage with and explore their passions for these experiences (Marsh et al., 2005). Teachers are either unfamiliar or unwilling to engage with children's culture, and there are ongoing calls for classroom walls to become more porous and for teachers to make children's everyday experiences and interests the starting points for learning.

This is crucial for children who struggle with literacy and who have dwindling self-esteem with regard to reading, writing and spelling. These children find the 'print culture' of our classrooms very difficult yet their problems with learning are not their fault. Teachers need to focus on helping children cope with their literacy learning and tackle their history of failure by adopting a more creative, flexible approach in order to build self-esteem. In 2010, Rose et al. took an interesting stance in an article where they fast forwarded to 2020 where they were presenting the presidential address for the International Dyslexia Association. In this address of the future they describe new landscapes for learning where it was 'nearly impossible to think of students with dyslexia as "learning disabled". In fact, these students taught us that our schools were "print disabled"' (p. 37). Smith and Scuilli (2011) describe how they used a popular text and its film adaptation to engage a group of teenagers who had experienced literacy struggles throughout their school careers. These young people had individualised education plans, did not see themselves as readers and were at risk of failing in literacy. The use of this text in their literacy lessons engaged these young people to be motivated to read both print and digital texts and to engage in both traditional and digital writing. Smith and Scuilli describe how this approach demonstrated the importance and power of focusing on children's and young people's unique interests.

 Example

In a recent research study (Dunn, 2013; Dunn et al., 2014), Dunn worked with a class of 6- and 7-year-old children using the *Toy Story 3* film to engage children in writing about their favourite characters. The children watched a clip from the film and then worked with the researcher in shared writing. The focus for the writing was Woody, one of the main cowboy characters in the film. A cowboy hat and Woody dressing-up clothes were used to allow some children to take on the role of Woody in the hot-seat and to give the class information about the character. The children were then given the task of writing about a favourite character from a children's film of their choice. The class teacher had already highlighted several children with particular needs within the class. One of these was Poppy. She was a reluctant reader and struggled to remember vocabulary and letter sounds. She found writing particularly frustrating and usually wrote very little. However, she was an avid fan of the *Toy Story* trilogy and it transpired that she had many of the characters at home. She chose to write about the cowgirl Jessie. She drew a picture of Jessie and her horse Bullseye. Her detailed drawing demonstrated her knowledge of the character. Her sentences contained some missing words, misspelled words and some repetition but the most encouraging thing was that she was engaged and interested and she was motivated to write. She was particularly proud of her finished character profile and wanted to read it to others at her table.

Resistance to popular culture in the classroom

The introduction of new technologies and new media can bring with it a range of 'moral panics' (Cohen, 1987). There are concerns that children's access to popular culture can motivate children to become hedonistic consumers and there are those that believe that children are vulnerable to exploitation by marketing. Kenway and Bullen (2001) warn that pervasive global texts invite children to identify with a range of media characters which mobilises feelings of connectedness, gratification, pleasure and excitement. But it can also provoke a sense of envy, yearning and anxiety. There are concerns about 'toxic childhoods' (Palmer, 2006) and 'remote control childhoods' (Levin, 2010). There is the view that the aim of schools should be to nurture 'educated people' and that this can only be done by using 'high culture' rather than a 'culture of fakes' (see Jones [2013] article in the *Guardian* on high culture versus pop culture). There is also unease about the suitability of certain forms of popular culture for young children. In a recent study of children's playground games and rhymes, Marsh and Bishop (2014) observed children re-enacting elements of the popular UK television talk show *The Jeremy Kyle Show*. They discuss how this programme, like many others in the reality TV genre, is often cast as 'trash TV' in which a particular representation of people from lower socioeconomic groups is embedded which generally features immorality and depravity. They suggest that such programmes are worlds away from the lives of many middle-class teachers but are closer to the worlds of some of the children with whom those teachers work. Therefore, they argue that play based on talk shows or reality TV should not be dismissed or derided but needs to be taken seriously as part of children coming to terms with their complex and often challenging social and cultural worlds.

Karen Brooks (2011) argues that resistance to popular culture and new media is futile. Digital technologies, new media and popular culture have revolutionised the way we live, interact and understand ourselves and the rest of the world. These changes provide stimulating and engaging experiences for children in their private lives and if schools do not move forward to embrace these changes then children's school lives are going to look very boring in comparison. Prensky (2005, p. 62) goes as far as suggesting that, in many schools, what is being deployed is 'yesterday's education for tomorrow's kids'. Yet, for many teachers, popular culture can be seen as a threat to their educational authority. They do not feel that they have the knowledge or the language to use popular culture and can feel overwhelmed by the sheer volume of material.

 Example

Janet has been teaching in primary classrooms for 25 years. These are her responses when asked about incorporating popular culture into her classroom activities:

I really don't know very much about what children watch on the television these days. There just seems to be so much. When my children were young, there were far fewer television programmes and television channels. I remember The Clangers, The Magic Roundabout *and* Andy Pandy *but children today wouldn't know about them. They would be very dull compared to all the special effects of today. And there seems to be a new film in the cinema every week. How on earth do you keep up? Everything is a fad; it is in one moment and out the next. I wouldn't know where to start. I would pick something that none of the children in my class had heard of. I really wouldn't feel comfortable with it; I would rather stick to what I know.*

Brooks (2011) takes the view that teachers do not have to make choices between old and new or traditional and modern. Rather, value should be drawn from both traditional teaching resources and contemporary popular culture to create what she refers to as an intertextual and converged learning environment. However, in order to do that, teachers need to be familiar with what children's popular culture is. Wohlwend (2013) suggests that the best way to do this is to note clues from children's school supplies (bags, lunch boxes, pencils), their classroom talk and their play. She believes that children are the experts and that we need to engage them in discussion and ask them about their favourite characters, television programmes and children's films.

Example

The author explains her approach to incorporating children's views in her research on the use of popular culture in the teaching of writing (Dunn, 2013):

I asked two groups of children to tell me what children's films they thought should be used in my lessons. I felt that this was a crucial element in my study since I wanted the films to be appealing to children and the only way to find that out is to ask the children themselves! These children were acting as an advisory group for the research project. The group contained

(Continued)

(Continued)

both boys and girls and the children were all in their third year of formal schooling and were 6 or 7 years old. I explained to them that I wanted films that would appeal to both boys and girls. The children were full of ideas and had lots of enthusiastic discussions with their partners before writing their ideas on sticky notes. Some of the children suggested films that might be considered to be more appealing to a particular gender (for example, some girls suggested Tangled *which is a Disney modern day version of* Rapunzel *and some boys suggested* Cars 2 *which is a Disney action film). However, many of the children suggested films which might be assumed to appeal to both genders such as* Toy Story, Finding Nemo, The Lion King *and* Shrek. *This activity was short and simple to carry out and provided me with lots of suggestions for my teaching. It also meant I could be sure that I was using films that would engage and interest children.*

 Exercise

Do you know what the latest children's films are at the cinema? Are you familiar with the wide range of children's television channels and popular television programmes? Do you know what the most sought after toys are for young children? Make a point of asking some young children you know well what their favourite films, television programmes, toys, etc. are to find out how in tune you are with children's culture.

▶ **Useful links**

The following links offer further useful insights into some of the aspects of popular culture discussed in this chapter:

Information and ideas on the role of popular culture in primary English: http://www.ite.org.uk/ite_topics/popular_culture_primary_english/011.html

An article by Donna Alvermann on popular culture and literacy practices: http://www.academia.edu/359745/Popular_Culture_and_Literacy_Practices

An article on practical ideas using children's comics to stimulate talk and writing: http://education.scholastic.co.uk/content/11848.

Accessing the views of children

For many years, children's views have been regarded as inferior to those of adults. However, the ratification of the United Nations Convention on the Rights of the Child (UNCRC) in the UK in 1991 represented a potentially dramatic shift in approaches to children's rights. Article 12 (para. 1) states that:

> States parties shall assure to the child who is capable of forming his or her own views the right to express those views freely in all matters affecting the child, the views of the child being given due weight in accordance with the age and maturity of the child. (UN, 1989)

In their annual Day of General Discussion on the Right of the Child to be Heard (September, 2006) the Committee on the Rights of the Child highlighted the importance of Article 12 and recognised the right of the child to express views and to participate in various activities, stating that this was 'beneficial for the child, for the family, for the community, the school, the State, for democracy' (UN, 2006, p. 2). One of the key recommendations that it makes is that children will be actively consulted in the development and evaluation of school curricula as they state this is conducive to increasing the involvement of children in the learning process.

Therefore, it can be concluded from this that consulting with children about the ways in which they would like to learn is a requirement placed upon all professionals working in education. However, despite this there still appears to be a divide between the rhetoric and the reality of listening to the views and interests of children. Indeed, it might be argued that many teachers continue to disregard children's views in their day-to-day practice. Adults may think they know what children need and may believe they know about childhood as they were once children themselves, regardless of how long ago that was and how the world and society may have changed since. Yet the only people who can understand what it is to be a child in the 21st century is the child who is living that experience. An underlying concern may exist that, in according children their rights, adults will have to relinquish their power and control. Lundy (2007) indicates three possible areas of concern for adults: scepticism about children's capacity in having something meaningful to say, an undermining of adult authority in the school environment, and a concern about wasting time and effort which would be better spent on getting on with education. However, whilst recognising these concerns, Lundy goes on to state that actively involving pupils in decision-making should not be seen as a gift from adults but as a legal imperative which is the right of the child. This includes children with special educational needs.

✎ Exercise

Consider Lundy's three possible areas of concern for adults when children are accorded their rights and given a voice (see above).

- How do you feel about the notion of listening to the views and interests of children in the context of their learning in school?
- How have you seen this happening (or not happening) in practice in any of the settings in which you have had some experience?
- What do you think are the factors that contribute to children being actively involved in decision-making in schools and what are the factors hindering this from happening?
- Have you seen any examples in practice of children with dyslexia or developmental literacy difficulties being asked their views about their learning in school?

In a recent research study, Long et al. (2012) used creative methodologies with a group of pupils aged between 9 and 11 years to elicit their views on themselves as literacy learners and how they might have more of a voice in how their needs might be addressed. All of these children had longstanding literacy difficulties. Long and her colleagues concluded from their research that there was a real need for children's voices to enable pupils to take more responsibility for their own learning. They also highlighted that this approach which empowers children should also empower teachers to then exercise their professional judgement and to tailor the teaching within their classrooms to the unique needs and wishes of children with special educational needs. See Chapter 2 – *Child-centred Literacy Pathways: Pupils' Perspectives*, for a fuller discussion on pupil voice and consulting with children and young people with special educational needs.

Despite this emphasis on children's voice, Prout (2000) points out that children are being governed more strongly than ever before and this is echoed by Jeffs (2002) who highlights the tensions between children's rights and what he calls the 'authoritarian, repressive and standardised school system' (p. 55). In this confusing situation it is essential to establish appropriate and effective systems for listening to young children and for their emancipation (Moss et al., 2005).

How can we listen to the voices of young children?

Listening to children can imply a passive process but Rinaldi (2001, p. 4) suggests that 'listening is an active verb, which involves giving an interpretation, giving meaning to the message and value to those who are being listened to'. This pedagogy of listening is central to the ethos of the Reggio Emilia pre-schools. Listening may suggest verbal interactions; however, with very young children this may not always be an appropriate way to access their views. Malaguzzi, the first pedagogical director of the pre-schools, created the phrase 'the hundred languages of children' (Edwards et al., 1998) which indicates the potential of children expressing themselves in a wide range of ways. Those that work with young children will know that children will express themselves through play, movement, dance, art, interacting with puppets, singing and a myriad other ways. What is required on the part of the adult is to observe children and learn to 'listen' and interpret what they are telling us through their actions.

Observation of young children has always been fundamental to Early Years practice and Nutbrown (1996, p. 55) emphasises the importance of this as an appropriate means of understanding young children's views: 'adults with expertise who respectfully watch children engaged in their process of living, learning, loving and being are in a better position to understand what it is these youngest citizens are trying to say'.

Clark and Moss (2001) have developed a well-known framework for listening to young children which they call the Mosaic approach. The principles of this framework are that it is: *multi-method*, in that it recognises the different voices of children; *participatory*, in treating children as experts; *reflexive*, including children's, practitioners' and parents' views in the overall interpretation; *adaptable*, within a wide range of settings; *focused on children's lived experiences* and *embedded into practice*, rather than seen as a bolt-on activity. The different pieces of the Mosaic include a creative range of approaches in listening to young children. These involve observation, child conferencing, using cameras to take photographs, tours led by children, map making by children and role play (Walsh et al., 2006). Clark and Moss recognised that there was a need to imaginatively re-think appropriate methods of consultation with very young children which would access their views in ways that were familiar, comfortable and engaging for them. This array of fresh and innovative techniques in accessing children's views accords with Article 13 of the UNCRC which states that children's right to freedom of expression includes the right to 'impart information and ideas of all kinds, regardless of frontiers, either orally, in writing or in print, in the form of art, or through any other media of the child's choice' (UN, 1989).

The challenges in listening to children

There are a number of challenges and dilemmas in relation to listening to young children and giving them a voice in the classroom. There are those that argue that children are very diverse and that we must be very cautious that we do not treat children as a homogenous group. We must be aware that the views of *some* children do not represent the views of *all* children. Therefore, engaging children in sharing their views about learning cannot be one-off experiences. Rather, they must be on-going to capture the multiple and changing perspectives of children. Dockett et al. (2009) urge adults to engage in ongoing, recurrent listening since children have diverse perspectives, experiences and understandings.

 Useful links

The following links offer further useful insights into accessing the views of children as discussed in this chapter:

A summary of children's rights from the UN Convention on the Rights of the Child: http://www.unicef.org/crc/files/Rights_overview.pdf

A short presentation by Professor Laura Lundy on the involvement of children in education decision–making: http://www.docs.hss.ed.ac.uk/education/creid/NewsEvents/38iv_ESRC_TT3_PPT_LLundy.pdf

---

Summary

The aim of this chapter was to explore the rapidly changing landscape of literacy. Young children's experiences of literacy at home have been discussed and shown to involve technology, media and a vast range of popular culture, yet these experiences are not often reflected in many classrooms. The world is changing, with boundaries between work and leisure beginning to blur, and the serious and the frivolous starting to intermingle (Merchant, 2006). Children's interests and passions need to be recognised and capitalised on if classrooms are going to be meaningful and engaging. This is even more important when teachers are working with children who are experiencing difficulties in their literacy learning and for whom school can be a very difficult and disheartening experience. Children themselves are the experts on being children in classrooms today and are in a unique position to tell us how they might learn better. Therefore, it is the responsibility of those involved in education to take their views seriously and involve them in activating change.

Recommended reading

Dunn, J., Niens, U. and McMillan, D. (2014) '"Cos He's My Favourite Character!" A Children's Rights Approach to the Use of Popular Culture in the Teaching of Literacy', *Literacy*, 48(1): 23–31.

Long, L., McPhillips, T., Shevlin, M. and Smith, R. (2012) 'Utilising Creative Methodologies to Elicit the Views of Young Learners with Additional Needs in Literacy', *Support for Learning*, 27(1): 20–8.

Merchant, G. (2015) 'Keep Taking the Tablets: iPads, Story Apps and Early Literacy', *Australian Journal of Language and Literacy.*

Wohlwend, K. (2013) *Literacy Playshop: New Literacies, Popular Culture and Play in the Early Childhood Classroom.* New York: Teachers College Press.

References

Ashton, J. (2005) 'Barbie, the Wiggles and Harry Potter: Can Popular Culture Really Support Young Children's Literacy Development?', *European Early Childhood Education Research Journal*, 13(1): 31–40.

Bates, D. (2011) 'Rise of the Silver Surfers: Grandparents Using Internet to Stay in Touch with Family in Record Numbers', *The Daily Mail*, 10 May, http://www.dailymail.co.uk/sciencetech/article-1385330/Rise-silver-surfers-Grandparents-using-Skype-Facebook-stay-touch-family-record-numbers-seen-before.html (accessed 7 February 2014).

Brooks, K. (2011) 'Resistance is Futile: Re-accenting the Present to Create Classroom Dialogues', *Pedagogies: An International Journal*, 6(1): 66–80.

Burden, K., Hopkins, P., Male, T., Martin, S. and Trala, C. (2012) *iPad Scotland Evaluation.* University of Hull.

Clark, A. and Moss, P. (2001) *Listening to Young Children: The Mosaic Approach.* London: The National Children's Bureau.

Cohen, S. (1987) *Folk Devils and Moral Panics: The Creation of the Mods and Rockers* (2nd edn). Oxford: Blackwell.

Davies, J. and Merchant, G. (2014) 'Digital Literacy and Teacher Education', in P. Benson and A. Chik (eds), *Popular Culture, Pedagogy and Teacher Education: International Perspectives* (pp. 180–93). London: Routledge.

Dockett, S., Einarsdottir, J. and Perry, B. (2009) 'Researching with Children: Ethical Tensions', *Journal of Early Childhood Research*, 7(3): 283–98.

Dunn, J. (2013) 'Children's Views on the Use of Popular Culture in the Teaching of Writing in the Primary Classroom'. Unpublished EdD dissertation, Queen's University Belfast.

Dunn, J., Niens, U. and McMillan, D. (2014) '"Cos He's My Favourite Character!" A Children's Rights Approach to the Use of Popular Culture in the Teaching of Literacy', *Literacy*, 48(1): 23–31.

Edwards, C., Gandini, L. and Forman, G. (eds) (1998) *The Hundred Languages of Children: The Reggio Emilia Approach – Advanced Reflections* (2nd edn). Norwood, NJ: Ablex.

Fisher, J. (2013) *Starting from the Child* (4th edn). Maidenhead: Open University Press.

Frey, N. and Fisher, D. (2010) 'Reading and the Brain: What Early Childhood Educators Need to Know', *Early Childhood Educational Journal*, 38: 103–10.

Healy Eames, F. (2002) 'Changing Definitions and Concepts of Literacy: Implications for Pedagogy and Research', in G. Reid and J. Wearmouth (eds), *Dyslexia and Literacy: Theory and Practice* (pp. 327–42). Chichester: John Wiley and Sons.

Holloway, D., Green, L. and Livingstone, S. (2013) *Zero to Eight: Young Children and their Internet Use*. LSE London: EU Kids Online Network.

Humphrey, N. (2003) 'Facilitating a Positive Sense of Self in Pupils with Dyslexia: The Role of Teachers and Peers', *Support for Learning*, 18(3): 130–6.

Jeffs, T. (2002) 'Schooling, Education and Children's Rights', in B. Franklin (ed.), *The New Handbook of Children's Rights: Comparative Policy and Practice* (pp. 45–59). London: Routledge.

Johnson, G., Davies, S. and Thomas, S. (2013) 'iPads and Children with Special Learning Needs: A Survey of Teachers'. Paper presented at the World Conference on Educational Multimedia, Hypermedia and Telecommunications. Available at : http//espace.library.curtin.edu.au/cgi-bin/espace.pdf?file=/2013/08/16/file-1/192194 (accessed 16 September 2014)

Jones, A. (2013) 'High Culture Versus Pop Culture: Which is Best for Engaging Students?' *The Guardian*, 20 February, http://www.theguardian.com/teacher-network/teacher-blog/2013/feb/20/pop-culture-teaching-learning-engaging-students (accessed 7 February 2014)

Katz, L. (2010) 'What is Basic for Young Children?', in S. Smidt (ed.), *Key Issues in Early Years Education* (2nd edn) (pp. 4–8). London: Routledge.

Kelly, K. and Phillips, S. (2011) *Teaching Literacy to Learners with Dyslexia: A Multisensory Approach*. London: Sage.

Kenway, J. and Bullen, E. (2001) *Consuming Children: Education-Entertainment-Advertising*. Buckingham: Open University Press.

Kissel, B.T. (2011) '"That Ain't No Ninja Turtles": The Prevalence and Influence of Popular Culture in the Talk and Writing of Prekindergarten Children', *NHSA Dialog*, 14(1), pp. 16–36.

Kress, G. (2003) *Literacy in the New Media Age*. London: Routledge.

Lankshear, C. and Knobel, M. (2003) *New Literacies: Changing Knowledge and Classroom Learning*. Buckingham, UK: Open University Press.

Larson, L.C. (2010) 'Digital Readers: The Next Chapter in e-Book Reading and Response', *The Reading Teacher*, 64(1): 15–22.

Levin, D. (2010) 'Remote Control Childhood: Combating the Hazards of Media Culture in Schools', *New Horizons in Education*, 58(3): 14–25.

Long, L., MacBlain, S. and MacBlain, M. (2007) 'Supporting Students with Dyslexia at the Secondary Level: An Emotional Model of Literacy', *Journal of Adolescent and Adult Literacy*, 51(2): 124–34.

Long, L., McPhillips, T., Shevlin, M. and Smith, R. (2012) 'Utilising Creative Methodologies to Elicit the Views of Young Learners with Additional Needs in Literacy', *Support for Learning*, 27(1): 20–8.

Lundy, L. (2007) 'Voice is Not Enough: Conceptualising Article 12 of the United Nations Convention on the Rights of the Child', *British Educational Research Journal*, 33(6): 927–42.

Marsh, J. (2010a) *Childhood, Culture and Creativity: A Literature Review.* Newcastle: Creativity, Culture and Education.

Marsh, J. (2010b) 'The Relationship between Home and School Literacy Practices', in D. Wyse, R. Andrews and J. Hoffman (eds), *The Routledge International Handbook of English, Language and Literacy Teaching* (pp. 305–16). Abingdon, Oxon: Routledge.

Marsh, J. and Bishop, J. (2014) '"We're Playing Jeremy Kyle"! Television Talk Shows in the Playground', *Discourse: Studies in the Cultural Politics of Education*, 35(1): 16–30.

Marsh, J., Brooks, G., Hughes, J., Ritchie, L., Roberts, S. and Wright, K. (2005) *Digital Beginnings: Young Children's Use of Popular Culture, Media and New Technologies.* Sheffield: Literacy Research Centre, University of Sheffield.

Merchant, G. (2006) 'A Sign of the Times: Looking Critically at Popular Digital Writing', in J. Marsh and E. Millard (eds), *Popular Literacies, Childhood and Schooling* (pp. 93–108). London: Routledge.

Merchant, G. (2009) 'Literacy in Virtual Worlds', *Journal of Research in Reading*, 32(1): 38–56.

Merchant, G. (2015) 'Keep Taking the Tablets: iPads, Story Apps and Early Literacy'. *Australian Journal of Language and Literacy,* February Issue.

Moss, P., Clark, A. and Kjorholt, A.T. (2005) 'Introduction', in A. Clark, A.T. Kjorholt and P. Moss (eds), *Beyond Listening* (pp. 1–16). Bristol: The Policy Press.

Nutbrown, C. (1996) 'Wide Eyes and Open Minds – Observing, Assessing and Respecting Children's Early Achievements', in C. Nutbrown (ed.), *Respectful Educators, Capable Learners: Childrens' Rights and Early Education* (pp. 44–55). London: Paul Chapman.

Pahl, K. and Rowsell, J. (2010) *Artifactual Literacies: Every Object tells a Story.* New York: Teachers College Press.

Palmer, S. (2006) *Toxic Childhood: How the Modern World is Damaging Our Children and What We Can Do About It.* London: Orion.

Prensky, M. (2005) 'Engage Me or Enrage Me: What Today's Learners Demand', *Educause Review*, 40(5): 60–4.

Prout, A. (2000) 'Children's Participation: Control and Self-realisation in British Late Modernity', *Children and Society*, 14: 304–31.

Rapeepisarn, K., Wong, K.W., Fung, C.C. and Depickere, A. (2006) 'Similarities and Differences Between "Learn Through Play" and "Edutainment"', *Proceedings of the 3rd Australasian Conference on Interactive Entertainment 2006*, Perth, Australia: Murdoch University, pp. 28–32.

Rinaldi, C. (2001) 'A Pedagogy of Listening: A Perspective of Listening from Reggio Emilia', *Children in Europe*, 1: 2–5.

Rose, D., Vue, G. and Halsey, M. (2010) '2020's Learning Landscape: A Retrospective on Dyslexia', *Perspectives on Language and Literacy*, 36(1): 33–8.

Shamir, A., Korat, O. and Fellah, R. (2012) 'Promoting Vocabulary, Phonological Awareness and Concepts about Print Among Children at Risk for Learning Disability: Can e-Books Help?' *Reading and Writing*, 25(1): 45–69.

Singleton, C. (2009) *Intervention for Dyslexia: A Review of Published Evidence on the Impact of Specialist Dyslexia Teaching*. London: DCSF.

Smith, C.A. and Scuilli, S. (2011) 'I Can't Believe We Read This Whole Book! How Reading for their own Purposes Affected Struggling Teens', *English Journal*, 101(2): 30–6.

Stenberg, G. (2006) 'Conceptual and Perceptual Factors in the Picture Superiority Effect', *European Journal of Cognitive Psychology*, 18: 813–47.

Street, B. (1997) 'The Implications of the New Literacy Studies for Education', *English in Education*, 31(3): 45–59.

UN (1989) *United Nations Convention on the Rights of the Child*. Geneva: United Nations.

UN (2006) *Committee on the Rights of the Child: Day of General Discussion on the Right of the Child to be Heard (CRC/DGD/2006)*. Geneva: United Nations.

Walsh, G., Dunn, J., Mitchell, D., McAlister, M. and Cunningham, J. (2006) 'Giving Young Children a Voice: Accessing the Views of 3–4 Year Old Children in Playgroups', *Representing Children*, 18(2): 79–95.

Wohlwend, K. (2013) *Literacy Playshop: New Literacies, Popular Culture and Play in the Early Childhood Classroom*. New York: Teachers College Press.

PART 4

CONCLUSIONS

CHAPTER 8

CONTEMPORARY CHALLENGES: LOOKING TO THE FUTURE

Sean MacBlain, Jill Dunn and Louise Long

Chapter aims

- To explore the implications for child-centred practice with children with dyslexia and developmental literacy difficulties in the 21st-century classroom.
- To identify key principles in providing for children with dyslexia in the inclusive classroom.
- To explore the importance of fostering and advancing partnerships between home, school, community, and the child.
- To examine issues central to the mentoring of teachers in training and the implications and challenges this will have for schools.

Introduction

Whilst the difficulties that children with dyslexia face remain constant the educational world around them is changing, and at a pace that, arguably, is unparalleled. Children and young people living today experience pressures that would be unknown to their parents and grandparents when they were at school. This said, we have come a long way in not only recognising conditions such as dyslexia, dyspraxia, ADHD and ASD but also understanding them. Whereas previously, children with dyslexia would have been viewed as lacking in ability, and in some extreme cases even moved to schools for children with moderate learning difficulties or emotional and behavioural difficulties, we are now much more informed.

Advances in our understanding of how children learn, and how different characteristics and elements of their thinking underpin learning has meant that many more children with dyslexia who might previously have gone unrecognised are now being identified. More specifically, as schools adopt more meaningful and relevant assessment, linked to purposeful interventions with clear identifiable outcomes, then many more children who would have previously been consigned to failure will benefit. More importantly, perhaps, is the unassailable fact that as teachers and Early Years practitioners have increasingly sought to understand the factors that lead to reading failure, so they have also increased their understanding of how failure affects social and emotional development in young children and, later, throughout their lives. This said, it also needs to be recognised that there exists, still, a legacy whereby few children who are experiencing difficulties with the acquisition of literacy have any real sort of identifiable voice. Too few, in effect, are never properly listened to, despite suffering frustration and anxiety, and even worse, in their adolescent years, depression and acute feelings of low self-worth and self-negativity.

The critique on 'pupil voice' in Chapter 2 demonstrates that the educational discourse surrounding pupil participation remains characterised by rhetoric. It is argued that many consultation practices are tokenistic and ineffective and fail to give children with dyslexia influence in the determination and planning of their learning. When children with dyslexia are outside the decision-making processes that define them as learners and as individuals, due regard is not given to their inner and outer social, emotional and academic worlds. In Chapter 2, Louise foregrounds the discussion on enabling methodologies for eliciting pupil voice by arguing that 'failure to involve learners with SEN illuminates the need to provide structured opportunities for those pupils who are being sidelined to convey their views and ultimately to influence the decisions that are made about their educational pathways' (p. 40).

Child centredness: implications for practice in the 21st-century classroom

Early childhood education has always been firmly rooted in the view that all children should have an education which meets their individual needs (Fisher, 2013). This child-centred approach goes back to Early

Years pioneers such as Rousseau, Pestalozzi and Froebel and it began to have an impact on practice in the UK partly due to its endorsement by significant official reports such as *Children and their Primary Schools* (CACE, 1967). This influential report, better known as the Plowden Report, specifically promoted a child-centred approach:

> At the heart of the education process lies the child. No advances in policy, no acquisitions of new equipment have their desired effect unless they are in harmony with the nature of the child, unless they are fundamentally acceptable to him. (CACE, 1967, para. 9)

Whilst the Plowden Report was published 47 years ago, this statement from that report is equally valid and compelling today. No advances in literacy will be made by policy, nor by the introduction of new pedagogical practices nor rapidly evolving technologies unless these policies, practices and technologies are acceptable, appealing and 'in-tune' with children. This includes children with dyslexia and developmental literacy difficulties.

Tina Bruce (2011) draws out commonalities between the most influential of the Early Years pioneers and presents these as the 10 principles of good Early Years practice. These principles can be read in more detail in many Early Years texts, however, her seventh principle is important to mention in this context. She states that what children can do, rather than what they cannot do, should be the starting point for a child's learning. This was developed from one of Froebel's most famous remarks 'Begin where the learner is, not where the learner ought to be'. This is essential for children with dyslexia and developmental literacy difficulties. They cannot be shoe-horned into a fixed and rigid curriculum that does not meet their needs and only serves to impact negatively on their self-esteem as learners. Their starting points and routes into and through literacy will be different based on their specific needs.

An essential element in this child-centred approach is the teacher who needs to 'have an appreciation of and respect for the ways of children' (Darling, 1994, p. 3). Vygotsky (1978) also recognised the educator as central to children's development. He posited that children operate at two levels: the present level and the potential level. He believed that the teacher's role was to move the child on from their actual level of understanding to the next potential level of understanding; to encourage children to do without help what they can only do with help at present. Since children with dyslexia and developmental literacy difficulties already show low achievement in many aspects of literacy, it is important that other risk factors that may further slow their achievement be identified. In a recent study, Hornstra et al. (2010) found that teachers working with children with dyslexia had implicit negative biases that they were not aware of towards this group of children, which negatively affected the achievement outcomes of children with dyslexia. They call for improved teacher education programmes on teaching children with specific learning needs but without stigmatisation. We need to have high expectations for what these children can do when they are given an appropriate curriculum, the correct support and creative approaches which may appeal to their different ways of learning.

The challenge of new literacies for teachers in contemporary classrooms

Chapter 7 in this book addresses new literacies in the classroom. It aims to explore the rapidly changing nature of literacy and what it means to be literate in the 21st century. It also presents the importance of being 'in tune' with what young children find interesting and the moral and legal imperative for listening, hearing and taking account of what children want to be included in their literacy teaching. The pivotal, crucial factor in all that is discussed within that chapter is the teacher. The McKinsey Report (Barber and Mourshed, 2007) observes that the quality of an education system cannot exceed the quality of its teachers. The central role for teachers in literacy is to provide high-quality teaching for all pupils. According to Merchant (2009), all teachers are concerned with creating a safe and orderly space for literacy instruction and want a harmonious learning environment. He argues that disturbing this 'fragile ecology' is a risky business and there needs to be both strong support and sensitive professional development to move beyond a narrow vision of literacy. These new literacies in the classroom require a quantum leap for some teachers from traditional books and paper-based education. There is a generation gap between teachers from a 'TV world' and students from a 'web world'. Mompoint-Gaillard (2013) suggests that this generation gap needs to be bridged where many teachers will have to learn to accept to take the risk of not being the one who knows best, or knows more. He suggests that relinquishing some of our power, empathising with young learners and accepting our 'illectronacy' is the first step in this process.

 Exercise

Some teachers find it difficult to move forward and embrace the opportunities that media and technology bring to the classroom. Hartley et al. (2008, p. 59) state that 'Formal education is often thought of as being in embattled opposition to media entertainment'.

> Discuss why some teachers adopt this approach and how they might be encouraged to create a converged learning environment which draws from both traditional and new literacy practices.

Moral panics

Jones and Hafner (2012) acknowledge that people have always had strong feelings when it comes to new media and technology and they go as far as suggesting that it is natural for people to feel insecure and worry that their ways of being, doing and thinking are being lost or marginalised. This is true for many parents and teachers who are concerned about the effects of digital media and the new literacies associated with them. There are concerns about the impact of digital media on children's language development, their ability to make meaning, their social relationships and the way they think. There are extreme views of 'technological dystopianism', that digital technologies are destroying our ability to communicate with one another meaningfully, and 'technological utopianism', that digital technologies will make us all smarter and the world a better place (Jones and Hafner, 2012). The reality is somewhere in between these polar views. We must acknowledge the opportunities that new technologies bring to learning but we must also remember that they are only tools and they must be used effectively to enhance learning.

Moving forward

The challenge for teachers in contemporary classrooms remains the same as it has done for many years and that is, how to engage all children in learning, including those children who have developmental literacy difficulties and other specific literacy difficulties such as dyslexia. There is a cacophony of dramatic predictions for the future of literacy within our primary classrooms and, in particular, the role of the teaching of writing. There is a sense of dramatic change on the horizon (Gundlach, 2009). However, Marsh and Singleton (2009) believe that, whilst developments in technology will mean that modes other than writing will become increasingly pervasive when undertaking everyday activities, writing will always be a significant mode of communication and 'the physical act of writing, whatever technology is used, will remain important' (p. 2). The challenge is to harness popular culture and new media technologies as innovative and meaningful tools in the teaching of writing (Brooks, 2011). This challenge is particularly important for children with developmental literacy difficulties and dyslexia who find writing a very difficult and onerous task.

In meeting the needs of a wide range of children, teachers must consider what is happening in the home environment and their out-of-school worlds. Some of the characteristics of children's positive home experiences are explained by O'Mara and Laidlaw (2011):

- Generally free, uninterrupted periods of time for exploration, discovery and creation
- Children following their interests and passions – driving their learning and their text production
- Most of the literacy activities are child motivated
- Sharing favourite digital texts and activities with others.

Indeed, O'Mara and Laidlaw argue that classrooms should incorporate some of these 'innovative freedoms' that children experience at home, and that teachers need to take up these new tools and use them in new ways within the classroom. In our primary classrooms today, we are educating children for the future. However, we do not know what that future will look like. No one can anticipate how the world will change in the next 20 or 30 years. No one could anticipate how the world has changed in the last 20 or 30 years, and it has changed immensely with the invention of the internet and many other technologies and the rise of computer use in everyday life. Literacies are not things we develop for the sake of it. Rather, we develop them to do certain things, create certain types of societies and become certain kinds of people. Digital media opens up a staggering range of possibilities for accessing and creating information, expressing ourselves and connecting with others (Jones and Hafner, 2012). How we adopt digital media and use it as a tool for learning for all children is our challenge for the future.

Key principles in providing for children with dyslexia in the inclusive classroom

It almost goes without saying that teachers working with children with dyslexia should, in the first instance, be sensitive to their emotional and social needs as well as their academic needs (McPhillips et al., 2012). Though this would appear obvious, it is sadly not always the case. Too many children, for example, who struggle with literacy and present with difficulties typically associated with dyslexia such as poor organisation and planning, weak memory, slow processing speed resulting in work not being completed on time, and problems with concentration, continue to be viewed by some teachers as, at best, requiring too much of their time and, at worst, something of a burden (MacBlain, 2014; Long et al., 2007). Moreover, as discussed in Chapter 2, many children and young people continue to remain distanced and excluded from decision-making processes within which they, themselves, are at the centre (MacConville, 2006; Noble, 2003; Todd, 2003). One is again drawn here to a most obvious, and sensible, declaration offered nearly two decades ago by DENI (1998, para. 2.28) cited earlier in Chapter 2, which emphasised that '... all reasonable efforts should be made to ascertain the views of the child or young person about his or her own learning difficulties and education, offering encouragement where necessary'.

Classroom environments come in all shapes and sizes and are dominated by social activities and relationships. It is within these classrooms, and Early Years settings that we learn to engage further with others. It is here that we lay down many of those important skills whereby we develop aspects of our personalities and extend our learning of how to become confident and effective members of society and the communities of which we are a part. From time to time, however, most children at primary and secondary school will experience feelings of unhappiness and even sadness. For children who have grown highly sensitive to their own limited progress compared with that of their peers, such feelings can become greatly amplified (Humphrey, 2003). The result, as we have seen in previous chapters, can be a deepening sense of failure, which, over time, becomes internalised and ingrained within those constructs they use to perceive themselves (Kelly and Phillips, 2011). 'I am really bad at spelling', 'I'm no good at reading', 'I'm not very clever', 'All my friends are better than me at reading' are phrases often heard from such children and not only indicate a strong sense of perceived failure but also a strong sense of learned helplessness. Teachers, therefore, must be alert in recognising such self-perceptions if they appear to arise and should take great care to identify factors that might contribute to the development of this type of thinking in their pupils and actively take steps to prevent it. At the heart of such recognition lies the importance of teachers giving careful, but purposeful, consideration to motivational and affective dimensions to reading and writing when making assessments of their pupils and adopting a holistic approach that goes far beyond simply teaching the mechanics of reading, spelling and writing (Long et al., 2007). In Chapter 2, the call is made for a new conceptual model of literacy learning that bridges the academic-holistic divide by embracing metacognition and emotional literacy. The case is made that creative approaches to eliciting voice could well help to generate teacher understanding of the importance of these concepts for informing the approaches and strategies they implement to teach literacy to children with dyslexia. However, Louise acknowledges the need for more research on the long-term impact of utilising creative methodologies that, 'takes into account the views of educational professionals and the views of young learners' (p. 54).

Recently, the late celebrated psychologist and academic, Professor Robert Burden (Burden, 2008) sought to raise awareness in regard to potential critical periods in children's learning development when children developed perceptions of themselves relating directly to success and/or failure in literacy and from which aspects of their personal identities might be formed. He wrote as follows:

> A number of studies appear to indicate that there may well be key periods at which dyslexic and learning disabled children may be at particular risk in the development of their learning identities ... during their early and middle school years children later identified as dyslexic are likely to call into question their intellectual abilities and to lose motivation as a consequence of their unexplained difficulties. Interview studies by Burden (2005) and Ingesson (2007) confirm that this period of trying to make sense of what may seem to be inexplicable difficulties prior to diagnosis can be quite crucial in a dyslexic child's life, and it is often here that the support and understanding of parents can make all the difference as to whether the child begins to give up or continues to keep trying ... (2008, p. 192)

Classrooms should be happy environments where children can feel confident in asking questions, explaining to their teacher that they find particular work difficult and taking time to understand how they learn best, what strategies work for them and developing those creative aspects of their personality. Structure will be important, as will planning and organisation, the efficient use of time, and opportunities for overlearning and reinforcement. These last two elements are central to the learning experience of children with dyslexia. Too often, however, teachers believe that they have to be actually with the child with dyslexia and 'teaching' them directly for the child to be learning. This should not be the case and children should be encouraged to develop their skills in working independently as well as with other children, for example, with a 'buddy' arrangement.

An important feature of inclusive classrooms for children with dyslexia in the future will be an appropriate emphasis upon the teaching and learning of phonics (see Chapter 1). This said, the teaching of phonics continues to divide the educational community and will, no doubt, continue to do so in the future. The extent of the controversy surrounding the teaching of phonics to young children, and especially beginning readers, continues to dominate much of the thinking in regard to reading and spelling in the Early Years.

> ▶ **Useful links**
>
> The following link offers excellent insights into how children with dyslexia should be taught. It includes, for example, such elements as multisensory teaching, early identification and assessment, planning and sequencing, the importance of overlearning, use of colour overlays and glasses with tinted lenses, handwriting, and developing and boosting self-esteem:
>
> Teaching the Dyslexic Child: http://www.youtube.com/watch?v=YkLjGlCfLRw

Central to the progress of children with dyslexia is the need for key adults in their lives to work in partnership. All too often, however, one hears professionals declaring how parents fail to back up their efforts with their own children, and parents decrying professionals who fail to listen to them when they feel, intuitively, that something is preventing their children from making progress. At times tensions between professionals and parents can be underpinned by a lack of communication whilst at others they can be down to a lack of trust. It is important that children feel supported by their family and their teachers and they know that both are working together to support them. Where other professionals such as Speech and Language Therapists, Educational Psychologists, Social Workers and Occupational Therapists are involved then it is also very important that they all work in a multi-professional way. This is especially important where children are experiencing significant problems that will ultimately work against them achieving their potential.

Sharing knowledge gained through formal assessment of intellectual functioning, observations of the child working on a range of activities and in different settings, early social and emotional development, language or medical assessments will be extremely helpful. This is not, however, always the case, despite governments, academics and policy decision-makers over the decades placing a high level of emphasis upon this way of working (MacBlain, 2014). A number of barriers have been identified over the years (Frederickson and Cline, 2002) such as professionals being socialised into developing specific vocabulary sets during their training to identify and explain conditions, which can present problems in communication. Other difficulties identified by Frederickson and Cline relate to tensions between different professional groups and the way in which different groups of professionals are funded, for example by local health authorities as in the case of Speech and Language Therapists or Local

Authorities as in the case of Educational Psychologists. New issues surrounding funding are now emerging as schools have taken on the role of Academies and with this new role the responsibility for allocating finances. A more recent barrier and one that can cause much difficulty is the need for confidentiality where, for example, some professionals are aware of particular difficulties experienced by a child but cannot share the information.

 Example

Alex and Natalie are young parents with two children, Martyn aged 8 and Hayley aged 5. They have been worried for some time about Martyn, whose language does not seem to be developing as well as they think it should. His reading and spelling are very poor and he is falling behind the other children in his class. He is becoming increasingly unhappy at school. Alex and Natalie have spoken to the SENCo at Martyn's school who has acknowledged that Martyn has been struggling since entering school but has indicated that if they want an assessment by an Educational Psychologist then they will have to arrange this privately and pay for the assessment themselves. The cost of such an assessment is in the region of several hundred pounds and Martyn's parents simply cannot afford this. They have also referred him through their GP for an assessment by a Speech and Language Therapist but have been told that they will have to wait for some time, perhaps several months, for an assessment and then there will be a waiting list on which his name will be placed, meaning that it might be 6 months before he begins any therapy or even longer. They are concerned that if Martyn is seen by a Speech and Language Therapist and, privately, by an Educational Psychologist that these two professionals will not meet with each other or even speak with each other, with the result that important advice in regard to setting up specific programmes for Martyn will not be passed on to the school. They have been told by friends that the reports they get from any assessments are likely to stay in folders and not be shared or acted upon by the school.

Mentoring teachers in training: implications and challenges for schools

As discussed earlier, teachers are increasingly being trained in schools whereas previously they have been trained in Higher Education Institutions

(HEIs). Whilst there is much agreement and disagreement about whether or not this is the best way forward, it is clear that there will be implications of this new way of training and preparing teachers. How, for example, will teachers who are being trained in schools develop the necessary knowledge and skills to work with children with dyslexia and from whom will they learn them?

In recent years much has been done to develop teachers' under-standing of special educational needs and to promote new and appropriate ways of working with children with dyslexia. Indeed, many schools have achieved, amongst many distinctions, the status of being 'dyslexia friendly'. With this there has come much more rec-ognition of dyslexia and the difficulties faced by children with this condition. However, too many children continue to fail, not only with reading and writing, but more worryingly with aspects of social and emotional development, and more specifically self-esteem and self-efficacy. This is despite the changes that have taken place in regard to the recognition that many children fail to access literacy because of specific learning difficulties.

 Useful links

The following link presents some very important messages for teachers through a humorous set of cartoons: http://www.youtube.com/watch?v=M1tA-5hfKJk

A further consideration for the training and mentoring of teachers work-ing with children with dyslexia is the proposed emphasis that is being placed by the current coalition government in England on the reinstat-ing of examinations as the primary means of testing children at 16. This will replace the existing system of testing and assessment where pupils undertake significantly high levels of course work. The implications of preparing pupils for examinations at 16 are, therefore, enormous and will require that teachers gain a much better understanding of factors that affect such key areas in learning as, working memory, processing speed, organisation and planning, comorbidity of conditions and the impact of this, pre-examination anxiety, and so on. To fail to do so, will almost certainly mean that many children with dyslexia and other spe-cific learning difficulties will be disadvantaged.

☐ **Summary**

This chapter explored the implications for child-centred practice with children with dyslexia and developmental literacy difficulties in the 21st-century classroom. Key principles underpinning provision for children with dyslexia in the inclusive classroom were identified and discussed, together with the importance of fostering and advancing partnerships between, home, school, community and the child. Issues central to the mentoring of teachers in training were identified and discussed along with the implications and challenges this has for schools now and in the future.

 Recommended reading

MacBlain, S.F. (2014) *How Children Learn*. London: Sage.

References

Barber, M. and Mourshed, M. (2007) *How the World's Best-performing School Systems Come Out On Top*. McKinsey and Company.

Bee, H. and Boyd, D. (2007) *The Developing Child* (11th edn). London: Pearson Education, Inc.

Brooks, K. (2011) 'Resistance is Futile: "Reaccenting" the Present to Create Classroom Dialogues', *Pedagogies: An International Journal*, 6(1): 66–80.

Bruce, T. (2011) *Early Childhood Education* (4th edn). London: Hodder Education.

Burden, R.L. (2005) *Dyslexia and Self-concept*. London: Whurr.

Burden, R.L. (2008) 'Is Dyslexia Necessarily Associated with Negative Feelings of Self-worth? A Review and Implications for Future Research', *Dyslexia*, 14: 188–96.

CACE, (1967) *Children and their Primary Schools (The Plowden Report)*. London: HMSO.

Darling, J. (1994) *Child-centred Education and its Critics*. London: Paul Chapman.

Department of Education Northern Ireland (DENI) (1998). *Code of Practice on the Identification and Assessment of Special Educational Needs*. Bangor: DENI.

Fisher, J. (2013) *Starting from the Child* (4th edn). Maidenhead: Open University Press.

Flavell, J.H. (1981) 'Cognitive Monitoring', in W.P. Dickson (ed.), *Children's Oral Communication Skills*. New York: Academic Press.

Frederickson, N. and Cline, T. (2002) *Special Educational Needs, Inclusion and Diversity: A Textbook*. Maidenhead: Open University Press.

Gundlach, R. (2009) 'Reflections on the Future of Writing Development', in R. Beard, D. Myhill, J. Riley and M. Nystrand (eds), *The Sage Handbook of Writing Development*. London: Sage, pp. 574–80.

Hartley, J., McWilliams, K., Burgess, J. and Banks, J. (2008) 'The Uses of Multimedia: Three Digital Literacy Case Studies', *Media International Australia*, 128: 59–72.

Hewitt, D. (2008) *Understanding Effective Learning: Strategies for the Classroom*. Maidenhead: Open University Press.

Hornstra, L., Denessen, E., Bakker, J., Van den Bergh, l. and Voeten, M. (2010) Teacher Attitudes Toward Dyslexia: Effects on Teacher Expectations and the Academic Achievement of Students with Dyslexia, *Journal of Learning Disabilities*, 43(6): 515–29.

Humphrey, N. (2003) 'Facilitating a Positive Sense of Self in Pupils with Dyslexia: the Role of Teachers and Peers', *Support for Learning*, 18(3): 130–6.

Ingesson, S.G. (2007) 'Growing Up with Dyslexia', *School Psychology International*, 28(5): 574–91.

Jones, R.H. and Hafner, C.A. (2012) *Understanding Digital Literacies: A Practical Introduction*. London: Routledge.

Kelly, K. and Phillips, S. (2011) *Teaching Literacy to Learners with Dyslexia: A Multisensory Approach*. London: Sage.

Long, L., MacBlain, S. and MacBlain, M. (2007) 'Supporting Students with Dyslexia at the Secondary Level: An Emotional Model of Literacy', *Journal of Adolescent and Adult Literacy*, 51(2): 124–34.

MacBlain, S.F. (2014) *How Children Learn*. London: Sage.

MacConville, R. (2006) 'Powerful Voices Conference Draws Out Pupil Opinion on Education and Services', *SENCO Update*, February 4–5.

Marsh, J. and Singleton, C. (2009) 'Editorial. Literacy and Technology: Questions of Relationship', *Journal of Research in Reading*, 32(1): 1–5.

McPhillips, T., Shevlin, M. and Long, L. (2012) 'A Right to be Heard: Learning from Learners with Additional Needs in Literacy', *Literacy*, 46(2): 57–64.

Merchant, G. (2009) 'Literacy in Virtual Worlds', *Journal of Research in Reading*, 32(1): 38–56.

Mompoint-Gaillard, P. (2013) *New Media and Education: How Will Educators Take Up the Challenge?* Olso, Norway: The European Wergeland Centre.

Noble, K. (2003) 'Personal Reflection on Experiences of Special and Mainstream Education', in M. Shevlin and R. Rose (eds), *Encouraging Voices: Respecting the Insights of Young People who have been Marginalised*. Dublin: National Disability Authority.

O'Mara, J. and Laidlaw, L. (2011) 'Living in the iWorld: Two Literacy Researchers Reflect on the Changing Texts and Literacy Practices of Childhood', *English Teaching: Practice and Critique*, 10(4): 149–59.

Todd, L. (2003) 'Consulting the Children', *Special Children*, September/October, 15–19.

Vygotsky, L. (1978) *Mind in Society*. Harvard, MA: MIT Press.

APPENDIX: USEFUL WEBSITES

ADHD Information Services

ADDISS is the national information and support service for ADHD. This service provides useful information on ADHD for parents, sufferers, teachers and health professionals.
http://www.addiss.co.uk/

American Speech-Language-Hearing Association

(Making effective communication, a human right, accessible and achievable for all)

This website has a literacy section that helps speech and language therapists to implement evidence-based strategies for advancing young children children's literacy development. This section includes journal articles, resources and useful websites.
http://www.asha.org/public/speech/disorders/LBLD/

British Dyslexia Association

This website offers a blended approach to raising awareness and understanding of dyslexia and provides useful information for parents and teachers. The website provides details of conferences that bring together key stakeholders in the field of dyslexia and inclusion including academics, researchers and teachers.
http://www.bdadyslexia.org.uk/

The British Psychological Society

The society provides helpful ethics guidelines for researchers, teachers and practitioners.
http://www.bps.org.uk/

Center for Appreciative Inquiry

This website provides information on applications of Appreciative Inquiry, a method for advancing people and organisations using the principle of positive change.
http://www.centerforappreciativeinquiry.net/

The Department for Education in England

This website is helpful for providing up-to-date information on policies and publications pertaining to the education of children and young people in England.
https://www.gov.uk/government/organisations/department-for-education

The Department of Education Northern Ireland

The DENI website provides information on the underpinning legislative framework for education in Northern Ireland. It provides help and advice for pupils and parents on a range of educational and personal issues. Information and advice that supports teachers' professional development in inclusive practice can be found at this website.
http://www.deni.gov.uk/

Education Scotland

The website, Education Scotland, provides information on the work of a number of organisations and teams pertaining to the education of children and young people in Scotland. The website gives details about a designated team that supports local authorities and learning communities to introduce and embed approaches to promote positive relationships and behaviour.
http://www.educationscotland.gov.uk/

The National Foundation for Educational Research

This is a good website to visit for contemporary and archived publications of research reports and summaries, policy papers, practical guides and professional development tools on SEN including international comparisons.
http://www.nfer.ac.uk/

North Eastern Education and Library Board TV

(Educational television for the web)

This website provides training packages, videos and resources that would be of interest to teachers and classroom assistants who are working with children and young people who have special educational needs.
http://www.neelb.tv/supporting-pupils-with-sen/

Northern Ireland Commissioner for Children and Young People

This website has a 'Policy and Research' section that is a good source of information on the advice that NICCY gives to Government on how to improve children and young people's lives and the outcomes from research about children's lives including schools and schooling.
http://www.niccy.org/

The Office for the Children's Commissioner in the UK

The Office for the Children's Commissioner in the UK promotes and protects children's rights. This website publishes findings from recent research studies on matters that affect children's rights.
http://www.childrenscommissioner.gov.uk/

Reading Association of Ireland

This website provides support and advice to parents and teachers on children's literacy development. Information is also provided on contemporary publications on advancing education in literacy and forthcoming conferences and events.
http://www.reading.ie/

Scottish Commissioner for Children and Young People

There is a section titled "Policy and Research" on the website that provides information on current research projects that relate to the lives of children and young people. For example, bullying and cyberbullying and young people's views on poverty and education in Scotland are some of the areas that the Office of the Scottish Commissioner for Children and Young People is researching in the field of education.
http://www.sccyp.org.uk/

The Standing Conference on Teacher Education North and South

This website provides information on how to obtain seed funding for cross-border research projects on the island of Ireland and has a 'Research' section that provides details of the outcomes from cross-border projects on a range of SEN.
http://scotens.org/

The United Kingdom Literacy Association

(The advancement of education in literacy)

This website provides information on high-quality international, national and regional conferences on policy, research and practice in literacy education. Details are provided on protocols for applying for research grants in areas that advance education in literacy. Information is available on resources and publications in cognate areas. UKLA is a great supportive professional network for teachers, teaching assistants, policymakers, researchers and teacher educators.
http://www.ukla.org/

United Nations Educational, Scientific and Cultural Organization (UNESCO)

This website has an online bookshop, library and database of documents, publications and archives in areas related to UNESCO's fields of competence, including inclusive education.
http://en.unesco.org/

INDEX

able pupils 30, 31, 72–3
academic performance 25, 41, 61
Academies 18, 29, 30, 32–3
acceptance 70, 132
accessibility, academised system 33
accountability 2, 32, 34, 132
achievement 8, 30, 41
  see also low achievement; underachievement
action 44
action research 138, 147
adaptability 72, 173
adaptation 112
additional support needs 40, 95–6
ADHD Information Services 194
adult support, overdependence on 43, 117
adult values 45
adult-directed activities 114
adulthood 145
aesthetic function 143, 144–5
affective dimension 42
affective process, self-efficacy and 75
affordances, new literacies 161–4
age-equivalent scores 104
aggression 76
Ainscow, M. 138, 140
alliteration 88
ambition 8
American Speech-Language-Hearing
  Association 194
Andrews, D. 134
anxiety 67, 75, 76, 84, 182
applications (apps) 161, 162, 163
appreciative inquiry 138–41, 195
Article 12 (UNCRC) 39–40, 52–3, 171
Article 13 (UNCRC) 173
assertiveness 72
assessment
  at age eleven 24–6
  best practice 115

assessment *cont.*
  child-centred approaches 2, 102, 115
  consulting pupils on 41
  culturally fair 2
  developmental literacy difficulties 1–2
  of dyslexia *see* dyslexia
  in the Early Years 86–9
  eliciting pupils' views on (case study)
    46–52
  flexibility in 96
  formal and informal 25, 84–6
  importance of using quantitative/qualitative
    elements 88
  language used in 103
  in primary school 89–93
  SEN pupils 112
  see also psychometric assessment; self-
    assessment
Association of Teachers and Lecturers (ATL)
  29, 70
Aston, H. 45
attainment 4, 20, 29, 32
attention deficit/hyperactivity disorder (ADHD)
  4, 99, 100, 101, 105, 194
Australia 134
authoritarianism 172
authority 168
automaticity 111, 163
autonomy 134, 146

Bandura, A. 75, 76, 77
Bar-On, R. 71–2
behaviour(s) 7, 67, 70, 76, 121
behaviour management programmes 105
beliefs, about human nature 139
belonging 116, 123, 132, 134
best practice 2
  in early years settings 3, 113–15
  in primary schools 115–20

best-fit learning and teaching 98
bests interests 53
Bigge, M.L. 6
bilingual children 95
Billingsley, F. 132
Bishop, D. 4
Bishop, J. 168
Blower, C. 35
Bousted, M. 29
Bracken, B.A. 104
British Dyslexia Association (BDA) 5, 9, 124, 125, 194
British Educational Research Authority (BERA) 49
British Psychological Society (BPS) 4, 49, 195
Brooks, K. 168, 169
Brown, A. 43
Bruce, T. 113, 183
Buckingham, D. 19
Buckler, S. 5
buddy time 116, 188
budgetary control 32, 35
built-in cameras 162
Bullen, E. 167–8
Burden, R. 121, 188
Butler Act (1944) 25

Cambridge Primary Review 10
cameras 162, 173
capacity building 44, 53, 132, 134, 149
Castle, P. 5
catalytic function 143, 145
central executive 99
Centre for Appreciative Inquiry 195
Centre for Social Justice 19
certificates 145
challenging behaviour 70
change 143
change management 140
Chapman, J. 19
child conferencing 173
child development 24
child-centred approaches
    addressing dyslexia needs 42
    assessment 102
    education plans 119
    eliciting pupil voice 49
    implications for 21st century classroom 182–4
    need for understanding of 8–10
    pupil-led 97
    for pupils with SEN and dyslexia 115
    raising awareness of need for 2
    social skills training 105
    to partnerships 123

child-directed activities 114
childhood 19–22, 145, 168
children
    as experts 169
    generation gap between teachers and 184
    see also digital child; pupils; unique child
Children and their Primary Schools see Plowden Report
children's interests, following 164–70, 184
choice 41, 146, 161–2
Circular 10/65 25, 36
Clark, A. 173
class (social) 29
classroom environments 103, 187, 188
classroom relationships 116
Claxton, G. 70–2
Cline, T. 189
Coalition Government 24–5, 33, 36, 123, 125, 191
codes of practice 40, 41, 85, 121
cognitive assessment 95, 103
cognitive processes 75, 99, 102
collaboration 33, 76, 112, 132, 133, 136, 137, 140
collaborative inquiry 134
    case study 140–8
    two modes of 138–40
collective action 140
collective dialogue 140, 148
Colverd, S. 76–7
commitment 76, 77
Committee on the Rights of the Child 10
communication 44, 61
community, features of 134
comorbidity 4, 99–105
competition 36
comprehensive system 25, 36
compulsory education 25
computer-based training 105
concentration 64, 67, 72
confidentiality 190
consultation
    barriers to 45
    child-centred assessment 102
    of children in curricula development 171
    metacognitive dimension to 43
    tokenistic 40, 182
    as a virtuous cycle of reflection 44
    see also pupils' views
contextual factors 10, 17–18, 97, 133
continuing professional development 124, 125
control, over learning 41
converged learning environment 169
conversations 44, 53, 119, 136, 137, 141, 147

cooperativeness 137
Cooperrider, D. 138, 139
coordination 111
Covington, M.L. 75
Creating and Sustaining Effective Professional Learning Communities 133
creative methodologies
    collaborative inquiry 140–8
    exploring pupils' views 45–55, 172
criminal records checks 49
critical periods 188
critical reflection 119, 137, 141, 147
criticism 74
Crombie, M. 87, 88, 89, 93
cross-curricular pedagogies 105
Cullis, A. 20
culturally fairness 2, 97
culture(s) 8, 10, 97, 133, 168
    see also inclusive cultures; popular culture
cumulative programmes/teaching 112
curriculum 23–4, 171
Curtis, K. 45

The Daily Mail 19
Daugaard, H.T. 96
Davies, J. 161
Davis, A. 26–7
decision-making 40, 41, 44, 53, 136, 171, 182, 187
decline of deference 70
defiance 76
Department for Education (DfE) 26, 28, 32, 34, 195
Department for Education in Northern Ireland (DENI) 120, 122–3, 195
Department for Education and Skills (DfES) 133
Deppeler, J. 136, 137, 148
depression 182
deprivation 29
Deprivation and Risk: The Case for Early Intervention 20
design (4-D model) 140
destiny (4-D model) 140
detached behaviour 76
developmental delay, in speech and language 94
developmental disorders, dyslexia and 99–105
developmental literacy difficulties 1
    assessment and intervention 1–2
    emotional intelligence and 68–9
    implications for the digital child 21–2
    pupils with
        benefits of consulting 41
        impact of new literacies on motivation of 159–61
        importance of experiencing success 120
        lack of attention given to social and

developmental literacy difficulties *cont.*
        emotional aspects of 60–1
        opportunities to demonstrate competencies/talents 116
    social contexts 17–18
Diagnosing Dyslexia 5
diagnostic assessment 103
diagnostic labels 4–5
Diagnostic and Statistical Manual of Mental Disorders (APA) 101
dialogical models, professional learning 146
dialogue 117, 119, 134, 140, 142, 148
dictionaries 162
dietary intervention 105
Digital Beginnings 165
digital child, emergence of 21–2
digital technology 10, 157–8, 168
    concerns about 185
    novelty effect 161
    potential of 7–8
    see also information and communication technology; media technologies; tablet devices
discover (4-D model) 139
distractible learners, strategies for 100
diversity 2, 95, 137
divorce 19
Dockett, S. 174
Dowling, M. 88
drawings, elicitation of children's views 46
dream (4-D model) 139
drill-and-practice 118
drug treatment 105
Dunn, J. 46, 167
Dweck, C. 43, 118
dyscalculia 4
dyslexia
    assessment
        at 11 years of age 26
        and comorbidity 99, 101–3
        EAL pupils 96, 97
        principles 1–2
    behavioural/social and emotional difficulties 7
    changing nature of childhood 19–22
    changing nature of schools 28–37
    comorbidity 99–105
    conceptualisation 1
    emotional intelligence and 68–9
    identification 4, 88, 100–1
    implications for the digital child 21–2
    inclusivity for EAL pupils with 95–8
    interventions
        and comorbidity 99, 104–5
        for EAL pupils with 97

dyslexia *cont.*
   meeting holistic needs 42
   principles 1–2
  knowledge development 2
  literacy *see* literacy
  perspectives on 3–6
  social contexts 17–18
  teacher understanding 7, 27, 41, 124
  usefulness of term 4–5
  viewed as a continuum 83–4
'dyslexia friendly' schools 191
Dyslexia-SpLD Trust 125
dyslexic pupils
  benefits of consulting 41
  child-centred approaches 42, 115
  educational experiences 109
  gifted 72
  home-school partnerships 121, 122
  impact of new literacies on motivation of
    159–61
  importance of experiencing success 120
  inclusive classrooms 186–90
  lack of attention given to social and
    emotional side 60–1
  with literacy difficulties, working with
    110–13
  negative biases of working with 183–4
  opportunities to demonstrate competencies/
    talents 116
  post-primary 42
  recommendations (example) 63–6
  selection process 76
  self-concept of 41
  support for 37
  see also pupil voice; pupils' views
dysphasia 4
dyspraxia 4, 61

e-books 161–2
EAL pupils, with dyslexia, inclusivity for 95–8
Early Years Register 23
Early Years settings
  10 principles of good practice 183
  identification and assessment in 86–9
  identifying best practice in 113–15
  play-based learning 114–15
economic costs, of poverty 21
Education (Additional Support for Learning)
  Scotland (2004) 40
education plans 41, 104–5, 119, 122, 167
Education Scotland 195
educational psychologists 45, 84, 102–3, 104, 190
educational reform 132
educational theories 6

edutainment 158
Elbro, C. 96
eleven, assessment at age of 24–6
Eleven Plus 25, 36
Eliadou, A. 46
emotional intelligence 66–74
emotional literacy 67, 71
emotional maturity 31, 60, 61
emotional needs, perceived as barriers to
  learning 42
Emotional Quotient Inventory (EQ-1) 71–2
emotional well-being 74, 117
emotions 6, 53, 59–60
empathy 42, 51, 72, 116, 144, 184
employment, single parents 19
empowerment 2, 3, 8, 40, 137, 143, 147, 148,
  172, 182
enabling environments 24
enabling values base 44–5
England 18, 24, 25, 26, 29, 34, 36, 41
English 30, 31
English as an Additional Language *see* EAL
  pupils
'engulfed', by emotions 69–70
episodic buffer 99
equality 95
equality of opportunity 8, 103
ethic of care 134
ethical intelligence 52, 53
ethics forms 49
ethics (research) 49–51, 141
Europe 158
Every Child Matters (ECM) 2
examinations, reinstatement of 191
experiential learning 114
experimental psychology 118
expertise 2, 18, 111, 121, 125, 136, 164
experts, children as 169
extended professionalism 123
extrinsic motivation 112

failure 3
  feelings/sense of 8, 85, 159, 187
  importance of not experiencing 112
  indirect effects of perceived 89
  lone parent families and academic 19
  low self-concept and 77
  lower estimate of ability 75
  to access literature 67
  understanding of effects of 76, 182
fairness, of academy system 33
Faith Schools 29
Falvey, M. 119
family context 18, 19–21

family support 19, 189
fear 67
feedback 104, 119, 120, 147
Fielding, M. 45, 116
financial hardship 19, 20
Fisher Act (1918) 25
Fisher, J. 164
Fitzgibbon, G. 104
flexibility 72, 96, 112, 136, 147, 166
fluency 102
Flutter, J. 41
forensic focus, teaching 33
formal assessment 25, 85, 86
formative feedback 119, 120
Foucault, M. 142
4-D model (AI) 139–40
fragile ecology 184
Frederickson, N. 189
Free Schools 18, 29, 34–5
Freud, S. 67
Froebel, F. 23, 113, 183
frustration 7, 60, 67, 70, 88, 101, 104, 122, 182
functional/personal differentiation 116
funding 29, 32, 190

Gardner, H. 72
Gardner, R. 35
GCSE 30, 31
Gellert, A. 96
General Comment no. 12 (CRC) 10
general mood 72
General Teaching Council (GTC) 133
generation gap, between teachers and
        children 184
Gergen, K. 143
gifted young children 72
Gillberg, C. 104
Gillingham, A. 3, 110, 111
Gillum, H. 102, 104
Goleman, D. 69–70
governors, academies 34
Grammar Schools 25, 26, 35–6
Griffiths, C. 121
Guardian 168
guidance, right to 53
guilt 74, 104

habits of mind, unsettling 143–4, 146
Hafner, C.A. 185
Hales, G.W. 42
Halsey, M. 166
Hammond, N. 45
handwriting 64, 102
Hansen, K. 20

happiness 72
'hard to reach' parents 122
'hard to reach' pupils 45, 46
harmony 134
Harris, A. 77
Hartas, D. 7, 31, 60, 61, 72, 88
Hartley, J. 184
head teachers 32, 35
Healy Eames, F. 162
Heneveld, W. 98, 115–16, 132
Hewitt, D. 43
Higgins, S. 138
high culture 168
high order skills 65
high quality learning 23–4
high quality teaching 2, 8, 115, 132, 184
high-attaining pupils 30, 31
higher education institutions (HEIs) 18, 49, 52,
        123, 126, 148, 190–1
Hodgkin, B. 76–7
holistic approaches 115, 141, 146
Holt, J. 67
home environment 186
home literacy experiences 166
home-school literacy gap 9–10
home-school-community partnerships 115, 120,
        121–3, 189
hope 140
hopelessness 75, 84
Hord, S.M. 134
Hornstra, L. 183
Howe, M. 75
human nature 139
human rights 8
humiliation 60, 88
humour 116
'hundred languages of children' 173
hyperactivity-impulsivity 101

Iceland 134
identification
    dyslexia and comorbidity 4, 88, 100–1
    in the Early Years 86–9
    in primary school 89–93
*Identifying and Teaching Children and
        Young People with Dyslexia and Literacy
        Difficulties* 4
identity 8
ill health 29
illectronacy 184
image-based research
    collaborative inquiry 140–8
        elicitation of children's views 46–55
imaginative function 143, 145

imaginative ideas, school improvement 144
Imperial College London study 10
impulse control 72
inattention 101
inclusion 2
    advancing for EAL pupils with dyslexia 95
    and challenging behaviour 70
    and meaningful participation 132
    transformative view of 137
inclusive classrooms 186–90
inclusive cultures 115, 119, 122, 136, 137, 143,
    146, 148
inclusive practices 2, 116, 137, 140
inclusive school 123
independence 162
independent schools 29, 30, 36–7
The Independent 29, 35
individualised approach 116
individualised education plans (IEPs) 41, 122, 167
inequality 29
inferior status 77
informal assessment 85–6
information, right to seek, receive and impart
    53, 173
information and communication technology
    64, 65, 92, 118–19
informed consent 49–50
Ingesson, S.G. 188
innovation 136, 138, 144, 147
innovative freedoms 186
insider perspectives 148
integrity (professional) 49, 96
intelligence *see* emotional intelligence; ethical
    intelligence
Intelligence Quotients (IQs) 71
intelligence tests 95
An Intelligent Look at Emotional Intelligence
    70–2
interactive multimedia technology 119
International Dyslexia Association 166
international education 133
interpersonal intelligence 72
interpersonal relationships 134
interpretation(s) 46, 67, 74
interrupted thinking 140
intertextual learning environments 169
interventions
    child-centred and culturally fair 2
    developing emotional intelligence 73–4
    developmental literacy difficulties 1–2
    dyslexia *see* dyslexia
    importance of early 105
intrapersonal intelligence 72
intrinsic motivation 112

intuition (professional) 53, 96
Isaacs, S. 113
Isle of Wight study 4
isolation 116

Jackson, L. 132
Jarvis, M. 7
Jeffs, T. 172
The Jeremy Kyle Show 168
Johnson, D.W. 137
Johnson, R. 137
joined-up approaches 115
Jones, P. 132, 147
Jones, R.H. 185

Katz, L. 165
Kenway, J. 167–8
Kershaw, A. 29
Knivsberg, A.-M. 101, 105
Knobel, M. 5
knowledge, collaboration and new 140
knowledge construction 45
knowledge creation 134
knowledge sharing 189, 190
Kortman, W. 121–2
Kress, G. 158

labels 4–5, 67, 104
Labour Government 25, 36
Laidlaw, L. 186
Lambert, N. 45
language
    in assessment 103
    capacity to generate new meaning 143
    developmental delay 94
    difficulties 99
    parental confusion over professional 122
    skills assessment 103
    social and emotional development and 61
    see also EAL pupils
language bias 96
language-based methods 45, 46
Lankshear, C. 5
Lawrence, D.H. 59
leadership 132, 134, 137
learned helplessness 43, 187
learning
    advances in understanding of 182
    barriers to 115, 140
    EYFS framework 24
    pupil ability to reflect on 42
    responsibility for 141, 172
    sense of control over 41
    strategies for managing 64–6

learning *cont.*
  through play 113–15
  see also literacy learning
learning difficulties
  characteristics 31
  increased understanding of 64
  see also literacy difficulties; specific learning
    difficulties
learning environments 8, 24, 71, 99, 103, 118,
    169, 184, 187, 188
learning experiences 28–9, 43, 188
learning profession 133
learning situations, increasing understanding of
    approaches to 64
learning theories 6
Learning to Learn (DENI) 23
Leitch, R. 45
Letters Form Words 65
letters of informed consent 49–50
Lewis, M. 134
life experiences 23, 49
listening comprehension 95, 102
listening to children 3, 48, 148, 172–4
literacy 1
  central role of teachers 184
  changing nature of 5–6
  DENI report (2011) 120
  digital child's need for 21
  engagement 120, 161–2
  entitlement to 8
  global economy and the need for 131–2
  growing gap between home-school 9–10
  new conceptual model for teaching 42, 53
  raising standards through assessment 25
  support *see* support
  testing 102, 104
  see also emotional literacy; home literacy
    experiences; new literacies; reading;
    writing
literacy acquisition
  difficulties in 8, 9, 18, 89
  emotional development and well-being 60
  phonics and 26
  regulation of emotions and feelings 69
literacy difficulties
  diversion of funding from pupils with 32
  early identification of 88
  emotional responses of children with 59–60
  implications for the digital child 21–2
  principles of working with dyslexic children
    with 110–13
  understanding sense of failure 76
  working memory impairment and 99
  see also developmental literacy difficulties

literacy learning
  affective dimension 42
  barriers to 132
  digital technology 7
  holistic model 141
  inclusive cultures 122
literature-rich learning environments 118
lived experiences 148, 173
local education authorities 25
location, of schools 29
Locke, J. 66
Lodge, C. 147
lone parent families 19, 20
Long, L. 42, 43, 60, 101, 104, 116, 122, 172
low achievement 41, 94–5, 117, 183
low income families 21
low self-concept 77
low self-esteem 7, 8, 61, 162
low self-worth 182
Ludicke, P. 121–2
Lundy, L. 44, 52, 53, 171
Lupton, R. 20

MacBlain, M. 42, 60
MacBlain, S.F. 32, 42, 60, 67, 93
McLoughlin, D. 104
McMillan, D. 46
McMillan, R. 113
McPhillips, T. 43
McPolin, P. 101, 104, 122
Malaguzzi, L. 113, 173
managing emotions 69
Marsh, J. 165, 168, 185
mastery 77
Mates, B. 119
mathematics 30, 31
Mayer, J.D. 67–9
meaning making 45, 166, 1162
media, phonics debate 26
media technologies 119, 185–6
memory 99, 102, 103, 111, 163
mentoring, teachers in training 190–2
Merchant, G. 161, 163, 184
metacognition 42, 44, 53, 117, 187–8
metacognitive ability 43
metacognitive awareness 120
metacognitive enrichment 44
metacognitive strategies 43
Miles, S. 138, 140
misrepresentation 46
mobile phones, health risk study 10
Moll, K. 99
Mompoint-Gaillard, P. 184
Montessori, M. 67, 87, 113

Moon, B. 133
moral panics 167, 185
Mortimore, T. 96, 97, 98
Mosaic Approach 173
Moss, P. 173
*The Most Able Students: Are They Doing as
    Well as They Should in Our Non-Selective
    Secondary Schools?* 30
motivation 41, 42, 75, 112, 159–61
Muijs, D. 137
multi-agency working 93
multi-component model, of working
    memory 99
multi-method approach, listening to
    children 173
multi-professional working 189
multimedia technology 119
multimodal texts 6, 164
multisensory approaches 65, 92, 105, 112, 163

National Association for the Teachers of
    English (NATE) 27–8
National College for School Leadership
    (NCSL) 133
National Foundation for Educational
    Research 196
negative self-image 70
Neil, A.S. 67
Neill, J. 140
neural connections 163
neurodevelopmental disability 5
new literacies 158–9
    affordances 161–4
    challenge of, in contemporary classrooms 184
    concerns about 185
    impact on children with dyslexia and
        developmental disorders 159–61
    multimodal nature of 6
new meanings, generation of, as central to
    change/transformation 143
Niens, U. 46
Noddings, N. 67
non-discrimination 53
non-selective secondary schools 30, 31
non-statutory services, awareness of 104, 122
non-words, phonetic 27–8
norm-referenced tests 95, 104
Norman, D.A. 118, 119
North Eastern Education and Library Board
    TV 196
Northern Ireland 18, 23, 26, 40
Northern Ireland Commissioner for Children
    and Young People 196
Northern Ireland Dyslexia Centre 122

Norwich, B. 121, 122
novelty effect, digital technologies 161
Nutbrown, C. 173

observation 88, 173, 189
Office for the Children's Commission in the
    UK 196
Ofsted 30, 90, 93–4, 112, 125–6
O'Mara, J. 186
Omelich, C.L. 75
'omnipresent flow of transmedia' 165
one-to-one teaching 105
openness 116
optimism 72
organisational development 139, 140
orthography 96, 97
outcomes
    of assessment, explaining to children 104
    from action research projects 138
    parental involvement and school 121
    PLCs and effective pupil 134
outreach programmes 122
outsider voices 148
overlearning 188

pacing 113, 116
Pahl, K. 160
paired reading 92, 116
parent-teacher relationships 121
parental anxiety, child's lack of progress 84
parental frustration 84, 101, 104, 122
parental involvement 93, 97, 101, 116, 121–2
parenting 23
parents
    awareness of non-statutory services 104
    listening to 3
    perceptions of dyslexia 3
    views on assessment 101
    working with 93–4
    see also home-school-community
        partnerships
participation *see* pupil participation
participatory approach 173
participatory research 51
partnerships
    HEI-school 148
    home-school-community 115, 120, 121–3, 189
    opportunities for pupil voice 97
    in reading 116
pastoral support 105
patience 116
Paton, G. 34, 36
pedagogy 105, 173
peer rejection 77

perceived failure 89, 187
perceiving emotions 68
percentiles 85–6, 104
performance measures 71
person-centred approaches 123
personal/functional differentiation 116
personality 74
Pestalozzi, J. 183
phonics 26–8, 89, 102, 111, 112, 188
phonological deficit theory 4, 102
phonological loop 99
phonological skills 103
phonology 96, 98
Piaget, J. 114
pictorial superiority effect 162
play, learning through 113–15
plenary sessions 43
Plowden Report (1967) 183
popular culture
    challenge in harnessing 185–6
    in the classroom
        resistance to 167–70
        value of 165–7
    literacy engagement 120
    study eliciting learners' view on 46
positive home experiences 186
positive relationships 24
post-code lottery 29
poverty 20, 21, 29
power 49, 184
praise 117, 118, 145
pre-school stage, identification at 88
Prensky, M. 168
primary schools
    identification and assessment in 89–93
    identifying best practice in 115–20
private schools 29, 36–7
problem-solving 72
processing difficulties 111
professional groups, tensions between 189
professional learning, dialogical models 146
professional learning communities (PLCs)
    133–7
professionals, knowledge sharing among 189
protection from abuse 53
protectionist values base 44
Prout, A. 172
Psychodynamics 67
psychological processes 75–6
psychometric assessment 95
pupil participation
    addressing barriers to 140
    eliciting pupils' views on (case study) 46–52
    empowerment through 40

pupil participation *cont.*
    inclusion and meaningful 132
    legislation and policy promoting 40
    removing barriers to 2
    SEN Toolkit 41
    teacher scepticism as a barrier to 44
pupil profiles 103, 104
pupil progress
    parental anxiety 84
    parental partnerships 122
    PLCs and 134
    targets for advancing, in literacy 97
pupil voice
    child-centred programmes 97
    critical literature on 41–5
    inclusive cultures and 146
    obstacles to 44–5
pupils
    isolation 116
    wellbeing and well-becoming 1, 6–8, 48, 60,
        74, 117, 118, 145
    see also able pupils; dyslexic pupils; EAL
        pupils; 'hard to reach' pupils; SEN
        pupils
pupils' needs
    centrality of 8
    non-acknowledgement of emotional 42
    see also additional support needs; special
        educational needs
pupils' views
    accessing 171–4
    commitment in giving voice to 40
    creative methodologies for exploring 45–6
        on assessment and participation (case
            study) 46–52
        implications for transforming practice 52–5
    misrepresentations 46
    right to express 40
    written representations 45

quality improvement processes 98

raising standards 2, 25, 44, 132
rapid automatised naming (RAN) 103
rapid serial naming/processing speed 102
reading
    assessing precursors of 96
    comprehension 65, 87, 96
    experiences 145
    outcomes of collaborative inquiry
        study 146
    skills, improving 65
    strategies, coaching in 118
    understanding factors affecting 111

reading *cont.*
  and well-being 1
  see also paired reading; recreational reading
Reading Association of Ireland 196
Reading by Six: How the Best Schools Do It
  125–6
reading comprehension 102
Reading Inventory 85
reality testing 72
Reason, R. 4, 83–4
reasoning with emotions 68
Reay, D. 121
reciprocity 134
recreational reading 119
Reed, J. 147
reflection 42, 44, 117, 119, 134, 136, 137, 138,
  141, 147
reflective dialogue 134
reflexivity 49, 173
Reggio Emilia schools 173
regimes of truth 142
Reid, G. 2, 4, 87, 88, 89, 93, 117
reinforcement, of learning 92, 188
rejection 77
relationships 24, 116, 121, 134
Remedial Training for Children with Specific
  Disability in Reading, Spelling, and
  Penmanship 110–11
remote control childhoods 168
Removing Barriers to Literacy (Ofsted) 94–5
Report of the Academies Commission
  (2013) 33
research, lack of attention given to 7
Research Ethics Committees 49, 52
resourcing 32, 35
respect 113
responsiveness 136, 137
review meetings 45
rhyming difficulties 88
rhythm 87, 98
Richardson, H. 26–7
Riddick, B. 41
Riehl, C.J. 137
right to withdraw, from research 50
rigour (research) 138
Rinaldi, C. 172
risk-taking 137
Robertson, C. 119
Rose, D. 166
Rose Review 2, 27
rote learning 118
Rousseau, J.-J. 23, 66, 183
Rowsell, J. 160
Royal Society of Arts 8

Rudduck, J. 41
Ryndak, D. 132

sadness 187
Salovey, P. 67–9
Samuelsson, J. 117
scaffolding 53
Schon, D. 138
school effectiveness 134
school improvement 143, 147
school leaving age 25
school readiness 164
school-community connections 137
schools
  dyslexia and changing nature of 18, 28–37
  'dyslexia friendly' 191
  training of teachers in 18, 123–6, 190–2
  see also home-school literacy gap
Schools Direct 123
Scotland 18, 40
Scottish Commissioner for Children and Young
  People 197
Scuilli, S. 166, 167
second language acquisition 95
Secondary Modern Schools 25
secondary schools, non-selective 30, 31
segregation 35
selection procession, self-efficacy and 75–6
self-assessment 117, 125
self-awareness 69, 72
self-belief 63, 66
self-concept 41, 77, 121
self-confidence 61, 65, 74, 76, 88, 92, 111
self-criticality 31
self-deprecating cycle 116
self-determination 119
self-efficacy 3, 8, 41, 74–7, 88, 111, 116, 117
self-esteem 7, 8, 31, 61, 63, 65–6, 72, 88, 111,
  116, 162, 166
self-image 70, 89
self-negativity 182
self-regulation 43
self-report measures 71, 72
self-worth 31, 182
semantics 96, 102
SEN Code of Practice (DfE) 121
SEN pupils
  child-centred provision 115
  consulting 44
  eliciting pupil voice 51
  failure to involve 40
  inclusion 2
  key elements of successful learning 112–13
  listening to lived experiences of 148

SEN pupils *cont.*
  metacognitive capacity 43
  participation 40
  role in review meetings 45
  tablet computers and increased motivation
    160–1
  see also dyslexic pupils; EAL pupils
SEN Toolkit 41
sequencing 103
sequential programmes/teaching 112
shared values 134
Shermis, S.S. 6
Shevlin, M. 43
Sigurðardóttir, A. 133, 134
Singleton, C. 185
Sipay, E.R. 77
small-scale action research 138
Smith, C.A. 166, 167
Smith, R. 140
Snowling, M.J. 4
social adjustment 31, 60, 61
social agents, children as 45, 146
social awareness 72
social contexts 17–18
social, emotional and behavioural
    difficulties 7
social and emotional development 1, 18, 60,
    61, 68, 182, 189
social intelligence 68, 72
social interaction 60, 61
social responsibility 72
social skills development 7
social skills training 105
socio-construction 114
socio-economic status 30, 77, 94–5
socio-emotional aspects, lack of attention given
    to 60–1
solution-focused principles 53
Sorensen, P.F. 139
sound/symbol correspondence 65
special educational needs
  Ofsted review (2010) 93–4
  parental confusion over procedures and
    language 122
  teacher training and 18
  see also SEN Code of Practice; SEN pupils;
    SEN Toolkit
special schools 124
specialist training 124
specific language impairment (SLI) 99, 100
specific learning difference 5
specific learning difficulties 5, 19, 61, 64,
    95, 124
speech delay 94

speech difficulties 98
speech and language therapists 189
speech sound disorder (SSD) 99, 100
speed of processing 102, 103
spelling 65, 92, 111
Spohrer, J.C. 118, 119
sponsors, of academies 32
sport 36
standard scores 86
standardised assessments 85–6, 96
standards-based school reform 148
Standing Conference on Teacher Education
    North and South 197
Stanine scores 86
Stanovich, K.E. 4
start-up grants 34
Statutory Framework for the Early Years
    Foundation Stage 23–4
Steiner, R. 23, 87, 113
Stenhouse, L. 138
Stillman, B.W. 3, 110, 111
Stoll, L. 134
Stothard, J. 4, 83–4
strategic innovation 147
stratified schools 29
stress 70, 75
stress management 72
stress tolerance 72
Strommen, L. 119
structured programmes 65, 92, 105, 112
subject knowledge 112
success 8, 41, 66, 76, 117, 120
support
  for dyslexic children 36
  as essential for educational reform 132
  for Free Schools 34
  for Grammar Schools 36
  for SEN pupils 112, 113
  vocabulary development 87
  see also adult support; family support;
    pastoral support
Sutton Trust 21
syntax 96, 102
synthetic phonics 27
'systematic enquiry made public' 138
systematic phonics 28

tablet devices 158, 161, 162, 163–4
target setting 41, 65, 119
task avoidance 76
teacher empathy 42, 184
teacher expectations 103, 113
teacher-pupil conversations 44, 53
teacher-pupil partnerships 97

teachers
  assessment of dyslexia and comorbidity 102
  central role in literacy 184
  and dyslexic children
    negative biases of working with 183–4
    principles for working with 110–13
  as essential to child-centred approach 183
  as facilitators 119
  generation gap between children and 184
  lack of attention
    given to education and learning theories 6
    given to research 7
  as members of a 'learning profession' 133
  non-acknowledgement of emotional
      needs 42
  perceptions of dyslexia 3
  rejection by 77
  relationships 116, 121, 134
  scepticism as a barrier to pupil participation 44
  shaping of the learning environment 8
  training in schools 18, 123–6, 190–2
  understanding
    of dyslexia 7, 27, 41, 124
    of emotions 68–9
    of metacognition 187–8
    of socio-economic/environmental/cultural
        contexts of children's lives 10
Teachers Standards 124, 125
teaching 33, 113, 116
teamwork 137
Technical Schools 25
technology see digital technology
Telegraph 34, 36
toxic childhoods 168
transformation, new meaning and 143
transformative view, of inclusion 137
transparent languages 97
triangulation 138
trust 134, 189
Twigg, S. 36

unconscious 67
underachievement 41, 95
unhappiness 187
unique child 24
United Kingdom Literacy Association 197
United Nations 8
United Nations Convention on the Rights of
    the Child 39–40, 52–3, 171, 173

United Nations Educational, Scientific and
    Cultural Organization (UNESCO)
    132, 197
Unsure Start: HMCI's Early Years Annual
    Report 2012/13 Speech 20–1
utility (research) 138

validity (research) 138
values 45, 49, 134
values base 44–5
variety 116, 146
verbal memory 102, 103
verbal texts 141
virtuous cycles 44, 147
vision 134, 137
visual discrimination/recall 87
visual texts 141
visualisation 43
visuals 162
visuo-spatial scratchpad 99
visuo-spatial skills 103
vocabulary, support 87
Vue, G. 166
vulnerability (social) 7
Vygotsky, L. 114, 183

Wall, K. 138
Waugh, D. 27
weak self-efficacy 76
Weinstein, B. 52
well-becoming 1, 6–8, 48, 145
well-being 1, 6–8, 48, 60, 74, 117, 118, 145
Westwood, P. 116
Whitebread, D. 6
Whitney, C. 139
Wilshaw, M. 20–1
wireless technologies 10
withdrawal from research 50
withdrawal from social situations 61
Wohlwend, K. 165, 169
Wood, E. 114
'word finding' difficulties 61, 88
word recognition 65, 96, 118
working memory 99, 102, 103, 111
writing 1, 64, 92, 102, 162–3
written representations, of pupils'
    views 45

Young, V. 104